T0247597

"Norman Hill and Velma's memoir reminds us all of the transformative power vested in a community organized from shared experience to bring about real change. The struggle for civil rights in the United States is not defined by any one moment, but by the collective stories of people across this country who put their lives on the line in hopes that America might one day live up to its promise. It is my sincere hope that the new generation of emerging activists and leaders will be inspired by this book as they chart a course forward to tackle the many challenges facing African Americans today."

—**Congresswoman Maxine Waters**

"Norman Hill and Velma Murphy Hill have written a compelling, richly detailed and thoroughly gripping account of their involvement in the civil rights and organized labor movements. It is so important, now more than ever, to remember the struggles that redefined the trajectory of American history, as we moved from the dark era of Jim Crow segregation and racism to a brighter era where we have come that much closer to realizing the ideals of freedom and dignity for all citizens. For the Jewish community, the missions the Hills took to Israel helped strengthen African-American support for the Jewish state.

—**Abraham H. Foxman**, National Director Emeritus, Anti-Defamation League

"Norman and Velma Hill began *Climbing the Rough Side of the Mountain* as young, idealist, warmly romantic students who were united around a common mission—to challenge the status quo of race relations in this country and to champion the values of their African American heritage. Theirs is a story of audacious youth who became tenacious partners in the risky and often unrewarding struggle to organize for social and economic justice against all odds. A must-read chronicle of a time in our history that offers a clear remembrance for those who lived it; and, serves as a platform on which future activists can stand. Bravo, Norm and Velma!"

—**Clayola Brown**, President, A. Philip Randolph Institute

"This book is about two people who fell in love with each other and with the movements for social and racial justice. It is a must-read for those who are committed to a society free of racial and gender oppression and to the right of workers everywhere to share in the wealth that we help to create every day. Norman and Velma are true heroes of the civil rights and labor movements, and their efforts helped build a better society for all."

—**Liz Shuler**, President, AFL-CIO

"Norman and Velma Hill's passion for justice—and for one another—is an inspirational story, and one that needs to be told. Their journey from idealistic young social justice soldiers to civil rights icons is quintessentially American and should be held as an example for the next generation of leaders."

—**Marc Morial**, President, National Urban League

"Their memoir tells a vivid story of struggle and perseverance, one that both illuminates a vital chapter in the history of American democracy and will inspire a new generation of activists to renew the never-ending effort to build a just society."

—**Carl Gershman**, President, National Endowment for Democracy

"Norm and Velma Hill bring history to life in their book, *Climbing the Rough Side of the Mountain*. Their story bears witness to the experience of countless civil rights foot soldiers, who were willing to risk their lives to realizing justice and freedom for all. This memoir should be a call to action to this generation of activists as they work to build upon the progress of icons like Norm and Velma Hill. Those working for progress should read and internalize this powerful testament to passion, persistence and moral courage in the face of injustice.

—**Congresswoman Barbara Lee**

"For over half a century, Velma and Norman Hill have been active in the struggle for equality in America. In their memoir *Climbing the Rough Side of the Mountain*, we see that their lives were lived focused on equality for all Americans. This book is a detailed testament to their work around social change in America. It is an important testament to the impact two individuals serving the cause of freedom can have on all Americans."

—**Congressman Robert C. "Bobby" Scott**

"From 1960 to today, Norm and Velma Hill have been at the forefront of the struggle for civil rights and economic justice in the United States. Their memoir is a valuable addition to the narrative of our nation's civil rights and labor histories, which they have helped author in words as well as action over the past fifty-five years."

—**Lee Saunders**, President, American Federation of State, County and Municipal Employees

"I know Velma and Norm Hill as two of the people who risked everything alongside Martin Luther King, Jr. during the march from Selma to Montgomery. During a demonstration decades ago, Velma was brutally wounded by a racist mob in Chicago, injuries from which she has never fully recovered. Norm picked up the torch of A. Philip Randolph and used it to shine a light on some of the darkest places in our nation.

"Norm and Velma Hill have made it their lifelong mission to build a fairer and more just America. Whether it's expanding civil rights, strengthening our democracy, or creating more opportunity for working families, the impact of their activism will be felt for generations to come. This book provides firsthand insight into their struggle, sacrifice, and service."

—**Richard L. Trumka**, Former President, AFL-CIO

"They both helped pioneer civil rights work throughout the labor movement; Velma even became my union's first civil rights and international affairs director when I was a young, openly lesbian organizer. I knew firsthand the daunting challenges she faced. Countless people who have been othered by our society will always be extremely thankful for her leadership. I am among them.

"These are just a few of the many ways that Velma and Norm have shown me how to fight for values that really matter to working people. With the courage of their convictions, they have been willing to put their very lives on the line to win justice.

"They have inspired me to risk my own privilege to win racial justice and to help working people to improve their lives. Those who read their story will find themselves just as powerfully motivated."

—**Mary Kay Henry**, International President,
Service Employees International Union

# CLIMBING THE
# ROUGH SIDE
## OF THE MOUNTAIN

# CLIMBING THE ROUGH SIDE OF THE MOUNTAIN

## The Extraordinary Story of Love, Civil Rights, and Labor Activism

Norman Hill and Velma Murphy Hill

**Regalo Press**
New York • Nashville
regalopress.com

Published in the United States of America
1  2  3  4  5  6  7  8  9  10

*To A. Philip Randolph and Bayard Rustin,*
*dear friends, mentors, brothers in activism,*
*and the architects of it all.*

*and*

*Michel Marriott, our dearest friend*
*who helped to make this book possible.*

# Contents

# Foreword

## By Vernon E. Jordan Jr. and Congressman John Lewis

*Author's note: Before their respective deaths in 2020 and 2021, Congressman John Lewis and former president of the National Urban League and civil rights attorney Vernon Jordan were among the friends and fellow activists given the opportunity to preview the manuscript of* Climbing the Rough Side of the Mountain.

I first met the Hills when I was a young man, not long out of Howard University Law School. I was in my hometown of Atlanta, Georgia, and involved in the Voter Education Project being led by the Southern Regional Council. This was the very early 1960s, and by then, Norman was already an experienced hand at organizing. He had, while a master's degree student at the University of Chicago, managed some major mobilizing of students for Randolph and Rustin, who would become longtime mentors to the Hills. Norman was a member of the National Association for the Advancement of Colored People and already held deep and trusted ties with trade union leaders.

To me, Norman Hill looked every bit the man who knew what he was doing; for me, that was an open invitation to learn as much as I could while working with him. It was soon after that I met his wife, Velma, a no-nonsense woman on a mission to change the world one picket line, one sit-in, wade-in, rally, and well laid-out plan at a time.

And over the years, no matter what I was doing, from leading the National Urban League, or the United Negro College Fund, or advising the president of the United States, I have remembered the fine and enduring work of Norman and Velma Hill.

—*Vernon E. Jordan Jr.*


I was lucky to have met Norman and Velma early in my life as well. I was always struck by their enormous patience and humanity. As busy as they were—and they were always busy running here and there around the country, meeting day and night, even hosting movement people in their home in New York—they always seemed to have an encouraging moment for you.

At that time, I was president of the Student Nonviolent Coordinating Committee. Hosea Williams of the Southern Christian Leadership Conference and I led 600 protesters that March 7 over the Edmund Pettus Bridge. History remembers that day as "Bloody Sunday."

But after we licked our many psychic and physical wounds, we decided to face down the threat of renewed violence against us and march again in the name of our fallen brothers and sisters, and for voting rights. Just wouldn't you know it, Norman and Velma Hill came to join us in that Selma to Montgomery march. And I applauded that. I appreciated them just as I had respected Norman's work helping Bayard [Rustin] organize the March on Washington for Jobs and Freedom two years earlier. Norman was nearby, too, when the march's elders, including [A. Philip] Randolph, the old lion himself, wisely talked me into delivering a less strident version of the speech I gave that day.

Today, from my House office as Georgia's Fifth Congressional District [representative] in Washington, I try my hardest to be just as attentive to my constituents as Norman and Velma were to the movement, a lesson well learned.

—*Congressman John Lewis*

# A Note to Readers

*C*limbing the Rough Side of the Mountain employs the distinctive voices of Norman Hill (his use of language—urbane, polished, and often professorial) and Velma Hill (colorful, passionate, and sparkling with the Southern idioms of her mother's small-town Mississippi origins). The Hills' memoir chapters clearly yet subtly shift the narrative in and out of two voices by one voice identifying itself by referencing the other. For example, in shared chapters, which most are, Norman's voice is identified by noting "Velma and I," and conversely for Velma when she notes "Norman and I." This avoids the rather clumsy and disjointed script style of identifying multiple voices. Italics are also used to indicate a shift from Velma's to Norman's voice and back again.

# Introduction

"Now is the time to make real the promises of democracy."

—MARTIN LUTHER KING JR.

It's a common mistake, one made so frequently when it comes to describing us over all these years that it is becoming easier and easier to understand.

Put simply, yes, we—Norman Hill and Velma Murphy Hill—are lifelong activists, both now in our eighties but hardly retired. We've worked as husband and wife for nearly six decades in the civil rights and organized labor movements. We have organized, marched, participated in sit-ins and wade-ins, and gotten ourselves arrested, yelled at, browbeaten, harassed, even bloodied. We have demonstrated and strategized from Chicago to Selma, from Montgomery to Mississippi, from Washington, DC, to Atlanta, from coast to coast; and then, around the world, including apartheid South Africa, Brazil, and Israel.

In those places and more, we have served under the banner of either civil rights or organized labor—and sometimes under both. So yes, perhaps it is reasonable that many people who know us, or just know of us, tend to mistake us as being strictly between those poles of protests and activism. Yet there was, at least to us, a clear overarching framework that bound those elements to each other, and then to us.

*Still, Velma and I did little to dissuade most people from characterizing us as strictly movement activists.* After all, on the second march from Selma to Montgomery in 1965, and before then, standing on the floor of the Lincoln Memorial overlooking the 1963 March on Washington for Jobs and Freedom, we worked closely with movement giants like Martin Luther King Jr., John Lewis, A. Philip Randolph, Bayard Rustin, Dorothy Height, George Meany, Walter Reuther, and Albert Shanker.

We worked hard as activists, at least six days a week for much of our lives, serving in influential groups like the Office of Economic Opportunity, where Velma worked while I was at the Industrial Union Department at the AFL-CIO. In time, we became part of the leadership of other major organizations, including the Congress of Racial Equality.

*Norman joined the A. Philip Randolph Institute (APRI) as its associate director in 1967, and by 1980, he was named APRI's national president.* It was a post he held for twenty-four years, the longest in the history of the fifty-four-year-old organization, which is dedicated to building bridges between organized labor and the Black community.

*Velma, after earning her master's degree in education at Harvard University in 1968, joined the United Federation of Teachers in New York and became an assistant to its president, and later was an American Federation of Teachers vice president.* Paramount was her sustained and successful effort to help unionize the public schools' thousands of paraprofessionals assisting teachers all over New York City.

Along with the UFT and its leadership, you created the model that led to new opportunities for thousands of "paras" to obtain college degrees and return to the classroom as full-time teachers. Some also made their way to the system's front offices as school principals.

*Norman and I feel very good about what we have been able to accomplish in the modern civil rights and labor movements.* Yet, we long realized that the root reason for our life of dedication to each other, and these epochal movements, was more than met most people's eyes.

In truth, we were, and will remain, crusaders for democracy.

And why not? It quickly became as plain to Norman and me as sunlight melts away the darkness that no meaningful outcome of the Great American Experiment of self-governance was possible if millions of people, by virtue of the color of their skin or economic status, were systematically excluded from participating in that experiment.

This realization informed practically everything we did and do today. The whole of our work, which we share in this memoir, was, in fact—even when we didn't always know it in the beginning—a struggle, in the words of Dr. King, "to make real the promises of democracy."

When many of the enemies of racial desegregation, like strongman Bull Connor of Birmingham, Alabama, may have thought of themselves as patriots in the 1960s, we harbored no doubts that they were enemies of American democracy. We saw the Ku Klux Klan, for example, as no less a domestic threat to democracy as we today think of terrorist groups like al-Qaeda and the Taliban posing severe threats to democracies worldwide.

*Any hateful ideology or campaign of racial rage aimed at limiting participation in democracy comes, Velma and I believe, at the detriment of democracy and its enormous potential for the good of the people.* We think England's 2016 Brexit referendum to leave the European Union, fueled in large part by a rising anti-immigrant populism there, is an example of the high cost of antidemocratic thinking and action.

Global shifts to the right have also been seen in the rise of what amounts to democratically elected dictators, including President Tayyip Erdogan of Turkey and President Rodrigo Duterte of the Philippines.

*Closer to home, Norman and I were greatly troubled by the open attacks we saw on the core institutions of our own democracy waged by the misadministration of President Donald Trump.* We were dismayed by his authoritarian and xenophobic tendencies, his blatant disregard for the rule of law, for truth. We were equally disturbed by his shattering of historically beneficial coalitions, domestically and internationally, and his open and frequent broadsides against America's free press—all anathema to a healthy and fully functioning democracy.

We are sharply concerned by patently antidemocratic practices on the rise. For instance, voter suppression in recent years severely limited the Black, youth, and senior votes in key elections. Most notable are the razor-thin electoral losses in 2018 of Democratic gubernatorial candidates Andrew Gillum in Florida and Stacey Abrams in Georgia. The fact that both candidates were Black also helps to underscore the persistence of entrenched electoral racism, which we see as decidedly undemocratic as Jim Crow poll taxes, literacy tests, and grandfather clauses. Of equal concern is the overturning of *Roe v. Wade*, and the assault on women's reproductive rights.

*Velma and I see the challenge of Trumpism as one that presents the need for more vigorous democratic action, one that calls on a wide-ranging coalition of Blacks and whites and of the LGBT community.* The outward manifestation of this may well look like a return to the rudiments of the civil rights and labor movements that we know so well. The Democratic Party's successful approach to recapture the US Congress in 2018's midterm elections bore witness to this. In 2022, the labor and civil rights coalition helped turn back the so-called Republican "red wave." We believe there is a need to continue to galvanize a coalition including minorities, trade unionists, the underserved, and men and women of good will to stave off looming authoritarianism.

Of course, when Velma and I first met in 1960 on a picket line in Chicago, we were primarily moved by the blatant injustices of racial discrimination we knew all too well as African Americans ourselves.

*In 1960, Norman was pursuing a master's degree in the school of social work at the University of Chicago, and I was a youth leader in the National Association for the Advancement of Colored People in my native Chicago.*

Months after organizing meetings, our first cause was leading effective demonstrations we called wade-ins to integrate Rainbow Beach. It was a lakeside public park and beach that by law, but not in practice, was supposed to be open to anyone regardless of their skin color.

Soon after our work at Rainbow Beach—a popular spot where the brother of the future first Black First Lady would have his new bicycle unlawfully seized by the police—Norman and I married each other.

Relatively quickly, we came to realize that our greater cause was to democracy, that the organizing principle of our work together was to help protect, perfect, and promote democracy. We never deviated from that path and its commitments.

*Velma and I firmly believe that democracy is, by far, the best and most humane system of governing in the world. Yet, like all systems, it has its flaws.*

For instance, how can a man or woman ever hope to secure a useful place in this country if he or she cannot exercise their vote, a chief right of citizenship? And what place can anyone, Black or white, have in this country if they cannot secure work that pays a living wage?

Too many people too soon forget that Dr. King's movement work when he was assassinated in Memphis in 1968 was principally about laborers' rights. He was there supporting the city's striking sanitation workers, who were mostly Black, mostly underpaid, and largely dehumanized.

*Norman and I can never forget the haunting images of the strikers bearing huge signs proclaiming "I AM A MAN."* I've long been certain that you, Norman, gained a special insight there into the close connections of race, work, and democracy.

*Yes, Velma. I was in Memphis at the time to assist the staff of AFSCME, the American Federation of State, County, and Municipal Employees, which was trying to organize the sanitation workers, who had no union to protect them. This* put me in close contact with Dr. King and his work there.

Make no mistake, Dr. King and much of the leadership realized that what we were doing there was to combine the discipline and passion of the civil rights movement with the hard-nosed practicality of organized labor, all to elevate Black men who had been too long held down.

Even before the bullet tore Dr. King from us, I could see how exhausted he was. There were many setbacks. Yet, he never failed to rally himself to press forward. Like when you, Norman, organized APRI affiliates in Louisiana to get out the Black vote when David Duke, the former grand wizard of the KKK, was running for governor there in 1991.

The idea there, Velma, was not only to help demonstrate how much power Blacks in Louisiana had to shape their own electoral destiny by way of the ballot box, but also to show them how to organize and mobilize themselves to make democracy work.

I remember how we similarly introduced Black workers to the tools of harnessing democracy as we helped them organize during our time as labor leaders. For many Blacks, trade unions were their first introduction to a democratic mass institution. And it provided many of them with a democratic experience from which they could learn.

*Norman and I saw this all the time.* When a person goes into a shop, whether a paraprofessional in a school or a steel worker in a factory, he or she begins to realize that they have no power. They learn that they serve at the whim of some agent or boss. Then something happens when they organize themselves into a union: They understand that there is power in a collective. In a union, they realize that they can exercise some control over their work life. This experience teaches them about their own power, and that power is democratic.

*Velma and I saw this phenomenon vividly at work in apartheid South Africa, which, ironically enough, had very strong trade unions for Black workers.* What the white-minority government may have failed to realize was that this organized labor experience helped to create the leadership equipped with the skills and tools needed to transform the country into a true democracy.

Case in point: South Africa's current president, Cyril Ramaphosa, has deep leadership roots in trade unionism as the founder and first secretary of the National Union of Mineworkers there.

We hope we are providing you with a double lens through which to read our book: seeing not only our personal love story but also our love for the work of civil rights and of organized labor, and always our love for democracy, which helped define and galvanize all that we did and attempted to do.

There is a quote of Dr. King's, often cited in fragments, that spoke to the need to work forthrightly in the name of democracy: "We are now faced with the fact that tomorrow is today. We are confronted with the fierce urgency of now. In this unfolding conundrum of life and history, there is such a thing as being too late. This is no time for apathy or complacency. This is a time for vigorous and positive action."

This is how we felt throughout our movement days, and throughout every day that has followed.

Given the current political climate dominated by Trumpism, we are challenged to engage in mass activism, developing a broader and deeper coalition of prodemocratic forces to hasten equality and economic justice in our nation.

# Prologue

What a time to be young, full of promise, and in love. It was 1960. The dawning of a new decade was beginning to illuminate our uneven path to racial equality. It was a journey of heart and conscience so many of us—millions of young Americans of African descent—were making. Along the way, we were finding new purpose. We were unabashed. We simply wanted to change the world and, in our youthful hubris, were convinced that the world would comply.

And why not? Evidence of monumental changes in the condition of our people, of oppressed people everywhere, seemed all around us. We could see it in the courageous sit-in movement for desegregation and in a swelling liberation movement loosening the colonial grip on Africa. We even saw it in the 1956 revolution of the Hungarian people, who removed a repressive regime, if only briefly, in favor of democratic self-rule.

A. Philip Randolph, the regal patriarch of organized Black labor, was taking on the trade union movement, pressing for the AFL-CIO and its affiliated unions to eliminate racial discrimination among its ranks.

Direct action was beginning to melt away the icy resolve of the segregationists, revealing the inevitability of racial integration in America.

The civil rights movement was on the march. We watched years earlier an unassuming Black seamstress say, with a rousing, quiet dignity, *no more*. We saw a young, little-known Baptist preacher in Montgomery, Alabama, step in to lead ordinary Black folks in a yearlong boycott of the city's bus system. Rosa Parks and Martin Luther King Jr. had started a wave that would wipe away decades of dehumanizing practices and customs.

1

Change was heavy in the air. It had a sound, from the silky, exuberant intonations of Johnny Mathis singing "Wonderful! Wonderful!" to the blues-infused stomp of Ray Charles pleading on the radio to have his heart unchained. You could see all this too in the sure-footed R&B elegance of the Temptations and the wigged, wide-eyed wonder of the Supremes, both straight out of Motown, the Black-owned record company founded and operated by Berry Gordy, a former Detroit autoworker. These stars glittered in black and white on tiny televisions, coast to coast, tuned to *The Ed Sullivan Show* on Sunday evenings. In 1960, Dizzy Gillespie was inducted into *DownBeat* magazine's Jazz Hall of Fame. Miles Davis and his trumpet were defining cool for a nation redefining itself.

And there it was too—success and ascendancy—splashed across the covers of *Ebony* and *Jet* magazines in the darkly enchanting faces of Dorothy Dandridge, Sidney Poitier, and Diana Sands. Abstract expressionism found a new, Black cast in the collages of Romare Bearden. In the early 1960s, he and others would form a civil-rights-oriented art collective called Spiral.

Lorraine Hansberry had already mesmerized Broadway in 1959 with her play *A Raisin in the Sun*, her bittersweet portrayal of a Black, urban family looking for a way to escape their hard-bitten lives. Ralph Ellison had won the National Book Award in 1953 for *Invisible Man*. James Baldwin was finding his way to *The Fire Next Time*.

These were days of abundance, of full skirts and skinny neckties. Manufacturing was king. Steel meant US Steel, and anything stamped with anything other than "Made in the USA" whispered substandard. You could see it in a new kind of soaring architecture, in its stripped-down stacks of glass boxes that screamed modern to passersby. You could see it in the cars with their projecting taillights and fins that made them resemble science-fiction spaceships while America was scrambling to chase the Soviets with the real things.

And people were talking issues, politics, big ideas again, debating in coffeehouses, in cafes, and on college campuses. In the wake of the McCarthyism of the early 1950s, the civil rights movement brought a new impetus to academic freedom. It really did. And it was a time when all kinds of young people wanted to get involved in social action to better others. There was a wave of activism that would power John F. Kennedy's Peace Corps and Lyndon B. Johnson's War on Poverty.

It was light-years away from the "Me" generation's preoccupations with itself. The '60s was the era of a Second American Revolution in this country. And we knew it.

In the midst of all that, we met in Chicago. One of us was a native of that Midwestern Oz for millions of colored masses who arrived there during the Great Migration. The other was born and raised in relative ease in Summit, New Jersey. And it was our commitment to activism that brought us together, sped us to the altar, and made us a team for the rest of our lives. No matter what we accomplished—or failed to accomplish— in The Movement, we always had each other.

Yes, 1960 would be our watershed, beginning with our work with the National Association for the Advancement of Colored People and the Congress of Racial Equality (CORE). Our lives would touch and be touched by the likes of A. Philip Randolph, Bayard Rustin, Oscar Brown Jr., Stokely Carmichael, Andrew Young, and Martin Luther King Jr., among many others.

We could feel the start of a general opening of opportunities for Blacks and other minorities that one day was bound to reach into all sectors of national life. We, the young and the motivated, had a lot to do with it because we, in effect, said we don't have to accept things the way they are and we can do something immediately, personally and directly, about the situation. In a way, we became the teachers in a sort of role reversal that showed the adults that we didn't have to accept the unfair, the unjust, or the status quo.

That was the spirit of the sit-in movement that started, for all intents and purposes, on February 1, 1960. Four Black students, freshmen from the Agricultural and Technical College of North Carolina, decided to challenge the "whites only" policy of the Woolworth store in Greensboro. They entered the store, sat at its lunch counter, and ordered coffee. When they were refused service, suffered insults, and had hot coffee poured on them, the Woolworth manager asked them to leave. They stayed until the store closed.

The following day, almost two dozen Black students from other campuses joined the sit-in. None were served. All were heckled and harassed. But soon the press began covering this nonviolent demonstration of resistance. Each day the number of demonstrators grew, from sixty to three hundred, and soon spilled over to other towns, including Winston-Salem, Durham, Raleigh, and Charlotte, then to Lexington, Kentucky; Richmond, Virginia; and Nashville, Tennessee.

While most people thought of the civil rights struggle as being a Southern thing, the movement had no geographical boundary. In 1960, we met on a picket line in front of a Woolworth on the South Side of Chicago. It was a demonstration held in solidarity with those sit-ins in the South. Our Woolworth up north was already integrated. But even in Chicago, people needed to be reminded of what was happening elsewhere.

We had such a bounce in our step, a glide in our stride that spoke of a renewed grace and confidence. There was fun, unguarded laughter, and a zest for the possible. And there was always a sense of mission, the serious business of belonging to a generation of Black people primed to transform everything that had come before it, to step up, speak out, and lift up, in unparalleled numbers and in unprecedented ways.

We were organized and organizers. And we were risk-takers in risky times. But we were also something else: fulfilled.

Sixty-three years later, we are still no less fulfilled and committed to each other and the hard work still to be done. There's no discount, no bargain basement clearance sale on freedom and opportunity. Despite having had Barack Obama, a Black man and adopted son of Chicago, in the White House, the struggle continues.

We have written this book, our shared memoir, in the spirit of telling the story of our involvement in the civil rights and labor movements. Both helped to further democratize this nation.

We offer a narrative that is as much a reflection of our souls and hearts as it is a product of our intellects. As eyewitnesses and participants, we hope that you discover some insight into a history that is much too often ossified by fussy footnotes, arcane academia, and "official" recollections. Nevertheless, we have, for this book, been exhaustively meticulous in researching the landscape and events of our lives together as husband and wife, and as civil rights and labor activists. We have done our homework, consulting pertinent documents, books, and publications to best clarify and verify our experiences and shared memories. And of course, we sought out and spoke with friends, colleagues, and associates whose living memories of our time proved greatly valuable in chronicling our own.

Our story of the movement is a living story, one with roots reaching deep, far below the topsoil of generations that have reaped so many of its benefits. Our story of the movement is one that, of course, looks back, but it also looks forward and is populated with consequences and demands that are as contemporary as the moment you read these words.

# CHAPTER 1

# Wade In the Water, Desegregating Rainbow Beach

It was 1960 and I'd come home from Northern Illinois University at DeKalb, an hour's drive but a world away from my family's home on the far South Side of Chicago. I had again done very well that semester. College suited me, a twenty-one-year-old Black woman-child, each day much more a woman than a child. I had a boyfriend now—a man, really.

He was twenty-seven years old, sophisticated, handsome, and as promising as a new day when you thought you had seen your last. But at this moment, I wasn't thinking about Norman. I was standing in the upstairs bathroom of my family's first home that we didn't rent, combing my hair, and letting a tiny transistor radio set the rhythm of my comb's strokes.

When I looked at my face in the mirror, I didn't so much see me—my smooth, richly brown skin, dark eyes, and effortlessly incandescent smile. No, I saw my Mississippi-born-and-raised mother, and all I could think was, *Ma is so proud of me.* I could read it in her generous, almond-shaped eyes that genetics deemed I should share with her. I could read Ma's eyes as plain as I could the headlines of the *Chicago Daily Defender.* Yet, I knew my mother was also worried about me. Part of it was my going to college out of her sight and reach. I was only seventeen years old when I had entered college. Too young, she thought, the baby of seven children. But I had eventually assured her that lots of kids start college at that age.

In time, Ma saw that I could handle it, that I was getting a good education, and that I was a good girl. Maybe too long a single mother with four daughters and two sons to raise on a factory worker's salary, my mother wasn't comfortable with men. Don't let me lie—Ruby Murphy had a *problem* with men. She didn't trust them. They made her nervous, suspicious. Lord have mercy, Mother was very strict when it came to boys. "Don't sit on no man's lap." "You don't let them touch you."

What she really cared about was education. Maybe it was because she never got a chance to finish high school. My older brother, Wallace, taught her how to read the newspaper. It was always assumed in my house that I would excel in school. One day I overheard Ma talking to someone on the telephone. "My baby is doing so well in college," she said with a glee in her voice that made me grin. "I think she's smart enough to become president."

On this late August morning, I wasn't thinking about education. My mind drifted back to another morning earlier that summer....

It was June. I combed my hair, put on a little lipstick, and hurried downstairs to do some errands. I had to get back home and get ready for the meeting of the NAACP Youth Council that evening. I had just been elected its president and was a little nervous. I was to chair the meeting and we had a guest speaker coming—as far as I was concerned, a very special guest. The council had been asked to join a coalition of groups to pressure both the Democrats and the Republicans during that presidential election year to include a strong civil rights plank in their party platforms.

The Democrats had scheduled their nominating convention for Los Angeles that summer, and the Republicans were meeting right here in Chicago in late July.

We had invited Norman Hill, that guy I had met on the Woolworth picket line just weeks earlier and a coordinator of the March on Conventions Movement, to address our gathering. It was a sweltering ninety-five degrees outside that evening, and the inadequate air-conditioning in a cramped room in our neighborhood community center made our meeting of fifty people feel twice as large in half the space. We were all dressed casually in shorts, T-shirts, and sandals. The meeting had already started when Mr. Hill walked into the room. I had talked to him only briefly when he was leading the picket line, so to me, he was still Mr. Hill. But this time, in this setting of mostly young people, he seemed shy and a little awkward. I immediately began feeling closer to him, sensing that he was someone I could be on a first-name basis with. I remember thinking how very uncomfortable he must be in that heavy suit. Nevertheless, he was striking. He was at least five years older than most of us in the group, yet his sensitive, coffee-colored face and gentle brown eyes seemed to close the age gap. He caught and held everyone's attention—especially the women.

As I listened to him speak, I thought, *I bet he's smart.*

*Although I had recently met Velma on the Woolworth picket line, this time, at the Youth Council meeting, I sort of saw her for the first time.* Velma's eyes were what I noticed first. They were dark and her gaze was direct, like they started speaking to you before her words did, and she spoke a lot. My mother, back in Summit, New Jersey, where I was born, would always be after me about the sort of woman I should marry. She used to tell my brothers and me that she didn't want us to bring any dark-skinned woman—darker than her light skin—into the family. I didn't pay that any mind. I was always drawn to attractive women but was always more captivated by what they had to say when they opened their mouths than the brilliance of their smiles. Nonetheless, Velma had, and still has, one sparkler of a smile. Shortly after I met her, she impressed me as a woman with a lot to say. Sixty-three years later, she still impresses me with what's on her mind.

That evening at the Youth Council gathering, I remember how she beckoned me to the front of the room and introduced me. By the summer of 1960, I had talked to so many roomfuls of energized Black people. I could feel how anxious they were, like me, to change the world, crack it open, and shake out its many opportunities for all people, Black and white. The year before, I had become the executive secretary of the Illinois

Socialist Party. I was an organizer, and after completing a short stint in the US Army in 1958, I became a graduate student in social work at the University of Chicago. Martin Luther King Jr. and labor and civil rights leaders A. Philip Randolph and Bayard Rustin had just asked me to help coordinate a march on the Republican National Convention in Chicago.

I thought speaking to a room of young NAACP members wouldn't be very difficult. I was confident that I could persuade some of them to follow me in a march on the convention in their hometown. But I noticed a slight but discernible disconnect during the beginning of my remarks.

*Norman was a wonderful speaker.* But back then, though, I noticed a pronounced New York or northeastern accent. I wasn't alone. My best friend, Bobbie, who sat beside me, leaned over and whispered in my ear, "What is he saying? Where did he come from? I don't understand a word he's saying."

I said, "Shhh, I think he's cute. I want to hear this." After a while, I didn't even notice his accent.

A new revolution began in the United States when young Negro students, some no older than most of you, went into an all-white restaurant in Greensboro, North Carolina, demanding to be served. That sit-in helped to ignite the flames that sparked demonstrations all over this country.

I was sent here by a civil rights leader whose name is A. Philip Randolph. Mr. Randolph has called for a march on both political parties to let them know that their platforms must reflect a firm commitment to racial equality and the needs of all. We want you to be a part of this movement for change.

As Norman spoke, I knew that I really wanted to be a part of this movement for change. I wanted to hear more about A. Philip Randolph. I wanted to know more about the civil rights struggles. Most of all, I wanted to know more about this Norman Hill. His words reminded me that social activism was always a part of my life. Demonstrating for change was natural to me. As a very young kid, I walked picket lines with my mother when her union was on strike. I remembered the songs, the signs, the solidarity, the overwhelming feeling that everyone was united and marching for something important. I saw a future in Norman's smile, and my college suddenly seemed very far away.

*It wasn't long after our initial meetings that Velma and I started dating and relating, doing our best to see each other a few times a week.* Sometimes I would take public transportation, but more often borrow a car from a friend to drive from where I lived in a rented students' apartment in Hyde Park to Velma and her family's house on West 92nd Street and Parnell Avenue. It wasn't a long drive. And I enjoyed seeing her, walking with her in this practically all-Black, tree-lined neighborhood known as Gresham. I was falling in love with her.

I can remember so clearly our first real date. She had extended an invitation for me to come to her house, to meet her mother, to have dinner with them. I don't know why it took at least a few invitations before I found myself actually driving to that house on Parnell Street. But the time I finally did, I was driving a friend's station wagon, as oversized a car as the suit I was wearing with a bright red, woolen necktie. I was going over in my mind what I was going to say to Velma's mother, Mrs. Murphy. This would be our first meeting.

*My mother and I were at the bay window in our house when we saw Norman drive up.* We watched him get out of the car. At that moment, my mother turned to me and said with skepticism, "Is that the man you were telling me so much about?"

"Be nice," I told her as I ran to open the door.

The dinner went well, and Mom behaved. Soon after, Norman and I took a long walk, hand in hand. It was so romantic, even though we talked more politics than romance.

*I remember how lovely, vibrant, and attractive Velma was in the early evening light on the far South Side of Chicago.* I leaned into her and asked softly, "Do you want to take a drive? Have you been to The Point in Hyde Park?"

*I told him yes, at first, with my eyes, and then I remembered to actually speak: "Yes, that sounds good. Let's go."*

That place on Lake Michigan was so glorious, the dark, gentle wash of waves, the sound of the lake's lips lightly brushing the rock, the lights of occasional ships passing slowly on a horizon too distant and black to see. We were alone. We never left the car. This was where we shared our first kiss. Glorious.

*Those moments with Velma were a special, moving experience of the heart.*

*For Norman and me, yes, I would have to say it was a whirlwind relationship.* It really was. I trusted him. And he had great legs. He still has great legs. We kissed and held hands. But I still don't fully understand why I had so much trouble getting that man to my house the first time. I mean, really!

The second time I broached an offer for dinner—the one that, thank the Lord, took—was after a rather serious talk we had about the still-emerging civil rights movement, the labor movement, and the state of social democracy all over the world. We had planned a vigil designed to get more young people involved in the movement. During the meeting, I whispered to Norm that I wanted to speak to him after the session was finished.

*I looked into Velma's big brown eyes and said, "Yes, fine."* I told her that I would meet her in the restaurant across the street. I had no idea what she wanted, but I was certainly interested in finding out.

*I don't know why but asking Norman to meet me like that made me feel a little anxious.* I left as the meeting was breaking up and ran across the street into the restaurant's bathroom. I checked my hair and put on some lip balm with a touch of color and walked out of the ladies' room to see Norm sitting in a nearby booth looking for me. He smiled when he saw me. I sat down across from him and said it had been a very good meeting.

*Maybe I nodded.* I told Velma that I thought everything was going on the right track, now.

"What can I do for you?" I asked her.

She smiled that big smile at me and said, "I want to do something for you. I know you are from the East Coast. Is it New York or New Jersey?"

I told Velma that I was born and raised in New Jersey, the son of a successful dentist.

"Well, it sure seems like you're a long way from home," Velma said, lowering the wattage of her smile a little. I don't know if I was smiling back. Probably not. She continued. "If you'd like a nice home-cooked meal, you're invited to my house either Saturday or Sunday of next week."

*We both smiled broadly and our eyes were shining as we agreed on Saturday.* He looked at me as if there hadn't been a previous invitation. I had made the first one when I met Norman on that picket line. Norman's baby brother, John, was there and heard me. "You sound a lot like my brother," he told me. "You should talk to him."

*My brother John found me on the picket line and said he had someone he wanted me to meet.* He brought me over to Velma and introduced us. Without skipping a beat, she asked, "I heard you're a socialist?" And I answered, "Why, yes."

*I looked at Norman right into his eyes and asked him if he wanted to come to my house for dinner.* I don't think he knew that I was still living at home and that if a dinner was going to be cooked, it would be cooked by my mother.

I asked Norman again, at the restaurant, because I wasn't sure he'd come, but he assured me that he would.

*At the restaurant that afternoon, I looked at Velma and became inexplicably serious, very serious, in fact.* I told her that I loved our talks, which I had looked forward to. I told her that I had to be completely honest with her.

*Then you took my hand, Norman. Remember?*

*I do, Velma, and I remember that my heart was in my throat.*

*And I noticed that you weren't wearing a wedding ring on that hand.* Then I braced for whatever would come next.

*I told her that I had been seeing someone, that her name was Yvonne Stevens.* But I quickly told Velma that since I had gotten to know her… well, I looked forward to seeing her sweet smile each day.

*Norm, you told me that I was smart and that you liked the way my mind worked and that you loved how I made you laugh.*

*And I said, stumbling around a little, that I didn't know what was ahead for us, but I did know that I had to end the other relationship and see if there could be more for us.*

By the end of the march on the Republican convention—which selected Richard M. Nixon to run against John F. Kennedy—we were officially a couple. After the demonstration at the convention, the NAACP Youth Council discussions turned to staging a "wade-in demonstration" to desegregate Rainbow Beach. It was a popular stretch of sandy beach along Lake Michigan from 75th Street to 79th Street, part of a string of similar parks and recreation areas managed by the Chicago Park District.

The district was, of course, supported by the city's taxpayers, Black and white. But more by practice than by law, these areas were segregated with Blacks having the least access to such lovely places. A vintage poster for the Illinois Central train line depicts Rainbow Beach. It's shown hugging the sweeping curve of the lake with Chicago's skyline soaring in the background. People in bathing suits and sun wear are frolicking there under the rubric of "The Vacation City." Everyone in the poster is white.

*Norman and I knew that Chicago, one of the most residentially segregated cities in America, has a long, tragic history of racial tension and turf wars.* On a Sunday, July 27, 1919, Eugene Williams, a Black seventeen-year-old, was swimming alone along the shore of Lake Michigan near the 29th Street Beach. Chicagoans knew that the 27th Street Beach was for Blacks, but not the beach two blocks to the south. When Eugene drifted across some invisible boundary that separated the white-only waters of the lake from the black waters, some white beach bathers took the unwritten law into their own hands. They began throwing rocks at the Black teenager until he drowned. No one was arrested for the incident, except for a Black man on the scene, probably upset by what he had witnessed.

That night, whites began attacking Blacks in the city as Chicago's South and Southwest Sides erupted into a full-blown race riot. The rioting didn't stop until thirteen days later when the state militia was called in. In the violence, 23 Blacks and 15 whites had been killed, and 537 others—342 Blacks and 178 whites—injured.

As late as July 30, 1960, on a Chicago beach, a Black police officer named Harold Carr and his wife and children were harassed by rocks and racist jeers hurled by a gang of white youth, according to an article published in the *Chicago Daily Defender*. It reported that Carr spotted a white

13

police sergeant nearby, but the officer did not come to his family's aid. Frustrated, Carr ran to his automobile and got his service revolver. But Carr and his family were forced to leave. The place was Rainbow Beach.

*The incident further persuaded the NAACP Youth Council that something had to be done.*

When Velma told me about plans for a wade-in to integrate the beaches, starting with Rainbow Beach, it sounded like a very good idea. I believed in direct action. Five years earlier, I had followed the Montgomery bus boycott in Alabama with great interest. I realized that Velma and her Youth Council were taking their cues from young people in the South staging sit-ins to push for integration of public places. But Velma's leadership had its detractors, especially among the adults in the NAACP chapter in Chicago. Velma brought me in as an unofficial consultant, an adviser for the planned wade-in. It was to be staged before the city closed the beaches for the winter on Labor Day.

*During the meeting, there were two major concerns: Would we defy the NAACP adult leadership who had discouraged all direct action?* And would whites be permitted to join our wade-in? I, with Norman's support, pushed to have whites included. That troubled some of our members. Youth Council members not only worked together, but also socialized, dancing and playing records together. Some of the members complained that whites wouldn't understand us. "They don't know anything about our music and dances," an objector said. "We don't want to change the way we do things for them," another said.

But Norman and I felt very strongly about presenting an integrated group to desegregate Rainbow Beach. It just made sense.

Howard Irving, an executive board member, spoke up. "We don't want whites going with us," he told the gathering. "We want to do it by ourselves! They will start coming to our meetings and our parties, and we'll have to change the way we act. They don't understand our culture. We just want the right to use that beach like anybody else."

My buddy Bobbie, whose full name was Barbara Jean Tiller, replied: "Let them come along. We should not be afraid that some group is going to change us so fast. They just want to help."

After a couple of hours of more talk, we decided to defy—for the first time in my memory—the NAACP adult leadership and demonstrate.

We had talked about carrying out the wade-in for a long time. The adults just did not want it because they were more for making change through the legal system, the courts. They were not for direct action. And they had also been compromised by the political machine of Chicago Mayor Richard Daley. The last thing they wanted was for us to do something that could embarrass Daley.

So when these guys said, "Velma, I think there are other ways to do this," we said—the audacity of youth speaking up—"We don't know any other way."

We also voted to let a group of liberal white youth from Hyde Park that Norman brought in join us for Chicago's first wade-in.

The demonstration took place on the morning of August 28. It was one of those hot, hot—oh, Lord—Chicago days. Going outside was like walking into a blast furnace. You could see the heat rising off the sidewalks, giving even the most brazen of barefooted bathers second thoughts. I put on shorts and a white blouse over my bathing suit. I had to use a towel to wipe off the perspiration streaming down my face. It was not just the temperature. It was also the anticipation of danger. Looking back on it, I was scared. I know you aren't supposed to say you were scared about something like this, but I was.

*I watched Velma slide into the car's backseat with me.* A bunch of us in a borrowed Pontiac drove to her house. Under my slacks, I was wearing some red swimming trunks that were trimmed with blue. I wore a shirt and held Velma's hand as we drove from West 92nd Street to 3111 West 77th Street, the entrance to Rainbow Beach.

*Thirty people—one-third white and two-thirds Black—showed up for the wade-in with their swimsuits, blankets, towels, and chess and checker sets.* We met in the park at the edge of the beach as a staging area, and we could feel that just about everyone was tense with the anticipation of danger and uncertainty. At times like these, you sort of know that what you're doing could get you hurt—maybe. But then you think, and I didn't know if Norman was thinking the same thing that I was, nobody's going to hurt us. They're not going to do it.

I thought back to when I left my house on 92nd Street. Ma stopped me and gave me a tight hug and said: "Velma, I want you to be very careful. Don't take chances and let me know that you are all right when everything is over."

I gave Ma a big kiss and told her not to worry. I laugh now when I think about it, but I told her that the police would be there and I'd call her when the demonstration was over. The naiveté of youth.

*My parents back in New Jersey didn't see much value in what I was doing with my life at the time.* In their eyes, civil rights didn't appear to be a shrewd career move. It looked more like rocking the boat, and they had managed to secure a pretty comfortable cabin on that boat. But I knew there was a higher calling in opening doors for those who have systematically had doors closed to them for too long. I was convinced that Velma was answering the same call even though she was six years younger than me. So I smiled at her when she got into the car headed to the beach and reveled in her passion to make a positive difference in the world.

*Norman's smile was comforting.* No, even better—it was reassuring. Still, I was struggling to not broadcast my worry. I said to myself: "Be cool. Be confident, and definitely do not throw up." I had to set a good example for the others. As we walked on the beach, Norman and I noticed that it was crowded. And everyone was white. People were playing volleyball, kids were running into the lake's edge, families were sitting on blankets and enjoying the afternoon. A group of men were sitting on a high seawall near the water. Everyone turned to look at us as we slowly walked toward Lake Michigan. As we approached the water, it seemed that all talking stopped and everyone on the beach was staring at our group.

I heard someone yell out, "You're on the wrong beach, niggers." I felt the nasty word slap me across the face. We all tried to ignore the hurtful stares and comments, found a place near the water, put down our blankets, and started to play checkers, chess, and cards. Some took out books and began to read, uneasily. There weren't any protest signs. I guess our bodies—Black and white—on that whites-only beach was evidence enough of protest.

Some of us took off our shoes; some peeled off their street clothes and started to swim. I glanced at Norman and didn't go too far into the lake. I just went in and splashed around because I thought I had to be there and watch everybody.

*I watched Velma.*

*The one thing we both noticed was that there were no police.* Anywhere. I told Norman that there were usually police around. There were lifeguards, but no police at the time. We sent one of the white demonstrators to call the police and tell them what we were doing with hopes that they would come. He trotted back to the beach, flashing a thumbs-up sign.

After about an hour, things got quiet, and the beach thinned out. No one was playing volleyball, the women and children had left, and the beach was almost deserted. I signaled the group that we should begin to leave. It was only 2 p.m., and Rainbow Beach was strangely still.

Then we heard it. It sounded like a drum banging. Boom. Boom. Boom. Boom.

At first the beat was slow, and then it seemed louder and faster. Everyone heard it, and you could see the fear flow over us like a fog. Norman and I didn't run. No one did. But we did pick up our gait. We started singing an anthem of the movement, "We Shall Overcome." We could see all these guys sitting on that seawall where the sound of that damn drum was coming from. Its beat was coming faster now, and all these white men, some young, but a lot of them older than Norman and my big brother, Wallace, who was with us, started jumping down from the wall and coming to surround us.

There must have been at least a couple of hundred of them. I'll never forget the face of one. He had icy-blue eyes that didn't convey even a spark of humanity, like an animal's eyes. His face was pinched and badly pockmarked; his skin was chalky, drained of color. Dead. I can see it to this day.

*I stayed close to Velma, who was leading the group.* I was trying to protect her when the rocks came raining down on us and the mob began to close in on us.

*I looked to Norman and could see the phalanx of men carrying chains and rocks and bricks.* The chalky man appeared to be a leader. We were surrounded by hatred on three sides; our backs were to the water. The only way out was to walk past this angry mob that was shouting profanities at us. I heard Bill Hart from the Hyde Park contingent whisper, "Let's get the hell out of here."

We were singing loudly now, and rocks were whizzing by us, falling hard into the sand with a thud. Someone got struck on his shoulder. Then, I felt myself falling. A sharp pain tore into the back of my head and blood warmly soaked my white blouse. A rock had found its mark. My brother Wallace went nuts at the sight of me bloodied and knocked senseless for wanting no more than what should have already been ours.

*I grabbed Velma and picked her up.* I don't remember being angry, just concerned about getting her out of harm's way and to safety. I heard her say one thing in the midst of all the chaos that day: "Where's Norman?"

I told Velma that I was right there as we all headed to a simple structure where people changed their clothes at the edge of the beach and nearby park land. It was several yards away. We locked the door, but we could hear the mob pounding, trying to get in. Suddenly we heard police sirens and then nothing. Someone outside yelled: "Open the door. This is the police. Is anybody hurt?"

*I was bleeding badly.* The police must have seen the blood on the ground leading to the door. An ambulance came. I think I passed out for a couple of minutes. Some of my memories around this part of it fade in and out. I do remember Norm was at my side, holding my hand at the hospital.

Some published accounts of that day said I just got "glanced," but I got seventeen stitches in my head. Other demonstrators had cuts and bruises. As I came out of the treatment area into the hospital waiting room, I was glad to see that everybody was there. We agreed to come back the next week, and every week until the beach was safe—and integrated.

On August 20, 2011, the Park District of Chicago unveiled a historical marker on the spot where Norman and I—and so many others—literally stood our ground for a purpose greater than our own. We attended a wonderful commemoration of the wade-ins that day, and Norman and I spoke about what those protests meant then and now. I believe the marker reflects our feelings remarkably well. It reads:

> Here on August 28th, 1960, an integrated group of thirty young Chicagoans led by the South Side NAACP Youth Council and its President, Velma Murphy (Hill), initiated the first "wade-in" at Rainbow Beach, braving mob violence to do so. This protest challenged de facto segregation that existed at most city beaches and parks in Chicago at the time. Further "wade-ins" at Rainbow Beach took place in the summer of 1961, spearheaded by the NAACP, with religious and labor groups, and other community leaders. These actions helped inspire Chicagoans to confront discrimination across the city, through the 1960's and thereafter.
>
> Chicago is now a more tolerant city, where all can participate in public life. This is a tribute to those 30 young activists and the values they championed: the audacity of youth, the power of non-violent direct action and its capacity to affirm the dignity of all brothers and sisters of every class and color.

As we left the hospital that day more than half a century ago, we saw Howard, the Youth Council member who had objected to an integrated group protesting at Rainbow Beach, helping one of the white Hyde Park youths who had been injured. Howard held the young man's arm and said, "Watch your step now."

The white youth replied, "I've never been so scared in all my life, but we've gotta go back." We did.

About a month later, Norman and I were wed. We were blissfully happy, but the trauma of that day of rocks and racism wasn't finished with us. It would strike again in a bloody fury and claim the most innocent of all victims.

# CHAPTER 2

# A New Beachhead

By the spring of 1965, we had become accomplished activists and dedicated veterans of the civil rights movement.

All around us, the stream of history rushed with powerful currents. So many of us were involved in a mass movement that was gripping America. It was giving Blacks, and progressive souls of all colors, reason to believe that a better day was on the nation's brightening horizon.

Lyndon B. Johnson was securely in the White House. In a landslide, the plainspoken Texan had won the presidential election the year before and in January of 1965 was sworn in to his first full term after assuming the presidency in the wake of Kennedy's assassination in the fall of 1963. Johnson had already signed the 1964 Civil Rights Act, the most comprehensive civil rights legislation in American history, which eliminated discrimination in virtually every area of public life.

Yet there was still much civil rights work to be done in Congress, and Johnson promised that the Voting Rights Act—a twentieth-century guarantee of a nineteenth-century promise of full Black enfranchisement—would be the law of the land in June.

It was in these transcendent times that Bayard Rustin, the chief strategist of the civil rights movement and prime planner of the 1963 March on Washington, asked us to leave Washington, DC. At the time, Velma was director of the DC branch of Americans for Democratic Action, and I was on the staff of the Industrial Union Department of the AFL-CIO, working as a legislative representative and liaison to the civil rights movement. Rustin wanted us to join him in the Deep South.

The Southern Christian Leadership Conference, led by Dr. King, was calling hundreds upon hundreds of college students to Atlanta to be trained to fight racial segregation and help Southern Blacks take the best advantage of the vote Washington was working to ensure them. Andrew Young, one of Dr. King's closest confidants and aides, asked Rustin to help coordinate this undertaking in a telegram:

> April 14, 1965
>
> We are in the process of organizing our executive steering committee for SCLC's summer project (SCOPE). Your name has been suggested because of the important role that you have played in the movement over the years. It is urgent that you meet with some of SCLC's top officials April 20, at 5:00 P.M. at SCLC's headquarters in New York 312 West 125th Street. Please give us your reply at the home office in Atlanta 522-1420 c/o Hosea L. Williams. Sincerely Andrew J. Young Executive Assistant to the President Southern Christian Leadership Conference 330 Auburn Ave Atlanta Georgia.

The SCLC mobilized the conference, in which Dr. King himself would address the attendees, under the banner of SCOPE, the Summer Community Organization for Political Education. Some of his first words to the students were: "This generation of students is found where history is being made."

The program was inspired by the 1964 Mississippi Freedom Summer. We would be trainers for the weeklong orientation that began June 14 on the leafy campus of Morris Brown College, part of a complex of historically Black centers of higher learning that included Clark and Atlanta Universities and Morehouse College, which Dr. King famously attended. The volunteers would stay with local Black families who were paid $15 a week for the students' room and board. Trainers like us were strictly volunteers.

Upon our arrival in Atlanta, we would also learn that we were being summoned to join a group of advisers gathered there to help Dr. King make a monumental decision regarding the very direction of the civil rights movement. But that would come later.

Bayard and A. Philip Randolph, the father of the modern civil rights struggle, were our mentors. They made sure that we understood what they were doing and why they were doing it, and that we had a role. Most of the time, when people mentor, they don't do that. But Bayard and Mr. Randolph were very conscious of who we were and wanted us to learn. They were not hung up on their own prestige or positions.

We were assigned to conduct workshops, as were many others who would also address the gathering. Among the trainers and speakers were Vernon Jordan of the Voter Education Project, years before he became chief executive director of the Urban League and a close friend to President Bill Clinton; Black historian John Hope Franklin; Michael Harrington, a democratic socialist and author of *The Other America*; John Doar, President Johnson's assistant attorney general for civil rights, and Ralph Helstein, president of the United Packinghouse Workers, a progressive union with a long and strong record on civil rights. And of course, Andrew Young and Ralph Abernathy of Dr. King's inner circle attended, along with lawyers, journalists, actors, religious leaders, and educators.

*Norman focused on teaching the students—mostly white Northerners, by the way—the importance of nonviolence.* I concentrated on teaching them how to register Blacks to vote and to better understand the Black community. Those young people got a real education and a real sense of the movement that summer. More than 1,200 of them would fan out and work in scores of targeted counties in six Southern states.

We were all very excited about the prospect of the passage of the voting rights bill, because we thought that this could really mean something in terms of changing the political complexion of the South.

*Velma and I were part of the cadre of resource people.* The sessions would last an hour or so, and the students were kept in relatively small groups, fifteen to twenty at a time, so that we could have meaningful interactions with them. I tried to convey the tactical necessity of nonviolence. I wasn't interested so much in the youth becoming pacifists as I was in their understanding that nonviolent, direct action was important and appropriate. We always felt, especially with Dr. King, that we were seeking the moral high ground. Since Blacks were both a numerical and racial minority, appealing to the better instincts of people by creating coalitions in the hope of building a majoritarian strategy for change was always our mode of operation. We thought, particularly since we had both trade union and civil rights people at this training session, that we could also talk about coalitions.

Mr. Randolph and Dr. King used to say that comparatively speaking, pitifully few Blacks were millionaires. Not many more owned or managed large businesses. Blacks, if they were employed, were employed as workers, laboring for somebody, someone, some firm, some company, some organization, some institution. And therefore, being the most historically exploited of workers, they had a direct economic, bread-and-butter stake in participating at all levels of the trade union movement. And in fact, the core, the essence of the coalition, was a partnership between organized labor and the Black community, between the trade union movement and the civil rights movement. Dr. King once said that Black people should be skeptical of anti-union forces, adding that the "labor-hater and race-baiter is virtually always a twin-headed creature spewing anti-Negro epithets from one mouth and anti-labor propaganda from the other."

Mr. Randolph put it much more clearly than I could when he said, "In concert with their fellow workers, Black people can take decisive control of their own destinies; with a union, they can approach their employers as proud and upright equals, not as trembling and bowing slaves. Indeed, a solid union contract is, in a very real sense, another Emancipation Proclamation."

That was the framework upon which Velma and I conveyed the essence of coalition politics and the importance of operating with a view toward building majority support.

*Norman and I understood that nonviolence was crucial to that end.* Violence would alienate potential allies. We were pushing for the Voting Rights Act, and we needed a majority. In order to get the legislation passed, in order to push Congress into that, we knew that violence would abrogate that effort. It was important for people who didn't feel the moral reason for nonviolence to understand the tactical reason for it.

But there was, of course, violence all around us.

A year before, in July 1964, Harlem erupted with racial rage on the heels of a protest march organized by CORE in response to the killing there of a fifteen-year-old boy, James Powell, by a white police lieutenant. Six days of rioting followed, eventually spreading to the Bedford-Stuyvesant neighborhood in Brooklyn. One person was killed, one hundred were wounded, and hundreds were arrested. Bayard was living and working in New York then. It was hard on him. Norman and I remember him going to Harlem every night and walking the streets up there all night during the rioting.

He would try to talk sense into people, but some didn't want to hear what he had to say. They would scream in his face, "We don't want your fucking nonviolence," and that kind of stuff.

And there would be more racial violence that summer, flaring up in Rochester in upstate New York, and in Jersey City, Paterson, Newark, and Elizabeth in New Jersey. Even Chicago and Philadelphia would not be spared.

Later that summer, the nation would be talking about another Philadelphia. Pressed into service by Robert F. Kennedy, then the US attorney general, the once reluctant FBI and US servicemen began searching for three missing civil rights workers. On August 4, 1964, they discovered their bodies buried beneath a muddy, earthen dam in rural Philadelphia, Mississippi. James Chaney, a Black twenty-one-year-old CORE activist from the state, had been tortured and then shot three times; Andrew Goodman, twenty, and Michael Schwerner, twenty-four, both Jewish and from New York, had also been shot. The three men had been working to register Black voters in the rural South's most resistant racist stronghold.

As a matter of fact, Schwerner was in CORE when we were in CORE. Norman and I went to New York when Norm was recruited to become East Coast field secretary for CORE in 1961, and I became the executive

director of New York CORE before joining its national staff. I was supposed to speak somewhere in New York and couldn't do it. My big
brother, Wallace, who worked on a special CORE task force that used
rent strikes to improve living conditions in New York ghettos, offered
to stand in for me.

There he met Schwerner, this nice young guy, and brought him into
CORE. Schwerner then went to Mississippi, where he was killed. It would
be forty-one years before Edgar Ray "Preacher" Killen, who everybody
knew was the ringleader, was convicted on three counts of manslaughter
for the murders. There's a beautiful, stained-glass window at Cornell University that honors Chaney, Goodman, and Schwerner. When Schwerner
went missing, I knew my brother felt so bad, so I didn't talk about it much
with him.

Then in the spring of 1965 there was the first Selma to Montgomery march, organized by the Southern Christian Leadership Conference
and the Student Nonviolent Coordinating Committee. It came to be aptly
known as "Bloody Sunday." Black voting rights were again the organizing
issue. For much of a century, Alabama—like other states of the former
Confederacy—had employed discriminatory ordinances, laws, and measures, in addition to violence, to turn Blacks away from the ballot box.
In Selma, where Blacks were half its population, less than 2 percent were
registered voters. The plan was to march the fifty-one miles from Selma
to Alabama's capital, Montgomery, to protest this injustice and to honor
Jimmie Lee Jackson, who had been shot to death weeks earlier by a state
trooper. Witnesses said Jackson, a twenty-six-year-old farmworker and
church deacon, was killed trying to protect his mother and grandfather
from police beatings during a voting rights demonstration led by the Reverend C. T. Vivian, a lieutenant and friend of Dr. King.

On Sunday, March 7, 600 or so protesters approached the foot of Selma's Edmund Pettus Bridge and prepared to cross it, despite throngs of
Alabama state police and deputies assembled on the other side to stop
them. The march was led by John Lewis, president of the Student Nonviolent Coordinating Committee and a future congressman from Georgia.
Hosea Williams of the SCLC was at his side. Both men were neatly dressed

in shirts and ties and overcoats that would soon be bloody and torn when they attempted to cross the bridge. Police, some on horseback, and led by the notorious Selma sheriff Jim Clark, descended on the marchers in a cloud of tear gas and nightsticks.

Many of the demonstrators were injured; seventeen were hospitalized. Among them was Lewis, who had been brutally beaten, leaving him with a severe concussion.

*Velma and I knew John well, and we knew that there had been great violence even as we prepared to join the second Selma to Montgomery march.* We knew the prospect of violence was likely, but somehow, for whatever reason, we didn't believe it would happen to us. You can't let yourself think it's going to happen to you. It will prevent you from going where you need to go.

*I always tell Norman that the mind is incredible.* In the movement, I don't remember being hurt. I know I was at Rainbow Beach in Chicago. I was hit hard. But I don't really remember the pain because in the movement it was like you were fighting for something that was bigger than you. And you may have felt something, but it was unimportant. The movement was my family, okay? I felt like all of us who were a part of it were actually changing the world. Right, Norm? What we were doing was important.

By the way, this is one of the things I would like young people to understand. I don't think young people in America today have that feeling about being part of a movement with clear objectives that makes a transition from protest to political action. And that's too bad. When we were marching and organizing and teaching, all kinds of people, Black and white, were involved. We, and they, were a part of a movement that passed groundbreaking, comprehensive civil rights legislation. We don't see much of that now.

But in recent times, we have seen violence associated with protest, like the forced removal of Occupy Wall Street protesters in Oakland, California, and more recently what anti-police brutality protesters faced in Ferguson, Missouri. But there is a difference; these were lesser degrees of violence compared with facing fire hoses, burning Freedom Ride buses, dogs, and "Bull" Connor.

I remember a policeman somewhere in the South grabbing me by my blouse and holding me by my neck. It was violent. But the point is, I thought at the time that he's not doing this to me. It had to do with how I was raised and a sense of belonging to the movement. I looked that policeman in the eye until he let me go.

But there were incidents that did have a way of focusing me on the very real dangers that we faced as activists.

Not long before going to the Selma to Montgomery march, I was down in Mississippi, working for the Office of Economic Opportunity, which was part of Johnson's War on Poverty. My job was to recruit Black students to go north to attend midsized, predominantly white colleges. It was the first time I was alone in Mississippi, the native land of my mother. I was interviewing students and making speeches for the OEO, and I was there without my husband, without my buddies, without my posse, without anything.

So, I'm walking along and felt I wanted a little something to take the taste of Mississippi dust out of my mouth, so I went into this little store. And there is this woman.

"Hi y'all," she said, eyeing me and all my deep brownness with no small degree of suspicion.

"Hello," I replied, pressing the best Mississippi accent I could to slide off my Chicago tongue. I told her that I wanted to buy a pack of chewing gum.

The woman—white, late middle-aged, and looking the worse for wear from working too long in a stuffy, old shop halfway between somewhere and nowhere—gave me the oddest look.

Then she asked, more sour than sugar in her tone, "Where y'all from?"

I didn't mean to, but I could feel my face grimacing. I think I said Washington or New York. I don't remember. Whatever I said seemed to choke her on its way down.

"Uh huh," she finally said as she gave me my gum and change. She looked right through me before she spoke again. "Y'all come back and see us some time."

I left knowing that she clearly didn't like me, didn't want me there. Now remember, in the movement I was fearless. But I walked out of that store and was walking down the road when all of a sudden, I got scared. It was the first time in the movement when I was really scared.

I threw up right there in plain sight.

It dawned on me just as suddenly that I was alone in a hostile land. I didn't have the movement with me. At the time, I wasn't working for the movement; I was part of the government. It just sort of got to me. My mother, Ruby Murphy, used to always stress to me that I always had family, a large one, one that would support me. When I was a little girl and my big sister took me to school for my first day there, she told me not to be scared. "Remember," she said, "there's a Murphy on every floor."

The movement was my family, a large family, too. But here I felt alone, unprotected.

A couple of days later I was supposed to meet Norman in Montgomery. I went to the airport, and there was this little plane, a fifteen-seater that I was supposed to get on. I walked up its stairs and through the door, looked around and sat down in a seat by the window. The first thing I noticed was that there were all these white folks. And they looked like they were Southern Klansmen types. You know, big rednecks. They had on suits, some of them, but none of them looked like any friends of mine.

I sat near the center of the plane. The days of Black people having to sit in the back of the bus were over, so I certainly wasn't sitting in the back of a plane flying to Alabama. Just as I settled into my seat, I heard these white men in the back talking loudly enough for me to hear every word.

"Yeah, that nigger, Martin Luther Coon," one said. "He's coming, he's coming to our neck of the woods."

Another one joined in, "And he ain't doing nothin' but tryin' to cause trouble. And they're sleepin' together in the fields, the Blacks and the whites."

Hearing all this made me really scared. I said to myself, *Oh Lord, well, they are going to throw me off this godforsaken plane. They're just going to get me.* In the South, let me tell you, *they don't play.* I just sat there, trying to be cool. I had a book in my hand. Then this white, middle-aged man comes up from the back of plane and sits in the empty seat beside me.

I kept looking at my book, then nervously out of the window, and then back to the book. But I noticed that he was reasonably well dressed.

"Y'all from the South?" he asked me.

"No," I said and kept looking at my book, thinking, *Here we go again.*

"Y'all going to that march?"

I swallowed *hard* before I answered him. If they find out that I'm going to Montgomery to take part in a civil rights march, these people are definitely going to throw me out of this moving plane. I'm thinking, *I'm going to die. What am I going to do?* I finally found enough moisture in my mouth to speak again.

"Yes, I am," I told him and braced for his reaction.

"I see," he said, then asked in a nicely mannered way, "Can I sit up here with you because I don't like them back there?"

Relieved, I nodded yes, then thought, laughing inside, *Hey, he's going to bring attention to me now that we've integrated the row.*

I made it to Montgomery without further incident. The man, whose name escapes me, said goodbye, and I never saw him again. I also made it to the demonstration but couldn't find Norman at first. I did find Don Slaiman, the civil rights director of the AFL-CIO, a dear friend. I plunked myself in the middle of Donny—a big man of about 200 pounds or more—and five or six building tradesmen, relieved to be among friends again.

I did worry about Norman, his safety, as he took part in the movement. Norman is sort of mild-mannered and sweet. I thought somebody would mistake his kindness for weakness. And I also didn't want him to be hurt. I didn't want anyone hurt.

*Velma? There were times when I worried about her, too.* But I also had a sense of confidence about Velma, that she could take care of herself. I was confident that she would find a way to not let herself be crossed, abused, or mistreated. That was a quality that I very much admired in Velma. In a very good sense, Velma was self-assertive. We always loved each other, but we were struggling in common, struggling to make things better, struggling to achieve something good in society. That, very much, was the glue of our marriage.

*I knew Norman loved that I was so confident and self-assertive.* But deep down inside, I tried not to let Norman know that I wasn't so sure of what I was saying or doing. My mother taught me to speak up; she used to say, "All you can be is wrong." I was young and a bit cocky. But it helped, in our years in the movement, that we had each other. We were always talking. Oh God, we talked a lot. We said, "I love you," a lot to each other. But we mostly talked about our work and how we were going to handle this situation, what are we going to do about that situation.

While we understood the role of nonviolence in the movement, neither one of us believed that nonviolence meant passive nonresistance. Velma and I always associated nonviolence with some kind of action: sitting in, wading in, marching, and picketing. You were doing something. Nonviolence, as Mr. Randolph taught us, did not mean just sitting back and letting whatever happens happen. You were, in fact, taking a stand, doing something, projecting yourself.

Norman and I didn't agree with pacifists like Bayard and Dr. King and others. We didn't think that love was going to solve the problem or that we were going to get those who oppressed us to love us. We were about strategy. We were about tactics. We were not violent people. Sure, we had our schoolyard fights growing up, and we both understood that human beings can be violent and that those impulses must be suppressed. Norman and I accepted nonviolence as a tactic, but for Dr. King and Bayard, it was a philosophy of life.

Norman and I didn't accept that love alone would address the problems of people who had been violently oppressed. If you waited for everybody to love everybody, you'd be waiting a long time. That was what we understood Dr. King to be saying, that you could convince your abuser to love you somehow. I want to restrain the abuser. I didn't become a therapist later in my life because I believed that the solution is to put everyone in therapy and overcome all of his or her problems of racism and misogyny. It would just take too long. I think Dr. King, and many of the people around him, felt that way, that you could overcome your abuser with love.

*While Velma was involved in her SCOPE workshops in Atlanta, in my workshops, I turned to training the students in the use of nonviolence.* And it was not a simple task.

At first, there were the practical matters, like teaching women not to wear long, pierced earrings because when faced with violence the earrings could be pulled and ears torn. A similar warning pertained to necklaces and chains that men might wear. When confronted by violence or arrest, people were instructed to go limp as a form of noncooperation.

We taught much of this by way of role-playing. At times some of the students resisted, perhaps reflexively, because the natural, instinctive reaction is to hit back. We had to put nonviolence in context, which was essential for the movement to achieve its objectives. The young people had to utilize and practice nonviolence if they were going to be effective participants. They had to abide by the movement's discipline.

We remember a march somewhere in the South when Stokely Carmichael, then a leader of SNCC, trained in the tactics of nonviolence, saw a police officer strike a young girl who was marching nearby. We watched him walk up to a tree and just throw his arms around it, squeezing it, squeezing all the violent feelings he had toward that cop into that big, old tree. Stokely was broken up by it. We understood that he understood. But eventually, he couldn't take the unanswered violence. Maybe that was part of his problem. He, like so many younger activists on the front lines, just got to a point where nonviolence didn't work for them anymore. Renouncing nonviolence, Stokely became a major Black Power advocate.

We, even those committed to a nonviolent struggle, had to deal with the ramifications of violence, especially when it is directed at the innocent.

*Norman might not remember this, but right after those four little girls were killed in Birmingham, when their church was bombed by whites in September 1963, I said, "If you are white, don't talk to me for a while." I* grew up knowing that there are bad white people and good white people. But that act was so violent and its victims so innocent, I just needed to be left alone for a while.

We wonder what Dr. King would have made of the tens of thousands of Egyptian demonstrators who gathered in Cairo in 2011 to call for the end of Hosni Mubarak's thirty-year rule there in favor of a democratic system of government. Nonviolence worked there. When the protesters were met with violence, they defended themselves but quickly reverted to nonviolence. Demonstrations led to some labor strikes. They clearly had built coalitions with workers, at least loose coalitions.

One of the things we learned from Bayard was how to form coalitions. When I was organizing paraprofessional teaching assistants in New York in the late 1960s, I would sit and listen to Bayard. He taught us something very important about building coalitions with diverse groups. Number one, first and foremost, we should seek support from groups with similar goals and interests. As we select coalition partners, we should remember, for instance, that if you want a coalition for quality, integrated public education, you should not go to individuals like a Malcolm X or the Black Muslims. Approaching organizations of this kind initially would create controversy and lead to unnecessary fights that delay the formation of the coalition. Number two, creating a mission statement with specific goals and guiding principles that all groups can agree with and sign on to will provide a positive framework for establishing the coalition.

Principled steps he taught me to consider were (1) commit to non-violent action. Violence will only alienate possible allies. (2) Commit to inclusion of all groups committed to your goals. For example, labor, civil rights groups, religious and fraternal organizations, women's groups, gay and liberal organizations and other groups represented by Hispanics and Asians, among others; each group in the coalition must have a vote. (3) Then develop a funding strategy and a plan of action; understand that coalitions are by their very nature temporary. They have a beginning and an end once you achieve your objectives.

Years later, while working with Albert Shanker, president of the United Federation of Teachers and the American Federation of Teachers, I learned something else about coalition building: If you want to persuade someone to join you, don't try to do it with just arguments about what's good for humanity. You can feel that, understand that, but in addition you need to try to find out where someone's self interest lies. If you can find that, too, Al taught me, and put your argument in those terms, you can persuade them. It was a valuable lesson.

We learned something else very important about coalition building at this stage of the movement: that it gave individuals in the coalition a sense of the power to effect change. This sense of some control, or power, helps people understand that they could have more control over their own environment. That sense is at the core of democracy. If you can bring others into that same struggle to control their environment, you come to realize that in concert with others, you can make meaningful progress. That means inclusion. That makes, for example, whites understand the need to include Blacks in the political scheme of things, and Blacks realize that partnership with whites is crucial to advancement. All of which, of course, furthers democracy.

The civil rights movement provided an essential means to accomplish this. That process provided the template for empowering Americans as diverse as workers, women, gays, and other minorities, like Hispanics and Asians. That is the nucleus of a majoritarian movement, which the civil rights movement certainly was at its essence.

In the summer of 1965, Dr. King was about to test the limits of the movement when he asked us to gather at the home of Reverend Andrew Jackson Young Jr. and his devoted wife, Jean. We were told to be prepared for a frank discussion. The house was comfortable, in a sort of pleasantly nondescript way: sofa, polished end tables with ample lamps hooded with ample shades. It was all very typically Black Atlanta middle-class, circa 1965.

*It was August when Velma and I accompanied Bayard to Andy's living room to join no more than ten people, all trusted activists and advisers to the movement.* We were all there to meet with Dr. King. The man himself had not yet arrived. We all sat and engaged in light conversation as we drank sweet iced tea and dined on barbecued ribs.

This was not the first time I would meet with Dr. King. Back in New York there was a group that was known as the New York Advisory Group. Bayard was an integral part of that group. Periodically, he would take me with him to those meetings. Dr. King would come to New York to meet with the group every couple of months.

*I can't say that Norman and I were in awe of Dr. King, but he was Dr. King.* By this time, he had won the Nobel Peace Prize. He had blessed history with his "I Have a Dream" speech at the March on Washington two summers earlier. He was, for all intents and purposes, the leader of the movement that was changing the world; he was a man who had grown up

Black, Southern, and yet unbowed. Dr. King had a kind of gravitas that didn't so much demand respect as cause you to give it to him willingly.

We were all talking and eating when he walked into the room. He was wearing dark slacks and a white shirt with its sleeves rolled up to his elbows. And even though the living room was quite warm—this was summer in Atlanta—he didn't appear to sweat. His face was calm and untroubled as he waved off invitations from longtime friends and advisers who offered to give their seats to him.

Dr. King sat on the floor, crossing his legs, like the Buddha. It was something about the way he sat there that sort of announced him. I later told Norman that it was like Dr. King was saying, I AM DR. KING AND I AM HERE.

The room quieted and came to order without being prompted.

We all knew that Dr. King was straddling a great fork in the road to freedom and empowerment for the millions of Black Americans who had for almost 200 years been largely denied both. We knew it was a serious meeting. We thought he wanted us there to help him decide whether to remain in the South, working to help Blacks take advantage of the upcoming Voting Rights Act, or take the civil rights movement north to Chicago, challenging inequalities and indignities that Blacks suffered there more by practice and custom than by law. So, the question sat heavy in the warm room: *which way now*, Dr. King?

Before any of us could weigh in, Dr. King spoke.

"I am not here to have a discussion," he said, his voice mellow, his words stretched like warm taffy. To our surprise he continued. "I have already made my decision and I have prayed on this. I have a message from the Lord, and He told me to go north. What I want to ask you is not whether I should go, but if you have any suggestions for me once I get there." Some SCLC members supported his decision.

*Velma and I thought that he was very matter-of-fact, abrupt really, in making his decision.* That was not like Dr. King. He'd never say, "I don't want you to talk to me about this. I've made my decision." I didn't understand this. I was thinking at the time, *This is really something.* I didn't know why we were called there. We came to realize that he only wanted to discuss tactics for his move to Chicago.

*I looked at Norman.* Then I looked at Andy, who seemed to be supporting Dr. King; he always supported Dr. King. I was sitting next to Bayard, and I heard him say in a whisper pitched to my ear alone, "Maybe I should give him a counter message."

I didn't say anything. I was still sort of shocked. It was like there wasn't any room for any real discussion. But Bayard was one of Dr. King's chief advisers. Dr. King trusted him, and most of the time when he advised him, he was right. And Dr. King knew that. Everyone would tell you that. Bayard taught Dr. King about nonviolence in Montgomery back in 1956. So when Bayard heard Dr. King declare that he was going north, to Chicago of all places, and concentrating the movement's activities there, he finally spoke up.

Bayard understood that we had been doing all this training and planning and were sending people throughout the South. He refused to hold his tongue. He told Dr. King that he believed that he should reconsider his decision. While both men remained seated, Bayard's backbone seemed to stiffen as he offered a very powerful counter presentation in his crisp, vaguely British-accented English.

He argued that Dr. King had a natural base in the South, that the role of Black ministers was unique and dominant in their communities. He pointed out that the Voting Rights Act would most likely soon become law; he explained that Dr. King also had a unique responsibility to mobilize the Black vote and engage it in mainstream politics to change the political nature of the South. If he went north, instead, he would find, especially in a city like Chicago, that Blacks could not only vote but also were an integral part of the political life of the city. As Bayard spoke, I thought about Rainbow Beach and the infighting I saw within the NAACP there and the entrenched political machine built and deftly operated by Mayor Richard J. Daley. It was a machine that also co-opted or suppressed much Black opposition through its close working relationship with William Levi Dawson, a Black longtime congressman. I wondered whether Dr. King could overcome any of that.

*Velma and I listened as Bayard told Dr. King that Black people in Chicago had more of a vested interest in maintaining the status quo than with working with Dr. King.* Bayard was very clear, very analytical, and very much to the point. But it had no impact on Dr. King.

He heard everything being said. He was a sweet man. He listened, but we could tell he wasn't going to change his mind.

In the New York meetings I attended with Dr. King, there was a free-floating exchange; there was open engagement. But in this Atlanta meeting, Dr. King was adamant, unyielding. I felt that he was, in effect, a different Dr. King. I had never seen him posture like this in a small meeting with those of us who were fellow activists in the movement.

"Is there any way that we can get Dr. King to change his mind, to reconsider his decision?" I kept saying this to myself. Bayard's logic was compelling and well thought out. And I had known Dr. King to be a generally rational person. I was sort of caught, somewhat immobilized, by Dr. King's stance and the inability of a person like Bayard, a man with such great intellectual force, a superb strategist, to have any impact on his decision. I was perplexed. I kept thinking while Velma and I sat with the others in that stuffy living room, how do you deal with this? Why did Dr. King think that he could do in Chicago what he did in Birmingham?

Like Velma, I said nothing. I really felt stymied during the meeting, which lasted no more than ninety minutes. I didn't know anything that I could say that would meet Dr. King within his framework, where he was coming from. I didn't see, at that time or at any other time afterward, any way of moving him or addressing him in a way that he would listen or even take into account any other opinions.

*Later, in the hotel where we were staying, Norman, Bayard, and I talked about how there was little anyone could have done.* Dr. King told everybody that he had conferred with God on the matter.

I'm from Chicago, and I knew something about Chicago, I was thinking. *I remember what happened to me at Rainbow Beach.* And I was wondering, *Does he know about how vicious white Chicago can be?*

At Rainbow Beach, Norman and I had begun an avalanche of protests that continued for a least a year into 1961, until Blacks could finally use the beach without fear. We had left behind a cadre of young activists who went on to various projects organized by CORE. One of the activists doing this work was a democratic socialist named Bernie Sanders, who had been working with my brother Wallace.

Sanders was part of an interracial team of CORE members testing the housing policies and practices of buildings owned and operated by the University of Chicago. For example, Wallace, who is a dark-skinned Black man, would enter a real estate agency managing university property, seeking to rent. Consistently, he would be told that there were no vacancies. Yet when Sanders made similar requests, property managers readily offered to rent to him. This was indicative of the sort of entrenched racism that we knew awaited Dr. King.

Dr. King discovered this soon enough. Chicago was, in some ways, more extreme than the South. When he was demonstrating in the summer of 1966 in those white-only neighborhoods like Gage Park, I'm sure he had some second thoughts because those people really…well, they really wanted to kill him.

While leading a march, what he called "creative tension," against housing discrimination in the all-white Marquette Park section of Chicago, Dr. King was struck by a lethal-size rock on his temple. The blow drove him to one knee, where he lingered before recovering his wits. He got a taste of what I had gotten when Norman and I were leading demonstrations on a Chicago beach. But Dr. King wasn't marching on a public beach; he was coming right into their neighborhoods.

We watched, like the rest of the nation, on the news as thousands of whites, many of them second- and third-generation ethnics—Poles, Italians, Germans, Lithuanians—erupt in an orgy of xenophobia. Everywhere you looked, there were Nazi flags, Confederate flags, accompanied by every racist sign and "nigger"-tipped spear of insult you could imagine, all amid fists and faces of unadulterated hatred. A *Chicago Tribune* article noted that one sign read: "King would look good with a knife in his back."

There is a black-and-white clip of film in which a shaken Dr. King is seen telling reporters at the scene that he had been "hit so many times,

I'm immune to it." But he added, speaking of the sheer ferocity of the violence directed at him and his 700 or so demonstrators, "I can say that I have never seen, even in Mississippi and Alabama, mobs as hostile and as hate-filled as those I've seen in Chicago."

Almost from the moment Dr. King arrived in Chicago in 1966, he and his contingent of Chicago-based civil rights activists—including Jesse Jackson, then the leader of SCLC's Operation Breadbasket; and Al Raby, a former public-school teacher who in the 1980s would manage the campaign of Chicago's first Black mayor, Harold Washington—were outfoxed by the Daley-Dawson machine.

We believed that Jesse, for his own reasons, wanted Dr. King to come to Chicago because it would help him and his efforts there. There was also the Coordinating Council of Community Organizations that Raby ran and helped found. It was beckoning Dr. King to come to Chicago. So there was pressure on him to go north. Besides, he was also battling a growing sense by some, especially young and more militant Blacks like Stokely Carmichael, that the movement was fast losing its momentum, even becoming irrelevant on the national scene.

In a speech delivered in July 1966 to a less-than-filled Soldier Field in Chicago, Dr. King touched on the need to push harder with a national agenda, not just a Southern one. "Now is the time," he thundered, "to get rid of the slums and ghettos of Chicago. Now is the time to make justice a reality all over this nation. Now is the time." He would sometimes call this agenda the "moral reconstruction" of America.

But we would learn more about his deepest dilemmas and contrasting motivations much later. Back on that day in 1965, in Andy's non-air-conditioned home, we found it hard to understand Dr. King's intransigence.

For a while I thought Dr. King was leaving the South because he had been threatened. Sometimes we would hear things, that the FBI had informed Dr. King his life was in danger.

Yes, some historians differ on whether Dr. King was successful in Chicago. Velma and I firmly believe, like most historians do, that he was not. He had a unique opportunity not only to oversee masses of Black people voting for the first time in the South, but also to educate them about the power of the vote and how to use it.

Instead, Daley yessed Dr. King and a coalition of local activists known as the Chicago Freedom Movement into paralysis. Dr. King left Chicago in the fall of 1966 with a City Hall accord of empty and unenforceable promises to eradicate slums.

We see Chicago as a clear defeat for Dr. King. We wish we could have convinced him to take another path.

# CHAPTER 3

# Norman—The Molding of an Activist

In 1933, Franklin D. Roosevelt was the newly elected president of the United States, and the Great Depression was clawing at the nation's throat. One in four American workers was jobless. Adolf Hitler was appointed chancellor of Germany. It was the year that construction began on the Golden Gate Bridge, and civil war in Cuba caused the closing of American businesses there. The Harlem Renaissance had ended. Dr. Carter Godwin Woodson, founder of Black History Week (which led to Black History Month), published *The Mis-Education of the Negro*. It became a literary weathervane that pointed to coming storms as Black Americans increasingly began questioning the systems that fostered our oppression.

In 1933 the average laborer earned $20 a week; gasoline was 10 cents a gallon—the same price as a can of Campbell's vegetable soup. A new car could be had for $500; ten times more could buy a decent house. Couldn't afford to buy a place? A house could be rented for less than $20 a month—if the renter was white. Blacks were likely to be paid much less than their white counterparts while having little choice but to pay more for the necessities of life, a life often defined and truncated by segregation and race-based hostilities.

In a sense, the Great Depression, which began in 1929, was nothing new for most Black people. A. Philip Randolph was supporting legislation that would have required US railroads to hire Americans only, a step to counter the company's use of Filipino workers to weaken his effort to unionize Black Pullman workers with his Brotherhood of Sleeping Car Porters.

And in 1933, on April 22, I was born, entering the world in a minister's parsonage, the home of my maternal grandfather, the Reverend D. M. Lockett. He was the pastor of the Fountain Baptist Church in Summit, New Jersey, then a moderately integrated commuter community of 17,000 to 18,000 people about twenty-five miles west of New York City. People who know me often seem startled when they hear that I was born in such a sanctified setting because I am not known—as an adult, anyway—for my religiosity.

If it puts anyone at ease, the circumstances of my first residence had less to do with piety than with practicality. My parents, Norman Spencer Hill Sr. and his wife, Bessie Dora Lockett, were a young couple living with my mother's parents until they could get on their feet.

And get on their feet they did. In short order, my father became the first, and for years the only Black dentist in Summit. His success earned the family, which would include Julian, born twenty-two months after I was, and John, ten years my junior, a solidly upper-middle-class lifestyle. As long as I can remember, we lived in material comfort, first in a house my father had built and later in a larger house in an otherwise all-white neighborhood on the other side of Summit.

We had come a long way from very humble beginnings. My father's father, for example, was a handyman who did odd jobs to support a big family. My father worked his way through Temple University in Philadelphia.

In our first house, a medium-size residence in a pleasant, mostly Black and Italian neighborhood, Julian and I slept in separate beds in a bedroom we shared. Of course, my parents had their own bedroom. There was also a living room and a dining room, a well-appointed kitchen, and a spare room. The house was tastefully and thoughtfully furnished, reflecting a kind of middle-class refinement and appreciation for fine things my parents tried to instill in their children. While my brothers, especially my baby brother, John, seemed to embrace this aesthetic, I was never drawn to objects unless they were a means to obtaining a substantial objective, such as meaningful change.

Yet even at an early age, I was sometimes perceived to have been materially blessed beyond what I deserved. When I was in elementary school in Summit, in the fourth or fifth grade, three white students ganged up on me. I was walking home from school and had no reason to suspect that I was about to be threatened. The boys surrounded me, and two of them held me while the other one used his handkerchief, stretching and folding it into a surprisingly sharp crease, to cut my face. I was helpless as he sliced this fabricated blade over my light-brown skin.

I knew the boys and can't say they had been unfriendly to me. But we were certainly not particularly close. I had only one good friend when I was going to Roosevelt Elementary School, and he was not at my side that day.

The boys taunted me, saying, "This kid gets every fucking thing he wants."

They were Italian. But I don't believe this unprovoked attack was about race so much as it was about class. They belonged to working-class families in Summit. Within our rather insulated Black, professional bubble, my family lived well. In fact, we were better off than many whites in the town. Some obviously found this intolerable.

My mother, who wasn't an especially demonstrative woman, got very upset when she heard what had happened. She went to see the principal, a white man named Hoff. She later told me that she was more upset by the vulgar epithets the boys spat at me than what had happened to me physically. Mother was the sort of woman most interested in maintaining proprieties. As far as I know, she never publicly registered her dismay over the incident.

In fairness, the fight hadn't lasted long. Once the boys saw my blood, they seemed to figure that they had gotten what they wanted. I was not hurt badly, but I was frustrated by my powerlessness. Sure, I felt angry, too. They were average-size boys but bigger than me. It was three on one.

And I was asthmatic. I never forgot the senseless injustice of the many against the few.

For the most part, though, there were no incidents of racial conflict when we all lived in East Summit. We had neighbors right across the street and across our backyard who were Italian. There were Blacks living in the next block. And I knew and played with the children of Italian families. There was at least one white boy who used to play softball and football with us in my backyard. Much later I would even babysit two young sons of a white architect who was my father's friend, occasional houseguest, and golf partner.

Racial tensions did rise when I was in high school. I was already becoming racially self-aware. My grandfather's congregation at Fountain Baptist, where his photograph still hangs, was all Black. And while I was in my early teens, my father moved us to the more prosperous West Summit. It was not as wealthy as nearby Short Hills, New Jersey, but in some ways comparable, with its lavish colonial, Victorian, and Cape Cod houses and manicured lawns. When we moved to the big house on Passaic Avenue, we were the only Black family in the neighborhood. The 1950s were approaching. Real change was in the air, but for some it was a malodorous breeze.

My father frequently told a story about how there was a community meeting, either when we had just moved in or were about to. There was a lot of heated discussion about whether our family should be allowed to live on this finer side of Summit.

Finally, a white woman stood up in the meeting and said of my father, "If he's got the means, what's wrong with their living here?" She went on to speak of my father's excellent education, his professional acumen, and apparent middle-class values. At the time my parents were also Republicans (they voted for Wendell L. Willkie over FDR in 1940) in a Republican town.

With that, the opposition dissipated. There were never any angry white mobs at our door, no bombing threats like those that struck at housing integration across the nation. That wasn't the way things were done in Summit. For the most part, it was a peaceful community for Blacks and whites. And our family, with its middle-class values and aspirations, seemed to fit right in.

In retrospect, I can see that we were not a typical middle-class family. From the outside, we may have appeared as a coffee-and-cream-skinned version of an all-American Norman Rockwell *Saturday Evening Post* cover: quaint bedroom community in the shadow of New York; hard-working father, rushing off to work at his dental office, where he treated whites and Blacks; mother, the bridge-playing homemaker with her three fresh-faced boys in tow; and those boys off to school to return home in the late afternoon to shoot basketball in an ample backyard shaded with maples and elms and alive with birdsong. At times, my mother and father would go horseback riding, too.

But there was an unarticulated chill in my home. There were few, if any, displays of affection among us. I never doubted that there was mutual respect, but I cannot recall ever seeing my parents hug or kiss. Physical expressions of love, of tenderness, were inexplicably muted. We had a Hill family sense of togetherness, but it was more like members of an organization rather than a loving family. It was almost Victorian. We knew our parents cared greatly about us, but we seldom, if ever, experienced the sort of reassuring gleam of pride and love that children look for in the eyes of their parents. In my house, Mother and Father never offered praise for my successes; at least I don't remember any. This extended from my childhood to their last days, which reached deep into my adulthood.

When I needed something, I instinctively asked my mother for it, never my father. When I left home for Haverford College, just west of Philadelphia, in 1951, I wrote my mother, albeit not very often. Never my father. Yet, he would do things, acts of generosity, for me without my asking. For instance, when I got my driver's license in high school, I came home to find a new Ford I didn't recognize in our driveway; my father announced that it was mine.

And there were the occasional times when my father would take my brother Julian and me to baseball games at Yankee Stadium in the Bronx and Ebbets Field in Brooklyn. He'd buy us hot dogs, and we would have a fine time.

My father enjoyed the fact that I knew the game and kept up with all the machinations of professional baseball. I had been a Brooklyn Dodgers fan, while he preferred the New York Giants. But when Jackie Robinson broke the color line and joined the Dodgers in 1947, integrating Major League Baseball, my father threw in with the Dodgers and me. My father and I could talk with greater ease about baseball than most other things. We seldom talked about his work, even though I would spend some summers working with him when his nurse was on vacation. I know he wanted at least one of his sons to follow him into dentistry. But none of us did. I found no attraction to it.

I can't say I was close to my father, who I resemble in his medium stature and reserve. He was slightly darker than I am and tended to dress better than I ever bothered to. Nevertheless, I didn't feel emotional ties to Father, or Mother. I was pretty much tone-deaf when it came to emotions in my childhood. Such feelings, or lack thereof, seeped into me and stayed with me long after I left home. Of course, a lot of that would change when I met Velma. She remarked recently that she could tell, once she joined the family in 1960, that my brother John idolized me. This was absolutely clear to her. I knew she was right, but I never acknowledged it to John.

This emotional distance carried over into my early relationships with girls. Growing up, I didn't have much of a social life. In high school, which was mostly white, I didn't date at all. I poured most of my energies into my studies. I was a very good student, and I liked sports. Despite playing soccer and being a respectably good third baseman for my elementary school's baseball team, I sort of struck out as an athlete when I reached high school. I tried out for the baseball, basketball, and football teams but didn't make any of them. Julian was the athlete of the family and much more socially outgoing.

I was a shy and awkward teenager. I was fearful of girls. I didn't go to the senior prom and had no regrets. To be honest, I felt relieved, unburdened, by the decision. The whole affair would have required me to reach out, to be outgoing, to be sociable in a setting in which I was ill at ease. I hung out with bookish friends who shared my disinterest in the whole thing. Besides, I was a poor dancer.

Women. I thought about them, but not a lot. Starting in junior high school, I kept myself busy and earned spending money with summer jobs. I started with bagging and delivering groceries for a local supermarket and worked as a general handyman for Bell Laboratories in nearby New Providence, New Jersey. I was also developing an interest in religion, first joining Wallace Chapel African Methodist Episcopal Church, which was walking distance from my first home in Summit. As a boy, I taught Sunday school there while my parents attended Fountain Baptist. No one seemed to care that I had found a spiritual home elsewhere. I studied my Bible and, for a time, seriously considered becoming a minister.

I was brimming with a sense of serving. I don't know how that notion was born. I had no epiphany; I had only the overwhelming need for mission, a purpose. It was very important to me and remains so. This sense of serving formed in me as if it were triggered by a dominant gene in my DNA.

By 1951, when I entered Haverford, a Quaker college, I decided that I would major in sociology so that I could study race and race relations.

From an early age, I was certainly conscious of race and how it weighted the game of living in America. I remember in high school a Black student was campaigning to be the first Black class president. I told my mother about this, and she strongly advised me to vote for him, to support him in his effort to accomplish that. Perhaps she realized that his would be an uphill struggle. I also remember my parents being active in integrating the town's YMCA. Race mattered.

I was also conscious of how my parents' faith helped them stand up to racial resistance and live a generally fuller life. At an early age, I decided that religion would illuminate my path. This belief was so strong that I got involved with a group of young whites who were interested in joining the ministry. They were what I would call evangelical and much more aggressively religious than the Quakers I met at college. Our group would go on weekend retreats and talk a lot about spiritually "recharging and redirecting" one's life. There was a great deal of discussion about translating a life experience into a religious awakening. I was right in the middle of it for about a year, before I began to drift away from the group during my sophomore year at Haverford.

In college, where I began as an average student rather than the over-achiever I had been in high school, I started to think a great deal more about the role race plays in American society. Then, almost on cue, I had my first hand-to-face slap of racism. It was delivered in a nearly empty, makeshift barbershop in the basement of Haverford College in 1951.

My old friend and classmate Stephen H. Sachs, the former attorney general for Maryland, recently recalled in an article published by the *Baltimore Sun* the incident in a speech celebrating the birthday of Martin Luther King Jr. in Baltimore:

> *The barber chair was empty as I entered. The barber, an employee of a shop in neighboring Ardmore, Pennsylvania, who made weekly visits to the campus, busied himself with his tray of assorted scissors, clippers and tonics. He ignored the skinny Black kid who was sitting quietly, waiting patiently. That kid was Norman Hill, a sophomore, one of the tiny number of African-Americans in Haverford's student body then.*
>
> *Norman's presence startled me. I was a child of rigidly segregated Baltimore. I had never been in a biracial barber shop. Shameful as it is to admit today, I'm sure I wondered whether sharing combs and brushes with Norman would contaminate me somehow. Notwithstanding my own casual personal hygiene back then, I probably worried whether Norman's kinky hair was clean. But when the barber motioned me to the chair, I said—haltingly, I'm sure—that I would wait because Norman had been there first.*
>
> *It's hard to pinpoint why I deferred. Perhaps the teachings of our Quaker college called up the instincts of fair play. Perhaps my progressive, liberal upbringing (albeit lily-white) was at work. Perhaps it was merely the pedestrian call of politics—my responsibilities as the elected president of the Student Association to a constituent in distress.*
>
> *At root, though, I know it came to this: I saw the hurt on the face of the forlorn Norman Hill. I had witnessed, and somehow shared the pain of, Norman's debasement. I simply couldn't bear to be a part of it.*
>
> *As I recall, the barber's explanation for not serving Norman—accompanied by apologetic shrugs and pleas for us to understand his position—was that his boss at the off-campus shop didn't permit him*

*to cut "their" hair. Besides, he added lamely, he didn't have the special talent he needed to cut "Black hair."*

*Although Norman and I scarcely knew each other—it is likely that we had never spoken—we left the shop together and took a long walk around the campus. I can no longer remember the details of our talk. But I'm sure I tried to be comforting, supportive. I almost certainly made an awkward attempt at empathy by saying that, as a Jew, I understood and had experienced prejudice. I hope I had the good sense not to equate my relatively benign brushes with anti-Semitism with the direct, personal hurt he had just experienced. I told Norman that I would report the episode to Haverford's president, Gilbert White.*

That is precisely what occurred. When President White heard what happened, he told me that I should go back to the barbershop in a few days, assuring me that I should have no further troubles there. I did as he asked, and he was right. The barber had apparently gotten the word, and I never had any more trouble getting a haircut at Haverford. All of this was done quietly, as if an informal arrangement between gentlemen. Things were looking up, including my grades as I got the hang of the academic demands of higher education.

I had also started dating. My first date was with Helen Coombs, one of the few Black students I had known while I was a student in Summit. Coincidentally, she had been a classmate in my elementary, middle, and high schools, and somehow ended up in Philadelphia studying to be a nurse. And there were others, but not at Haverford because it was not yet coed. I made good friends there, Black and white, and graduated in 1955 with a bachelor of arts degree.

I quickly enrolled at George Williams College in Chicago to pursue a master's degree in social work—again, hoping to serve people. But George Williams proved to be academically uninspiring. I quit.

At about that time, Uncle Sam had a different idea about me serving. In June 1956, I was drafted into the US Army and sent back to New Jersey, Fort Dix, for basic training. I was then assigned to Fort Sam Houston and was shocked—for the first time—by WHITES ONLY signs as I got off the plane in Texas. Of course, I knew what would come to be called the civil rights movement was well underway.

My father had worked tirelessly to desegregate the membership of the YMCA in Summit. Rosa Parks, for instance, was a shining symbol of dignified resistance in Black households all over. The Montgomery bus boycott she ignited was rolling toward a year, starting in December 1955 and ending on December 20, 1956. The refusal of the city's Blacks to be treated like second-class citizens, to be forced to the back of the bus, had propelled the names of Martin Luther King Jr.—whose home had been bombed in Montgomery months earlier—and Ralph Abernathy into the national debate about race and rights and integration.

In the end, the United States Supreme Court found that the Alabama and Montgomery laws that required buses to be segregated were unconstitutional. The implications reverberated nationwide. But for me, the skinny, Black college kid stuck in the Army, racial segregation still stalked in Texas. I was stationed at the fort for three weeks and never left its grounds to take my chances in Houston. I simply didn't want to endure anti-Black discrimination that surely waited in a place as much of the South as it was of the West. I faced no similar threats on base. All the facilities were integrated there. And I knew my stay in Texas was temporary and I would soon be reassigned.

Next, I was sent to Ford Ord in Monterey, California, about eighty miles south of much more racially tolerant San Francisco. I was made a social work technician in an Army mental hygiene clinic on base. It was meaningful work. I conducted intake interviews with soldiers who were having problems adjusting to military life. I especially recall working with a soldier who lived in my barracks. He told me that he was a homosexual. I told him, decades before the policy of "Don't Ask, Don't Tell," that I would help him get out of the Army. I recommended a general discharge, basically saying he did his time in the Army. It all worked out for him.

I made some friends in the military. One was Raphael Hanson, who served in the same mental hygiene clinic that I did. He was a good-hearted character. But many found him a bit strange. He had an odd way of walking. While most people's heels strike the ground first when they walk, Raphael had a way of striding toe-heel rather than heel-toe. He had a large head, and it sloped from its crown and graded downward like a ski jump, concluding at his relatively short forehead. And he was a person who would walk into a restaurant and order a glass of water and bring his own sandwich. But we got along very well. We used to play tennis on the post and go to track meets on weekends. He liked the world of ideas in much the same way that I did. We would talk for hours about education and the condition of society.

These were good times. California was far ahead of many states in terms of its politics regarding race. For instance, there were no policies demanding segregated public accommodations there.

Raphael was also a professional student. He attended the University of California at Berkeley for more than a decade, doing postgraduate work. One day, he said to me, "There's a girl I think you'll find interesting at the university."

He gave me her name and telephone number. I called her up and got to San Francisco on a weekend pass to see her. Her name was Sue Keisker, and she was about my age, a student, and involved in civil rights and other political movements. She was also white and would, for all intents and purposes, become my first real girlfriend. I didn't give much thought to dating a white girl. I didn't think it was dangerous or playing out some hidden desire or exotic taboo. Besides occasionally sitting next to white girls as a schoolboy back in Summit, I had had very little interaction with them. Remember, my college was all-male, so there were no white women on campus.

Sue was intelligent and well read. She wore glasses and had very straight, light hair, but not very long, stopping just at her shoulders. She had sharp features and was not classically pretty. But she had a way, and I was romantically interested in her. She loved jazz, modern jazz, bebop, which I could listen to for hours. We went out quite a few times when I was in the Army. We would enjoy the many after-hours joints that lined San Francisco's Fillmore Street, then thought of as the Harlem of the West. There was much jazz in those little clubs dotting both sides of Fillmore.

They were the kind of places that opened at 2 a.m. and you didn't leave until dawn.

One night that melted into morning, Sue and I couldn't get enough of saxophonist Edward "Sonny" Stitt, the "Lone Wolf." He played his driving style of bebop-hard bop until the place closed. I was off on most weekends, so I could leave the base and see Sue. We talked, but not so much about politics, a subject I enjoyed. I think I got a genuine interest in it from growing up around my father. In time, and in his way, he became quite progressive in his outlook. He was interested in civil rights and the plight of Blacks—much more than my mother was. She had more of a let's-leave-well-enough-alone attitude when it came to race relations.

My father would have discussions on the issues of the day, the problems, the politics. This usually happened during social gatherings, when people came to the house to visit, and tended to involve fellow Black professionals. There were exceptions, like the white architect whose children I sometimes babysat. I enjoyed the banter, and it made me feel as if I lived in a world larger than that cozy corner of it in Summit.

When I got discharged from the Army in 1958, I moved back to Summit and lived with my parents for a while. It was at that time when Sue, who clearly hadn't forgotten me, called and asked me to join her at a conference to be held not far from Summit. I accepted her invitation, a decision that opened the way to my future. It would be the beginning, the prime move that set in motion the most important aspects of my life—even meeting Velma two years later.

The conference turned out to be a gathering of the Young People's Socialist League (YPSL), the youth arm of the Socialist Party. It was an anti-communist and pro-democracy group that fought for greater democracy in the US and in foreign lands, and Sue was a member. The conference was the first real introduction I had to democratic socialism.

But in America, at the time, socialism and communism were considered the same. The Red Scare and McCarthyism of the 1950s had warped much of the nation into seeing red, of seeing threats and intrigue in any ideology that wasn't considered homegrown. Socialism was radical. Drive-in movies were spilling over with alien-invasion B-movies in which the boogeymen and monsters were thinly disguised communists. Most Americans considered communists the enemy. The Soviet Union was communist. Mainland China was communist. And in the minds of too many Americans, socialists were a close second on the enemies list. In fact, any political activity that appeared left of center in America in those days was fraught with dangers.

But I wasn't afraid of ideas. And I didn't think I was taking any risks attending a gathering of socialists near my hometown. I went to my first socialist meeting while in the Army, a talk at Berkeley that explored the question of whether the Soviet Union was a socialist state. At the YPSL conference with Sue, I first heard Bayard Rustin speak. I had never heard anyone speak like that. I was enthralled by his eloquence, his keen sense of analysis, and his militant approach to the struggle for racial equality. In a very clear and dramatic way, in his clipped cadence, he told of his participation in the first Freedom Ride for racial integration in 1947. He talked about his arrest for simply entering the whites-only section of a bus, then being sentenced to a North Carolina chain gang, for something that was a crime only because his color had been criminalized by a specious law.

Bayard explained why discrimination existed, talking about how even the poorest Southern whites had a stake in racism because it enabled them to feel superior to someone, to us. But he just didn't talk about problems. He addressed the conference with a plan, a course of action mapped out to arrive at solutions. He talked about using civil disobedience, as a means to end discrimination and segregation. I was impressed and grew excited at an opportunity to speak with the man.

In the mid-1930s, Bayard had joined the American Communist Party, but by the time I heard him speak in the late 1950s, he had long left the party and had been working closely with A. Philip Randolph and helping him to move against the forces of racism and injustice. Rustin was mesmerizing.

He told a small group of us that gathered around him after the conference that he would take us to meet his mentor, Asa Philip Randolph, the founder and president of the Brotherhood of Sleeping Car Porters. He was already a flesh-and-blood legend, having unionized Black Pullman porters. Mr. Randolph, who had come to be known as the "Old Lion," had also secured the nation's first equal-employment policy (integrated the civil service) after threatening President Franklin D. Roosevelt with an all-Black march on Washington in 1941.

After Hitler invaded the USSR in the summer of 1941, communists in the US shifted a great deal of their attention and commitment from pushing for racial equality at home to pushing the US to join the war in Europe and supporting the Soviets against Germany. At the time, Rustin was a member of the Young Communists League. Consequently, he turned away from communism and toward democratic socialism and eventually to Mr. Randolph, the leading Black labor leader—and socialist—in the country and one of the most prominent Black leaders in America. It was an alliance that lasted until Mr. Randolph's death, in 1979.

Rustin was a man of his word. Before I realized it, he was taking me and a few other young people to Mr. Randolph's office in Harlem. By no means in a modern building, it was a worn and rickety place whose creaking elevator reeked with a familiar unpleasant smell. When we arrived at Mr. Randolph's office, I was struck, perhaps even saddened, to see its threadbare furniture, its dingy state. Yet, Mr. Randolph met us with a radiant dignity. He had a deep, resounding voice and spoke with the authority of a Shakespearean actor playing King Lear. Indeed, Mr. Randolph had a regal bearing that lifted us all above the mundanity of the crumbling headquarters, foul elevator, and less-than-plush office.

He greeted us warmly and then spoke with Bayard with a calm urgency about school segregation that persisted despite the US Supreme Court's 1954 decision that found it unconstitutional. Mr. Randolph and Bayard talked about organizing a youth march in Washington, DC, to call for the integration of the nation's public schools. Rustin explained to us that it was important that young people be involved because they would be the chief beneficiaries of desegregated schools.

I was inspired.

That fall, I moved and enrolled in the University of Chicago's School of Social Work. I also regularly attended meetings of the Young People's

Socialist League. I made friends. I discovered a more comfortable social and political environment among fellow socialists than I had ever known. After a few meetings, a YPSL activist asked me if I wanted to join. I did, and again, felt no sense of risk in this. I was taking a step toward fighting for democratic socialism, fighting to make America as good as its promise. I would never do anything to harm my country. This was a kind of socialism that couldn't be imposed, only chosen, voted for.

In the midst of all this work, I realized that my calling was not for social work or the ministry but for organizing in the struggle for racial equality and economic justice.

One day, I happened to notice in the *Chicago Sun-Times* that Mr. Randolph's plans had come to fruition. The article referred to his first march for integrating public schools. I also noticed that Bayard was scheduled to speak at the University of Chicago. In the winter of 1958, he came and was just as analytical, electrifying, and charismatic as he was when I first heard him in New Jersey.

He indicated in his talk that he and Mr. Randolph were organizing a follow-up youth march for integrated schools in the spring of 1959, also to be held in Washington. After his speech, I walked up to him and asked, "What can I do to help?"

He turned to me and said, "Organize Chicago."

*Organize Chicago.* I was stunned by the formidably tall order. I had never organized anything more than my own affairs. So I turned to my socialist friends in Chicago. They told me that I might be able to get assistance from the United Packinghouse Workers of America, which is now part of the United Food and Commercial Workers. They were right. I was given some office space and a telephone. On the advice of my socialist friends, I started going to after-school get-togethers, to student talks about politics, and social events where I knew I was likely to find students who were sniffing out change and broadening possibilities all around them.

I went to Chicago high schools and colleges looking for young people willing to sign up and go to Washington to march for the end of racially segregated schools.

These were heady times, and I found that I was an effective organizer. I was able to fill eight buses with high school and college students, quite a good number for those early days of mass demonstrations. Days before the buses were scheduled to depart, I received a call from Bayard, asking me to come to Washington. My airfare would be paid and my accommodations taken care of. Then he astonished me by asking me to speak to the marchers. I was not a public speaker. The phrase "unaccustomed as I am to public speaking" never applied to anyone better than it did to me then.

Yet, I made the trip and I found myself in front of 10,000 demonstrators. To this day, I don't know what I said. I doubt there are any recordings to refresh my memory. But I do know that I was very well received and whatever I said elicited rounds of applause.

I returned to Chicago a better man. I wanted to be an activist for political justice, for political and economic change, as much as I wanted to breathe. Social work was out, and out with it went the University of Chicago. I started to work full-time for the Illinois Socialist Party in Chicago. And soon I learned that there was a vacancy in the party for the post of executive secretary.

I began organizing for myself. I canvassed some of the key people in the party and gained their support. Later that year, in 1959, I was named to the post. I also joined the Chicago chapter of the NAACP. Months later, I would join the Negro American Labor Council (NALC), founded by Mr. Randolph to press the AFL-CIO and its affiliated unions to eliminate discrimination in the ranks of labor.

Proud of my accomplishments, I wrote my mother to tell her of my change in plans, about leaving school and taking on a big, new job. True to form, she never responded. Nor did my father.

Rather than dwell on my disappointment, I launched myself into my new job with directed intensity. I started recruiting people to join, depending on their age, from the YPSL and the Socialist Party. I started organizing education meetings. I also urged students to form informational picket lines at area Woolworth stores in support of the student sit-ins that had started at segregated Woolworths in the South.

In 1960, I attended the founding convention of the NALC in Detroit, where Mr. Randolph was pushing the group to challenge racially discriminatory policies in organized labor. When I returned to Chicago, I joined Bayard and Mr. Randolph in organizing a March on the Conventions Movement in the summer of 1960. I was able to work with my friend Joan Suall, who would become a dear friend and confidant to Velma. We were recruited by Mr. Randolph and Bayard and charged with the mission to urge the Democratic and Republican National Conventions to include significant civil rights planks in their party platforms that presidential election year. The Republicans were meeting in Chicago in July.

I spoke to anyone who would listen, this group and that. With the help of trade unionists and fellow socialists, we were able to mobilize some 3,000 people for a rally at the Republican Convention. My brother John participated. At a meeting preparing for the rally, he happened to strike up a conversation with the young president of the Chicago NAACP Youth Council.

He told her that she should meet me, that, in his words, "we spoke the same language."

Later that month, on one of those punishingly hot and humid Chicago days, she and I bumped into each other. It was on one of the Woolworth picket lines I had helped to organize. I was twenty-seven years old.

She came right up to me and said, "I understand you're a socialist."

"Yes, I am," I replied.

"Oh, that's very good! You want to come to my house for dinner?"

Suddenly I found myself speechless in front of this beautiful, twenty-one-year-old activist who seemed to be, in form and manner, wonderfully and delightfully all forward motion.

I accepted Velma Murphy's invitation. In that moment, I had unknowingly taken another leap into my future.

# CHAPTER 4

# Velma—A Path Well Chosen

It was a time when most clocks still ticked. There was nothing electronic about the alarm bells that roused me from a troubled sleep. It was 8 a.m., and I didn't feel like myself. I was in the fifth month of my first pregnancy. It was early April 1961, and I was still a newlywed.

The pregnancy wasn't planned. My mother was unsophisticated when it came to telling me anything about sex. I was the baby of the family, and Ma was slow to see me as a grown woman. She didn't even want to acknowledge that as husband and wife Norm and I were having sex. Thankfully, my sisters were nurses, and they helped in explaining the essential mechanics, but I still didn't know as much as I should have known.

I was a virgin on my wedding night in 1960. I had gotten a diaphragm and had my doctor show me how to use it. Apparently, I didn't know what I was doing. I got pregnant before I had time to learn how to make—without Ma's help—a decent Sunday dinner for my husband.

While I didn't know much about making babies, I knew something was terribly wrong on that Chicago spring morning. My head was seized by a tremendous thunder of a headache. When I stood up and tried to make it to the bathroom, the room spun and I stumbled. Then I saw it, a trail of bright-red blood. My fear detonated like a terrorist's bomb. *Oh Lord, I'm bleeding.* I couldn't walk. I collapsed.

I tried to call Norman but couldn't get him. I didn't know where he was. I tried to call my mother, too. I don't remember some details after that. My brain was like a record player getting bumped by a clumsy dancer. There are skips. I do recall thinking that I was supposed to go to my job. It's silly now, but I was worrying about being late. I had a part-time job at the University of Chicago, only blocks away. My supervisor was Milton Davis, a wonderful man. Years later he would become the first Black president of the South Shore Bank in Chicago.

Weak and frightened, I could only lie there by the phone near the bed. The next thing I knew, Milton was coming into the apartment. To this day I don't know how he got in. He said he called me on the telephone. When I didn't answer, he felt something was wrong, that I wasn't the type of woman who wouldn't come to work without calling in to say why. Milton picked me up and carried me down the four flights of stairs. Then he drove me to the hospital. If he hadn't, I'm sure I would have died that morning.

Doctors at Cook County Hospital said I had suffered an arterial embolism; a weakened blood vessel in my head had burst. They repaired the artery, but the damage caused some paralysis on my right side. My arm, my leg, my everything, on that side of me was numb, lifeless.

It was as if half of me belonged to someone else. That frightened me terribly. But what came next shook me to my core. I learned that I had lost a great deal more than feeling and mobility. I knew this before anyone in a white coat and a face full of sympathy could tell me. I had lost the baby.

The doctors told me that our baby did not survive and had to be removed. I have the maternal scar. They also told me, in no uncertain terms, that I should never get pregnant again, that I should never have children. The strain of childbirth would be too great on that artery that had been first weakened, doctors said, by the rock to my head when I was leading the protests at Rainbow Beach. Bringing a new life into this world would cost me my own.

I was depressed, but I wasn't angry. I wasn't mad about Rainbow Beach and what we did there. I was mad that I wasn't going to have children. I was twenty-two years old. I wanted a lot of babies; I wanted to be like my mother. Norm didn't. He was interested in changing the world. And I figured I could change the world and have a couple of babies too. But in a sense, I am glad I didn't have those children. If I had, I know I wouldn't have been able to accomplish what I did in the movement, what I accomplished in my life with Norman.

When my mother found out what happened to me, she rushed to the hospital. She was very upset, of course. And believe it or not, she was very upset with Norm because he had gotten me pregnant. As soon as I was able to leave the hospital, my mother and my sisters brought me to the house on the South Side, 9216 Parnell Avenue, where we all had lived together in a kind of socialist commune where Ma was the boss. Norman was no longer welcome, so he returned to our apartment in Hyde Park and became depressed living in our first home together without me. Doctors said I would not be permitted to go back to the apartment until I was able to walk up the building's four flights of stairs. That would take a while.

I was settled into an upstairs bedroom near the bathroom in my family's house. Lying there, resting and recovering and getting such loving attention, I couldn't help reminiscing about how Ruby Murphy, a single mother, and her six children landed in that handsome, split-level house in an elm-shaded neighborhood of lower-middle-class Black strivers, and some white ones. The area was known then, as it is today, as Gresham.

Before that, we lived in a crowded and crumbling Chicago ghetto on La Salle Street near Comiskey Park, the famous home of the Chicago White Sox. It was built in 1910 on the site of a city dump by the team's owner, Charles Comiskey. In 1937, Joe Louis fought there, defeating the heavyweight champion, James J. Braddock, known as the "Cinderella Man." The fight ended with an eighth-round knockout, crowning Louis, the pride of Black people just about everywhere, the champion and probably one of the first African-American national heroes shared by Blacks and whites.

I was born the next year.

One of my earliest memories is that grass wouldn't grow where we lived. The yards...everywhere that wasn't concrete was just dirt. There was no grass in front of our place, a two-bedroom, cold-water apartment in a four-family building. There was no grass along our whole street. It was as if all our grass had been gathered up in the dead of the night, carried off a long time ago, and used to pave this great field of emerald green once known as the "Baseball Palace of the World." On some warm nights we could hear the cheers of the tens of thousands of people jammed inside, behind the stadium's high walls, to see the likes of Luke Appling and Ted Lyons.

Two houses separated our apartment building from a vacant lot that was filled with sand, the backyard of a sandblasting company on the adjacent street. Sometimes the blowing sand gave our streets an eerie gray cast. But the lot was the neighborhood children's Sahara Desert, our bikes were camels, and we were Arab conquerors at war. Sometimes, depending on our mood or what adventures we last heard on the radio, we'd be Vagabond Kings. Sometimes I'd even sing the radio serial's theme song:

*Men of toil and danger*
*Will you serve a stranger*
*And bow down to Burgundy*

Across the street, there was a Mack Truck open-air parking and docking facility. It had a small, wooden attached office with a hulking, craggy, unkempt man inside who watched over the trucks like a gambler counting his chips. This place of sand, of fumes from the heavy scent of gasoline and choking smoke from the trucks, was our playground.

There were so many kids. And like my siblings and me, so many kids had fathers as absent as the grass. I didn't know where all the daddies were. I only knew that my own, Wilson Murphy, had died weeks after I was born. For a long time, I lived with half-a-joke of a notion that when I was born, my daddy took one look at me and said, "Oh, boy," then dropped dead from disappointment.

My father was from Texas and was traveling in Mississippi when he met my mother. Ruby Truss was born in Kosciusko, Mississippi, a small town of fields and few flush toilets at the time. It was also where Oprah Winfrey, another Black girl who would make Chicago her home, was born. My parents got married in 1928, and my father soon after brought her to Chicago in the Great Migration, joining millions of Southern Blacks moving north in the hopes of starting new, more promising lives. Ruby never lost her honey-thick Southern accent. She was twenty-eight years old when I was born. My father was fifty.

I know very little for certain about my father, mostly just what I have been told. I do know, of course, that he and my mother had four girls and two boys and another child who died before I was born. Through much of my childhood, I was told that my daddy was a minister. I found out soon enough that he had been a bootlegger, selling liquor out of our back door. And I found out too that he was not a man to be trifled with.

Once, a man in our neighborhood, I was told, insulted my mother. When my father heard about this, he went right up to the man's house and banged on his front door. Just as the door opened, my father punched the man right in the face, ka-POW, and that was that.

A heart attack took my father too soon to leave us with much more than colorful stories and fading memories of him. My mother told me that she cried and cried when Daddy died. She didn't know what she was going to do without him.

His death left Ma, a quiet-natured woman who wore her hair in a long, single braid that fell past her shoulders, to raise and provide for all of us. And she did, even if there were times when I had to plug holes in my shoes with newspaper. But I didn't feel particularly poor, even though we definitely were. I never remember being hungry, for instance. In fact, one of my most vivid memories is of the delicious invitation of Ma's biscuits baking in the oven. That aroma…oh my goodness. We all loved her biscuits. They were firm, with a thin brown crust on the bottom, just-beige-enough tops and fluffy, soft centers. They were so good—great for sopping syrup or gravy or eaten dripping with butter.

My mother had a reputation for not tolerating nonsense, but we knew she had a generous spirit. Some of the kids who lived around us seemed afraid of her. But that didn't stop some of them from slipping through our back door and stealing a handful of hot dogs my mother simmered in a big pot over a low flame. She pretended she didn't see them. They loved those hot dogs as much as they loved the thrill of escaping being caught by Mrs. Murphy.

Bobbie Jean Tiller was my best friend in those days and would remain a dear friend her whole life. Bobbie joined the NAACP Youth Council in Chicago and joined me in the wade-ins at Rainbow Beach. Back then, in the late 1940s, she lived in the apartment behind ours. Many decades later she lived in a building in the same high-rise co-op complex in Manhattan where Norman and I live today. Bobbie passed away in 2002, and I miss her terribly. She was sixty-five years old.

Back when we were kids, she and I rode our bikes across the great sands of the vacant lot. And we transformed my living room into a make-believe jungle where we played Tarzan with my youngest brother, Wilson. Ma would sometimes make her go home, which was a quick exit through our back door to her front door.

I can hear Ma now. "Bobbie Jean, you and Velma are making too much noise. It's late and you have to go home now."

My mother liked Bobbie, who was my age. But Ma always seemed to find a reason not to associate with Bobbie's mother—or any of the other mothers on our street.

"Bobbie's mother," she'd say, "drinks beer, has parties with liquor, and plays blues records. She also has male visitors."

All of that constituted major no-no's with my mother. Ma discouraged men from hanging around the apartment, especially around her blossoming daughters. I must have realized, even as a child, that men noticed my mother. She was beautiful, tall and slender and had a penetrating look in her eyes that frightened some men and entranced others. My mother was impossible to ignore. And she remained impossible to ignore until her last days as a stern yet sweet woman of remarkably self-made substance.

Yet, with all of my mother's strength, she was very cautious, perhaps even fearful, when it came to men. And drinking? I don't remember much alcohol of any kind around her or our home when I was growing up. She favored classical and religious music and would sometimes turn to country stations on the radio.

Ma's word was law, so I didn't go over to Bobbie's house much. And I liked her mother. She always gave me lots of hugs and kisses. But that was just the way things were. My mother was always looking out for what she thought was best for the Murphys.

She always told us to "stay together and stick together. The world outside is hard and dangerous, but you have your family. We have to depend on each other. Be nice but don't let anybody push you around." Her parting words each school day were, "Now, get a good education and don't do anything to make me have to take a day off work to come to school, or you'll be in real trouble."

We all knew that "real trouble" meant a nasty date with a long, black belt that she kept on a hook on the kitchen door.

Ma was a punch-press operator in a Near South Side factory and a trade unionist. This meant that she often left my oldest sister, Wardine, in charge. We called her Dino, and she made sure that we got cleaned up and got to school on time and that the house was locked up when the last of us left. Ma and Wallace were the first to get up. Ma put on large pots of water for us to wash up with before school, and Wallace walked our dog, Butch, and went to the bakery to buy sweet rolls and milk to eat with our morning oatmeal.

The nights before, I would watch Ma comb her long, natural hair beside the black potbelly coal stove. She often would sing or hum songs from church. The coals burned down as we slept, the boys and girls in separate rooms off the dining room, where Ma slept on a folding bed by the stove. My sister Thelma, who I always thought was the smartest among us, would read to me and tell me stories about Greek gods. She would read some, and then she'd make up her own stories about Zeus, Apollo, Poseidon, and their lives on Mount Olympus. Because I was the youngest, my sisters took turns babysitting me. It all helped us fulfill my mother's chief directive: stick together.

We were together, whether we were sitting on the floor or on old chairs listening to radio programs like *Grand Central Station, The Inner Sanctum, Symphony of the Air,* and *Grand Ole Opry.* The radio was big in our home. We all liked *Let's Pretend* and the Lux Radio Theater weekly presentations of *The Vagabond King*. We were together when we marched to the public library or the movies singing songs we heard on the radio.

I always fell behind because my legs were so short. We were like stair steps—each a little taller than the other because we were all born about one or two years apart. I was always running to catch up, trotting to a chorus of "C'mon, try to keep up, Velma."

Looking back, I have to say I was a darling little brown girl. Some in my family called me their "little chocolate drop." But by the time I got to school, I was surprised to hear that some of the other kids called me chocolate drop too. *How did they know?* Soon enough, I learned that in their bitter mouths the term was not one of endearment. Not at all. The sad truth was that even among Black kids, any skin darker than their own was a target for ridicule and mockery. Racism's wound of Black self-hatred was just that tragically deep.

When I was a young girl, I remembered hearing two little boys arguing in the playground. One called the other a "black motherfucker," and he angrily responded, "I ain't black!" The wound *is* that deep. But not only was my skin brown, it was also thick. I just went on about my business, secure in my mother's words to all her children, "You are all beautiful in every shade."

I had this smile that, when I was a kid, I thought had something magical about it. It didn't. It was just a big, friendly smile, and when I flashed it, even people I didn't know would stop and say hi and offer me their own smiles.

Even today when I walk down the street, strangers, see my smile and say hi to me. And I always say hello back to them.

When I was in elementary school, I witnessed something that dimmed my smile and put just about everything my mother instilled in me—self-reliance, self-confidence, courage, and the utmost respect for truth—to the test.

I went to Webster Elementary School, a predominantly Black school that featured a large mural of the Black 54th Massachusetts Regiment that fought in the Civil War, depicted in the film *Glory*. But most of Webster's teachers and administrators were white. One day, while standing with my classmates at the top of a stairwell, I saw a principal get irritated with a boy who wouldn't stand still in line. The next thing I knew, the principal pushed the boy, who was Black, down the stairs. He even called him a name, something like "little monkey."

The boy got hurt but not seriously. I knew I wasn't the only one who saw what happened. The boy's mother lodged a formal complaint; I found myself suspiciously the sole eyewitness. The principal had tracked down the parents of all the potential witnesses and persuaded them not to let their children say a word. I don't know if he promised anybody anything for their silence. I just know that when he got to my mother and me, we refused. I saw what I saw, and I knew it was wrong. I could not be moved. I was in the fourth grade.

I was called to testify at a hearing that was not held at the school, not in a courtroom either, but I remember it being very official. I was scared as I walked to the front of this big, stuffy room to say exactly what I saw. Everybody was looking at me. I was holding my mother's hand as I walked, and she was squeezing my hand. That let me know that everything was going to be okay. She told me to just go up there and tell the truth. That was Ma. A man started asking me questions, and I smiled. But my smile had no magic that day. The man didn't smile back. In fact, no one was smiling at me—except Ma. I told the man what happened, and someone later asked my mother if she thought I was telling the truth. "If Velma said it happened, it happened. My Velma doesn't lie," she replied without hesitation.

The principal didn't lose his job, but something bad must have happened to him. I had trouble with him for the rest of my years at Webster, which was long ago torn down along with our old house on LaSalle Street. When I was about to graduate to high school, I was told that I had been named the eighth-grade class valedictorian. I was elated. I was a very good student and was looking forward to delivering the valedictorian speech, which was part of the honor.

But soon I was told that no, another girl—a light-skinned girl everyone called Piggy, not for her size (she wasn't overweight) but for the huge, thick pigtail she wore—would have the privilege that year. I knew that the principal was behind the scheme. But I wouldn't stand for that. After all, Piggy was second in the class, and the Murphys were going to be in the audience and they expected me, the first in the class, to speak. After some protests, the school reversed its decision, and I gave that valedictorian speech.

I was a precocious kid. I guess I couldn't help it. I spent so much time with my older siblings and, through them, was exposed to so much, like discussions of civil rights and Pan-Africanism. I babysat for my sisters' friends. They were communists. The result was an expanded vision. I realized, for example, that the world was much bigger than what I could see day to day in the ghetto.

My sisters Thelma and Alice were very politically involved. They were always trying to integrate things. Our neighborhood bordered another that was mostly Italian and Eastern European and strictly off limits to Blacks. There was a movie theater there that didn't allow Blacks inside—unless, I guess, they were there to clean the bathrooms or something. My sisters were part of a group called the Civil Rights Committee, an integrated local group that was trying to break down segregation in the area. The committee was believed to be a front group for the Communist Party, which was quite serious about helping Black people getting into those restricted theaters as patrons.

At the time, dealing head-on with the "Negro question" was important to the communists. During these attempts to open the theaters to us, people sometimes got beat up for their efforts. I would want to go on these integration missions too, but my sisters never let me, telling me that I was too young and the work was too dangerous.

Nonetheless, they inspired me. When they weren't looking, Bobbie and I would sometimes sneak across that racial divide. One time someone set their dog on us. We ran back to our side, laughing and feeling some satisfaction that we had kicked, in our own way, at the bricks of racial segregation.

My mother tended toward activism herself. As an active member of the Mine, Mill and Smelter Workers Union at her factory, she was no stranger to picket lines. She used to take me to the demonstrations and other kinds of labor activities when I was young. I remember people singing labor songs; I remember those feelings of solidarity, of a cause. Perhaps I had no choice in becoming the kind of woman I became. Activism was in my blood and in my life as far back as I can remember.

When I was eleven years old, I was giving speeches in Washington Park in Chicago. I was talking about the revolution coming. I didn't know what I was talking about. Yet people would come by and listen to me. I thought I was saying something.

Because my mother's union was pretty much run by communists, I got to know a lot of so-called radicals. This was in the late 1940s and early 1950s, an era in America when communists were seen as scary, un-American, thinly disguised Soviet agents (and some actually were). This was when the Cold War was moving toward its most frigid phase. It was not unusual for members of the Communist Party to be involved in the labor movement, especially in large American cities like Chicago. I had free and open conversations with these people, whom I enjoyed probing. Paul Robeson, the Black activist and international icon of stage, screen, and song, came to our home in Chicago once. He had this deep, rumbling voice even when he spoke to you.

As handsome and commanding as he was, I did not admire him. I didn't like his politics. He and other communists we knew were hard-liners. I could not find any rational basis for Robeson's unwavering support for the communist leadership of the Soviet Union, in one moment applauding Joseph Stalin's alignment with Adolf Hitler at the predawn of World War II and then calling for the US to support the USSR once Germany stabbed the Soviets in the back by invading them, opening one of the bloodiest fronts of the war. Even closer to home for me was Robeson's blind allegiance to the Communist Party when it shifted its advocacy for Black civil rights in America to an all-out defense of Stalinism.

I would ask Robeson and his fellow communists questions that they didn't want to answer, like, "Who's Trotsky?" And somebody in the room would invariably say, "Oh, he was a disrupter," following the Stalinist line, even while knowing that Stalin had Trotsky, a political exile, assassinated in Mexico. I could never accept the kind of intellectual tyranny that the communists embraced so tightly. I was much more the free thinker. My mother encouraged this in me and told me all the time that I would do great things for my people, for my country. Maybe become a doctor. Maybe something more.

I'll tell you about another handsome man who walked into my life and turned my head—oh, good gracious, he was so fine. He looked as though he had just stepped out of a Hollywood movie.

When I was twelve years old or so there was this nice woman who had a big house within walking distance on the South Side. She was Southern-born like my mother, from Louisiana, I think. She was classy, well-educated, and into the arts, especially African and African-American arts. She went on to become quite famous in Chicago as Margaret Taylor-Burroughs, the cofounder of what is now known as the DuSable Black History Museum and Education Center.

That all started in 1961 in her living room on South Michigan Avenue, with her husband, Charles Burroughs, a teacher and poet who spoke fluent Russian. Before that, she created an arts program for young people in the community. In the mid-1950s, I was one of those young people.

Mrs. Burroughs seemed to know everybody. Through her, I met the distinguished singer and songwriter Oscar Brown Jr. and Lorraine Hansberry, another Black girl from Chicago, before she recast Broadway with her seminal play, *A Raisin in the Sun*.

My best friend, Bobbie, two of my sisters—Alice and Thelma—and I, with a few older girls around my sisters' age, were among the many young people attending Mrs. Burroughs's art program. It exposed us to so much. There was poetry, music, and dance in classes that included the rumba and the tango. We'd sing and talk about civil rights, art and history too. We called ourselves the Ebonettes. Mrs. Burroughs gave us a chance to do in the ghetto what most kids didn't get to do in the ghetto. It was wonderful.

She held special breakfasts for us at her house. We'd sometimes meet there for a meal and to sit around and talk with her. She always asked us what we wanted to do with our lives. She always talked about possibilities. One Sunday morning at her house with the other Ebonettes and a few other people, I was eating breakfast and saw this blindingly good-looking young man standing in the kitchen's doorway. He was the color of caramel and wore a smile so perfect it should have been framed.

I remember being so struck that the scrambled eggs and Canadian bacon I was chewing fell out of my mouth and onto the kitchen floor. Here I was just a little girl, and standing before me was this grown man sweeping me up in something I didn't understand. I couldn't take my eyes off him.

"Say hello, girls," I heard Mrs. Burroughs say like she was speaking from another world. "This is Harry Belafonte."

I'm sure Mrs. Burroughs said more than that, but I don't remember anything more than looking at my sisters and the rest of the Ebonettes looking up at Harry Belafonte just as I had seconds ago. They were dumbstruck—literally. He said, "Hello," and none of them said anything. He was that gorgeous, standing there in slacks tight at his narrow waist and a shirt that accentuated his manly shoulders and arms. There might have been a button or two undone at his chest, too.

By the time we got back home, my sisters and I were all abuzz about "Harry." Mrs. Burroughs told us that in a few days he was going to perform in her living room, and that we were all invited to hear him sing. My sisters and I were all so excited and were quickly obsessed with getting new outfits. We all had an instant crush on Harry Belafonte and dreamed, not so privately, about catching his eye and marrying him—every one of the Ebonettes.

Poor Ma. We pestered and pestered her to buy us new clothes and get our hair done for the concert.

She didn't seem to understand what all the fuss was about. "You are all very beautiful just like you are," she said.

But my sisters and I dismissed that out of hand. "We really have to look good," my sister Alice insisted.

"Okay," my mother relented. "Let's see what we can do."

We all arrived at Mrs. Burroughs's home looking very, very pretty in our new dresses, blouses, and shorts and hairstyles. We were seated and almost vibrating with excitement. Then Harry Belafonte strolled in on a wave of applause. He sat at the piano and began to sing. My sisters and I were all swooning and smiling. I think Bobbie giggled a little. Harry's voice was intoxicating.

He sang three songs. The one I remember most is "Suzanne (Every Night When the Sun Goes Down)." I was captivated. And then, in a single moment, the spell was broken.

Harry spoke directly to the audience and asked *his wife*, Marguerite Belafonte, to stand up. She did. And I was crestfallen. We were all almost in tears.

No one, not even Ma, told us that he was married. I should have done my homework on that one.

I went to Wendell Phillips High School in the nearby Bronxville neighborhood of Chicago. It was, and remains, a beautifully imposing, dark brick building designed in the classical revival style. When it first opened its doors in 1904, it had only a smattering of Black students. But by 1920, Phillips had become the city's first predominantly Black high school.

Somehow that seemed right. The school, which takes up a whole city block along East Pershing Road, was named for a leading abolitionist who criticized Abraham Lincoln for moving too slowly to emancipate enslaved Africans in America. Wendell Phillips High School quickly established a solid academic reputation and a penchant for winning basketball games. In the 1920s, the school had a series of winning basketball teams that, according to the school's historians, created the nucleus that led to the formation of the Harlem Globetrotters.

So many African Americans who would contribute so much to the world passed through Phillips High and its expansion schools, including entertainment legends Nat "King" Cole and Dinah Washington; John H. Johnson, the founder of Johnson Publications; and Alonzo S. Parham, who entered West Point in July 1929 as the only African American in his class (he did not graduate from the academy, however). Some years before I arrived at Phillips in 1952, Maudelle Brown Bousfield ended her long tenure there as the first African-American principal of a Chicago public school.

I knew very little of any of this when I got to Phillips. I mostly knew that the school was known for preparing the college-bound. And from a very early age, I knew I was college-bound. Bobbie and my brother Wallace went to Dunbar Vocational High School. I made new friends quickly at Phillips and became popular. I found my way into musical theater, acting and singing. I even got a scholarship to the city's Goodman Theater. But an acting coach told me in confidence that I shouldn't expect, given the backhand of racism that most Black entertainers faced in the 1950s, to get the sort of roles my talents deserved.

I was awarded a scholarship and decided to go to Northern Illinois University, about sixty miles and a telephone call from home, and majored in political science and speech. Once I arrived on campus, I looked every bit the young, respectable collegian. My family saw to that, pooling their resources to buy me beautiful things, like cashmere sweaters and fitted pants. I looked nice. I felt nice. And I could always go home for the weekends if I wanted. My family also saw to it that I never had to take the bus to Chicago. Either Wallace or Dino drove (my mother never learned to drive) to the DeKalb campus to get me and return me on Sunday evenings.

After a couple of years, I decided to move closer to home and finish my undergraduate degree at Roosevelt College, now Roosevelt University, in downtown Chicago near Grant Park. It was chartered in 1945 in hopes of opening higher education to groups like Blacks, Jews, and immigrants who were often victims of restrictive quotas at many colleges and universities. I once bumped into Eleanor Roosevelt at the college, which was named for her late husband, Franklin D. We rode in an elevator together. Mrs. Roosevelt, very much a humanitarian and equal rights activist herself, used to come to the campus quite a bit in those years to support and encourage its mission of opening higher education to *all* students who qualified.

I flashed my smile at her, and she said "Hello, dear." And I said hello back and smiled some more. I never forgot that, especially while I was working so hard at the college, studying and working and coming home late at night to a dinner of oatmeal. Everyone at home pulled together to help me be the first college graduate of the family. But actually, I didn't graduate; activism called. Much later, I would go on to earn a master's degree in education at Harvard University.

Pooling the family's resources had long become an effective way of life for the Murphys. When I was a teenager, my mother lost her job at the factory after a labor dispute. So many were fired. We all told her that she shouldn't work anymore. The girls headed for Michael Reese Hospital on Chicago's Near South Side on South Ellis Avenue (it is also now demolished), where we all got jobs. I didn't have the medical training my sisters had, but I could carry trays, whatever, in the afternoons after school. My brother Wallace got a job in Argo, Illinois, lifting one-hundred-pound bags at Corn Products Corporation.

We all knew that our mother really wanted to have her own house, and we decided it was time. We gave Ma our paychecks every week, and she would dish out what monies we needed. She saved and knew how to bust a nickel. Somehow, she found a way to come up with a down payment on the house on 92nd and South Parnell Avenue. We all moved into it when I was fifteen.

It was a lovely place, far away from the industrial grit and grime of LaSalle Street. And grass grew everywhere, on lawns and in backyards and sweet little parks of trees and flowers throughout the Gresham neighborhood. When we moved in it was a mixed community of mostly Black and a few white homeowners. But like the changing of the seasons, there seemed a certain sort of inevitability about whites moving out when they were not the majority. In time, they moved out of the ever-darkening Chicago South Side so fast that you'd swear moving vans could fly.

It was in this family home on Parnell that I lay in bed in the spring of 1961, doing my best to recover from the miscarriage. But I realized that I had my own home in Hyde Park, my apartment with my husband, my Norm. I was getting better. And I missed Norman so much. While recovering on Parnell, we talked on the telephone just about every night. There were occasional visits; there was always his gentle voice of hard reason and sweet encouragements. But I needed to be with him, physically. I needed to be his wife, his partner, back in our apartment. To accomplish that, I realized that I had to find a way to get strong enough to prove to the doctors that I could climb those damn stairs.

I realized that it would be a process. Every day I would drag myself to the bathroom. In retrospect, I shouldn't have done that because it probably messed up some nerves or something. To this day, my right leg is weaker and slightly shorter than my left. I walk with a discernable limp.

But back then in May 1961, I finally got to where I could move around a bit better. I was able to walk reasonably enough. Even climb stairs.

I went home to Norm, and we soon resumed out lives together, trading our shared personal struggle for an ever-deepening commitment to a national one. We were preparing, husband and wife, to climb just a little higher together.

# CHAPTER 5

# For Jobs and Freedom

There is little reason for Velma and me to believe that late August was any kinder a thousand years ago in the swampy wilderness that hugged a bulging curve of the Potomac River than it was in the early years of the sixth decade of the twentieth century. By 1963, the swamps were long gone. So were the area's original inhabitants, Native American tribes, who most likely greeted whites as they first made their way into the region in the early seventeenth century.

In 1963 Washington, DC—at least the parts the tourists saw—was at once majestically American as the nation's capital and yet very much European in its presentation, in its penchant for the monumental, dressed in tons of limestone, granite, and marble, in fluted Grecian columns, in pedestals and porticoes, accented with manicured baroque landscapes, vistas common to London and Paris. The actual design of the District of Columbia, which in 1790 was deemed by its namesake to be the Federal City, was principally the work of a French-born American, Pierre Charles L'Enfant.

The original vision called for broad, long avenues radiating from the Capitol building. One of those avenues never materialized and instead evolved, largely as a consequence of neglect, into a long, grassy front yard. It became the National Mall, the people's parade grounds for pageantry and protests, for presidential inaugurations, rallies, and celebrations.

On the cool early morning of August 28, 1963, I walked those grounds with Bayard Rustin, strolling along the edge of the reflecting pool on the far western end of the mall. We were not far from the stony glare of Abraham Lincoln seated stiffly in his memorial. Except for a gaggle of news reporters and photographers, we were practically alone. I was not certain what Bayard was feeling, although I learned later that he was terrified. I was more than a little concerned.

This was the day for what we hoped would be a great Washington march. While I and most of its other planners and organizers publicly avoided any predictions of numbers, we all not-so-secretly hoped that the march would bring tens upon tens of thousands of people streaming into this part of the mall. We wanted it to be big.

Velma and I knew that reputations were at stake, perhaps even the future of the civil rights movement and its alliance with labor.

When reporters approached Bayard sometime after dawn and asked where all the marchers were, I watched my fifty-one-year-old mentor, a clear-eyed, first-class thinker and the deputy director of the march, straighten his back and speak right up. Dressed in an off-the-rack business suit, dark tie, and crisp white shirt, he grinned and acknowledged the question while reaching into his pocket for a piece of paper. Then he took out his pocket watch. He studied the two, taking a long moment, looking at one and then the other, and back again. Finally, he addressed the press with a single pronouncement: "Gentlemen, everything is going according to Hoyle" (in other words, as it should).

The reporters seemed satisfied, or perhaps mystified. Either way, they walked away. Bayard turned to me and showed me the paper, with an impish gleam behind his horn-rimmed glasses.

The paper was blank.

Of course, the people came. They came by way of 2,000 buses and regularly scheduled transportation in addition to nearly two dozen special trains, ten chartered airliners, and untold fleets of cars. Some even hitchhiked, and others came by foot. By most estimates, at least a quarter of a million marchers, nearly one-third of them white, crowded from the base of the Lincoln Memorial and stretched eastward to the Washington

Monument for a single afternoon that history is unlikely to ever forget. I know Velma and I will not.

The Washington march, which fell on the centenary of the Emancipation Proclamation, became a defining moment for the Black struggle in America. It was a crowning achievement for A. Philip Randolph, its architect and, at seventy-four, the much-respected dean of the modern movement. It propelled Bayard to unprecedented prominence (the following month Mr. Randolph and Bayard shared the cover of *Life* magazine). The peaceful march helped to persuade President John F. Kennedy—who had opposed it—to redouble his efforts to push Congress harder for pending civil rights legislation. In fact, we are convinced that the march galvanized supporters of the bill that Kennedy had called for in June of that year, making it a stronger bill and thus a stronger law when it was enacted some eight months after Kennedy's assassination in November.

Over the years, of course, the Washington march made Martin Luther King Jr. and the "I Have a Dream" speech he delivered in the waning minutes of that glorious gathering nothing less than legend. We are also convinced that the march represented much more than the thumbnail sense of it that many Americans, of all colors, carry in their collective memories, in selected schoolhouse recitations of what was said that day, in occasional glances at grainy, gray videos of its most famous faces and largely anonymous crowds. The Washington march was, as Dr. King himself said from its podium, "the greatest demonstration for freedom in the history of our nation."

Yet it was still more in what it accomplished that day—and didn't.

The march was conceived by Mr. Randolph as a means to bring all the major civil rights organizations together, bringing the movement into a broader one with organized labor. For instance, he repeatedly talked about how there needed to be an alliance based on common political interests like fair and full employment, quality integrated education, affordable housing, and universal medical care. That's one of the aspects that made Mr. Randolph unique. He was both a civil rights leader and a labor leader.

*Norman and I listened to Mr. Randolph and Bayard talk about the civil rights movement evolving to embrace these issues of economic, political, and social relevance to the Black community.* At that time, most people in the movement were talking about just race. At that time, they were not talking about changing institutions in any really deep and fundamental way. It was more about opening existing institutions, pretty much as they were, to Blacks. But there is an important difference between pushing through a front door and building a new structure with doors that open equally and welcome all inside. This difference is what the Washington march was trying to illuminate.

Today, whenever the march is brought up, people always mention Dr. King. Indeed, Dr. King and the march are synonymous in many people's minds. And Norman and I don't mind them mentioning him. We had great respect for Dr. King. But he was hardly the only figure involved in the demonstration that day; his message was hardly the only one heard by the quarter of a million people assembled on the mall and millions more listening on the radio or watching on television. The march was about more than Dr. King's dream—and its goals deserve to be remembered more than they are. So let's put the March on Washington in context.

*Velma and I clearly understood why the march wasn't simply called the March on Washington, as it is mostly known today, but was actually the March on Washington for Jobs and Freedom.* The complete name wasn't an accident. For us, along with Mr. Randolph and Bayard, the economic component was essential in obtaining freedom and equality for Black people.

In retrospect, some seemed to believe that the March on Washington for Jobs and Freedom had a certain inevitability, that it was a natural culmination of all the sit-ins and boycotts and picket lines calling for justice and equality for Black Americans that had come before it. Ralph Abernathy, Dr. King's closest friend and associate, wrote in his 1989 autobiography that the march "was an idea that recommended itself."

It didn't seem that way to us, certainly not at its inception. Velma and I knew that Mr. Randolph, in his fullness of strength as founder and president of the Brotherhood of Sleeping Car Porters, threatened Franklin D. Roosevelt with a "call to Negro America to March on Washington for jobs and equal participation in national defense on July 1, 1941." The issue then was race-based barriers that prevented hundreds of thousands of Black workers from getting jobs in the defense industries as the country anticipated assisting its allies during the coming world war.

As summer approached, Mr. Randolph began predicting that some 100,000 people would participate in this march. The Roosevelt administration feared such a gathering, which might elicit racial violence in the nation's capital, would undermine the president's authority, and embarrass the nation before the world. All efforts to persuade Mr. Randolph to cancel the march failed. As the date of the demonstration approached, Roosevelt finally blinked. In June, Mr. Randolph, along with the NAACP's Walter White, T. Arnold Hill of the National Urban League, and New York Mayor Fiorello La Guardia, met with President Roosevelt in the White House. Mr. Randolph told him that he wanted a solution that was "something concrete, something tangible, definite, positive, and affirmative." Roosevelt reluctantly issued Executive Order 8802, which banned racial discrimination in hiring for defense industries as well as federal bureaus. This, of course, included civil service jobs, which became an avenue for Black upward mobility. The order created the Fair Employment Practice Committee (FEPC) to receive complaints, investigate charges of discrimination, and take action—though it possessed no enforcement powers—to resolve outstanding problems. No action was taken on the demand to integrate the armed forces; too many white military officials, sharing the prejudices of the day and refusing to "experiment" in their branches of the service, drew the line in the sand.

That issue would be postponed until after the end of the Second World War with Harry Truman in the White House. And not surprisingly, Mr. Randolph—with Bayard—would be at the center of a campaign to boycott the draft. As a result of that threat, Truman issued Executive Order 9981, which began the desegregation of the nation's armed forces. Of course, Mr. Randolph then called off the boycott.

By the winter of 1962, Mr. Randolph, again with Bayard at his side, was considering another march on Washington. But this time it was to pressure and call attention to America's still unkept promises to its Black citizens, now one hundred years out of chattel bondage, yet still burdened with glaring economic, political, and social inequalities. It was early the following year, and in this atmosphere, that Velma and I were summoned to Mr. Randolph's office in Harlem.

He told us that he wanted us to join a planning group for a great march on Washington, tentatively set for August. He said we would be working with him and Bayard and a young socialist intellectual and writer we knew, Tom Kahn.

When Mr. Randolph called, you came, and you came willingly.

*Norman and I were in such awe of Mr. Randolph. In fact, we always called him Mr. Randolph; even people very close to him, like Bayard, did too.* Mr. Randolph had this great presence but was also approachable. He spoke with a rich baritone and the broad "A," like the lord of the manor. Yet, he was so warm and considerate. He used to recite poetry and was a kind of Shakespearean actor; he had memorized passages of so many of the great tragedies. He also used to hurry home at night to his wife, Lucille, who had once been a hairdresser and supported Mr. Randolph emotionally and financially. He never made very much money doing the work of the movement. An Associated Press obituary notes that when Mr. Randolph died in 1979 in his sparsely furnished, fifth-floor New York home, the "only signs of luxury in the apartment were two black-and-white television sets." Commentators over the years noted that he was perhaps materially the poorest labor leader in America.

Material success was not what drove him.

Mr. Randolph would read poetry to Lucille before she went to sleep. He was such a wonderful, romantic man. Sadly, his wife died just three months before the march. In spite of his grief, he wanted the Washington march to go on as scheduled, and it did.

Asa Philip Randolph radiated integrity. He could not be bought, and his word was always his bond. People knew this. During the Depression years when he was organizing the Brotherhood of Sleeping Car Porters, the nation's first Black trade union led by Blacks and recognized by a major company, some attempted to buy him off. The Pullman Company, which leased and operated many of the nation's most popular passenger trains, used middlemen to offer Mr. Randolph $10,000 to abandon this mission to organize the thousands of Black men who served the company's mostly white train passengers. He didn't accept the bribe. That was the kind of man Mr. Randolph was.

*The first task for Velma and me was to help Mr. Randolph find ways to bring all the major civil rights groups together for the march—or figure out what it would mean if this was not possible.*

We agreed with Mr. Randolph and Bayard that if the march was to succeed, it was important to gain the support of what he called the Big Six. And that meant bringing in the NAACP, the National Urban League, the Congress of Racial Equality, the Student Nonviolent Coordinating Committee, and Dr. King's Southern Christian Leadership Conference. The sixth organization was Mr. Randolph's newly formed Negro American Labor Council.

Mr. Randolph was also in a different position from where he had been in 1941. Back then, he was the most prominent civil rights leader in the nation. But by '63, other leaders had emerged. In '41, Mr. Randolph could use his union as his base and resource to put on a march. By the 1960s, the Brotherhood of Sleeping Car Porters was in decline as American railroads were shifting to cargo-carrying trains that were thought to be more profitable than passenger trains. Mr. Randolph needed the other groups, particularly the NAACP, which was the largest and oldest of the civil rights organizations. It was also the one with the greatest resources and infrastructure of branches throughout the country.

Mr. Randolph wanted the left and the right of the movement. He wanted the entire movement on board, plus—and this was crucial—the labor movement. He wanted a coalition. SNCC and CORE were the vanguard of the left wing; the NAACP and the Urban League were the right wing. Dr. King was in the middle. He didn't have the youthful, risk-taking exuberance that characterized much of SNCC's membership, and yet he understood that direct action was very important.

I'd say that Dr. King was closer to where Mr. Randolph was, but Mr. Randolph, a longtime democratic socialist, was a little farther to the left of Dr. King. Mr. Randolph understood the essential role of labor in developing a thrust that would solve the economic problems. He also understood the dual problems of race and class that Blacks faced.

We also were concerned about how to prevent groups like the Communist Party and the Socialist Workers Party from overly influencing the march. It was agreed that the march would focus on domestic issues. It would not be about foreign policy. It was not going to be about Africa, and it was not going to be about Cuba or anyplace else. So we decided to control all the signs and placards displayed at the march.

All the signs had to be centralized, made at headquarters, with slogans and wording that reflected the themes and demands of the march. And they were. None of that homemade stuff. No one seemed to take issue with this decision.

Brokering the cooperation and participation of these groups proved difficult. The NAACP and Urban League were, by their nature and approach to civil rights reform, more traditional in style than the others. Neither of them wanted to be associated with a march that in its initial planning would use direct civil disobedience as a tool of pressure on the federal government. Early plans for the march included sit-ins and demonstrations aimed at the White House and the halls of Congress, where the civil rights bill was pending and facing a probable Southern-based filibuster in the Senate.

On the other hand, SNCC and CORE—where we worked—were more militant and balked at the notion that the march would refrain from using the very tactics that had come to define the civil rights movement. Direct action came up in the early planning meetings. I believe Bayard was the first to raise it.

The Southern Christian Leadership Conference and Dr. King were at first cool about supporting Mr. Randolph's march. Dr. King said he and his supporters, based primarily in the South, were considering their own march on DC.

*But because it was Mr. Randolph calling, the leadership of each group listened to him and eventually came to support the march. But not without compromises.* Norman and I knew that only Mr. Randolph could have brought all these people together. Even Dr. King couldn't have done that.

When Mr. Randolph started talking, people got still. We all knew he had been visiting American presidents in the White House for decades. Over the years, he kept up frequent letters and conversations with Marcus Garvey, whom he met in Harlem in 1916 while both were delivering soapbox oratory. W. E. B. Du Bois, who would die on the very eve of the march, also kept up a correspondence. The United Nations' Ralph Bunche and the NAACP's Roy Wilkins, and most of the Black leadership at the time, gravitated to Mr. Randolph, despite his major philosophical disagreements with Garvey and Du Bois.

The Woodrow Wilson administration, which had little patience for racial integration at home or aboard, had called Mr. Randolph the "most dangerous Negro in America."

*During the march's early planning meetings, Velma and I listened to Bayard, who did much of the talking, especially during the meetings that Mr. Randolph didn't attend.* We would talk about the recruiting base, about the logistical challenges. Part of the discussion was always about bringing the movement together or whether the march could really take place with just the militant wing, which was composed of mostly SNCC and CORE.

There were a half-dozen or so meetings held every few days in the spring of 1963. Each lasted a couple of hours. At these meetings, the idea was to build coalitions and cooperation.

*Norman and I don't remember any heated debates during these meetings.* We were all social democrats. Most of the meetings took place in Bayard's uptown Manhattan apartment. It was such an interesting place, filled with beautiful things. He really loved art, especially African, Christian, and other religious art. He had these high-backed wooden chairs and this old medieval cabinet. He would pull out a drawer, and there would be beautiful stuff in there. He was a collector of fine canes.

Bayard was an amazing man. Sometimes he would just stick out that jutting jaw of his and start singing Elizabethan ballads. He had a splendid voice and a sort of playful, even outrageous, aura about him. And he had tremendous courage. Once he saw two people fighting on the street in

Harlem and tried to play peacemaker. When police arrived and began to arrest the bickering parties, they moved to arrest Bayard, too.

He stopped the police officer with a statement: "I am Bayard Rustin."

The cop replied, "Rustin, Smustin" as he threw Bayard right into the police wagon.

Along with the work, the meetings at Bayard's would often turn into a bit of a social thing. We would have a glass of wine or something and schmooze. Tom Kahn was as smart as a whip and had such a natural ease with everyone. He was tall and attractive, and looked very Waspy. He had attended Howard University, one of the few whites who graduated from that venerable Black institution at the time. While there, he worked with groups of politically sophisticated Black students, Stokely Carmichael among them. We liked Tom. It seemed that everyone who knew him respected him.

At some of the strategy meetings, Bayard would indicate that he wanted something in the plan, and Tom would write it up. And then we would all talk about it some more. For the most part, we all got along very well. Norman and I, of course, were very close to Bayard. And I remember Mr. Randolph saying something like if he had a son, he would have been Bayard, and if he had a grandson, he would have been Norman. That made me feel so good, like we were connected in a deeper way than simply shared politics and a shared vision.

But some of our march meetings were tense. Very often I was the youngest person in the room. Everyone understood that while Norman and I shared the same politics, they also realized that he and I were very different people. I was the more creative, emotional type. Norman was more cerebral and self-directed. I came at things much more working-class. I wanted to go out and talk to regular Black people and discover where they were on issues and what they were thinking. Then I wanted to integrate their ideas with ours. That sort of stuff. I had a more grass-roots orientation. Sometimes I was wrong; sometimes I wasn't. It never bothered me if they thought I was wrong.

And there was Bayard's assistant, Rachelle Horowitz. She was politically compatible with us, having roots in the Young People's Socialist

League. Shortly after the meeting of the Big Six, Bayard named her coordinator of transportation for the march. She later became an effective political director of the American Federation of Teachers and the wife of Tom R. Donahue, the secretary-treasurer and later the president of the AFL-CIO.

Tom Kahn went on to become a lifelong activist for civil rights and labor causes. He eventually moved to Washington, where he became the director of the AFL-CIO's International Affairs Department after serving as a special aide to Lane Kirkland, the federation's president. Tragically, Tom died of AIDS in 1992. He was fifty-three.

*One of the chief obstacles that Velma and I realized was that Mr. Randolph and the committee had to manage relations among the various groups in the civil rights movement.* We had a sense that SNCC and CORE would immediately support the march, especially if it remained as militant as early plans called for. But we knew the NAACP and the Urban League would be reluctant. We also knew that Dr. King, who could be frustratingly deliberative in making up his mind, was once again in the middle.

The NAACP, founded in 1909, was the most widely known civil rights organization in the United States. Its executive director, Roy Wilkins, was extremely proud of the NAACP's watershed victories in the courts, which included, of course, *Brown v. Board of Education of Topeka*. As a result of that 1954 US Supreme Court decision, not only was the *Plessy v. Ferguson* doctrine of "separate but equal" struck down as it related to America's public schools and race, but it also laid the legal and philosophical groundwork for challenges to racial discrimination in almost every sphere of American life.

*Nonetheless, Norman and I knew that the NAACP had its critics, even among the other civil rights groups Mr. Randolph had called together for the march.* There was a feeling that the NAACP, founded by a diverse group that included Du Bois and Ida B. Wells, was too attached to legal approaches as a means to gain full rights. Wilkins was opposed to civil disobedience and consequently pressed for the elimination of such militant tactics as part of the march.

And CORE, which was founded in 1942, strongly favored direct action in those days. Its members had shown extraordinary bravery and determination in organizing the Freedom Rides through the South in 1961. They were directly challenging racial segregation in interstate bus travel with their bodies. We understood the power in that.

Under James L. Farmer Jr., CORE's principal founder and national director, riders boarded buses on May 4, 1961, in Washington, DC, and planned to travel more than 1,000 miles to New Orleans. The riders, Black and white, never got there. Along the way, they faced storms of angry whites who beat them, police who jailed them, mobs—most likely working with the Ku Klux Klan—that vandalized buses and burned one of them, hoping to kill riders momentarily trapped inside.

That summer, President Kennedy and his brother, Attorney General Robert Kennedy, were drawn into the events. The violence forced the White House to take a stronger public stand in support of the Freedom Riders and soon the civil rights movement in general. In the end, the Interstate Commerce Commission issued a desegregation order that covered interstate travel.

Jim Farmer, who could give a good speech, was always committed to direct action. The National Urban League, while having its own issues with the NAACP, had more in common with his organization. Some were critical of the Urban League, then led by Whitney M. Young Jr., saying it was too close to the business community. It was founded in 1910 by Ruth Standish Baldwin and George Edmund Haynes. Its birth came about in the blending of two distinct groups with similar missions: the Committee for the Improvement of Industrial Conditions Among Negroes in New York and the National League for the Protection of Colored Women. Its roots lay in the need to help multitudes of Blacks streaming out of the South and into the North in search of jobs during the Great Migration. The Urban League's branches in cities like Chicago, Detroit, and New York distributed information to newly arrived Southerners during and after the First World War. According to Isabel Wilkerson's history of the migration, *The Warmth of Other Suns*, the Chicago Urban League distributed information to the newly arrived Southerners shortly after its founding.

Among its admonishments, which included cautions against talking loudly on public transportation, were: Do not loaf. Get a job at once. Do not keep your children out of school. Do not send for your family until you get a job.

A hallmark of the National Urban League has always been pushing for racial progress by way of job training, job placement, and college scholarships, and encouraging minority business and home ownership.

In contrast, SNCC was forged straight out of direct action. In February 1960, a group of Black students at the Agricultural and Technical College of North Carolina (now North Carolina A&T State University) refused to leave a Woolworth lunch counter in Greensboro, North Carolina, where they had been denied service. Soon, a tide of similar sit-ins spread across other Southern college towns where Blacks were denied service. Two months later, SNCC was created at Shaw University in Raleigh, North Carolina, to coordinate the sit-ins, support their organizers, and publicize all the events.

In 1963, SNCC was led by John Lewis, who became a congressman from Georgia and a recipient of the Presidential Medal of Freedom. SNCC most often found itself aligned with CORE. That left Mr. Randolph and Dr. King to help pressure a deal among all the groups.

The thirty-four-year-old Baptist preacher, following his successes facing down segregation in the South, had become the bright new face of the movement by 1963. Few other civil rights leaders wanted to appear out of step with him. And Bayard, a master at coalition building, skillfully used these kinds of openings to help Mr. Randolph bring and hold these groups together. It didn't hurt that Bayard was instrumental in the founding of both CORE and the SCLC. He was perfectly positioned to do the practical engineering Mr. Randolph's march required.

But Bayard wasn't merely dealing with organizations. Norman and I realized that we were dealing with human beings with all their accompanying baggage that comes along with that. As with all groups of people, there was infighting, competition, hurt feelings, the tenderness of toes believed stepped upon. For example, Wilkins often felt that

Dr. King was riding a crest of national support and recognition on civil rights victories that had largely come by way of NAACP landmark work in the courts.

And at CORE, Jim Farmer was wary of Bayard and his obvious brilliance. Jim was competitive with Bayard, and Bayard never felt competitive with anybody. The two of them had had problems before.

To Jim's credit, he continued to pay Norman's salary as CORE's national program director after he loaned Norm to the march. Bayard quickly named Norman staff coordinator of the Washington march.

*One of the advantages of working for CORE was that Velma and I had the flexibility to meet to plan the march.* We had the kind of leeway in terms of our jobs that if anything was civil rights related, we could be involved. It helped in our hands-on participation. We did not have to clear our calendars to do this work because this *was* our work.

Velma was based pretty much in New York while I did a great deal of traveling. As staff coordinator, I was expected to travel through much of the Northeast, Midwest, and upper South to identify and coordinate the local organizers for the Washington march. By early July, we were feeling a great sense of urgency. The march was now set for August 28, an endeavor large in effort and scope. I would work the local chapters and branches of the civil rights organizations supporting the march, the Big Six. That would be expanded to the Big Ten by adding the National Council of Churches, the National Catholic Conference for Interracial Justice, the American Jewish Congress, and the United Auto Workers.

Once a city strategic to the march was targeted, I would place a telephone call to people we knew on the ground there, saying, "I am calling at the urging of your national leadership, and I would like you to pull together a representative group of civil rights leaders and activists, including labor and churches, for an initial planning meeting to set up a structure for generating and mobilizing participation in the March on Washington from your city."

By this time, I had become quite experienced at this sort of organizing. Of course, I had been constantly organizing for marches and rallies since my days in Chicago. But at CORE, I had the excellent experience of building and organizing its chapters around the country. I carried that knowledge into building participation for the March on Washington for Jobs and Freedom.

I usually had only days between the time I called for the meetings and the time I arrived in cities to speak at those meetings. I packed light and seldom stayed longer than overnight. I arranged the meetings like a band leader might, flying from city to city, being careful not to double back or zigzag, wasting time and money.

For example, I remember flying into Louisville, Kentucky, where there were branches of the NAACP and the Urban League. Someone from the NAACP met me when I landed at the airport. I stayed at the NAACP president's home.

Wherever I went, I could feel the enthusiasm for the march. So it wasn't difficult for me to convey that this was something big, something important, and that all who could be a part of it must. I depended on the local people to contact and encourage broader support, including religious, labor, and other allied organizations, Black and white.

While in a city organizing, I would contact other leaders in other cities, repeating my refrain for support and indicating that I was coming and what day I would be there. The leadership on the ground would determine the best place to hold the meetings before I arrived.

*Norman isn't very musical, even though he played the trumpet when he was a boy back in New Jersey.* But when I think of that march and all those people climbing into buses and planes and cars to get to Washington, it makes me sing. I used to sing a lot back then, civil rights songs, gospel songs, and play my guitar.

"Get on board, O Lawd. Get on board, get on board."

When Norman was traveling—and he traveled a lot during our marriage—I was at the CORE headquarters in downtown New York, near the Brooklyn Bridge. I was trying to help Jim Farmer understand that Bayard and Norm were allies, not enemies. Other people were telling him that we were the bad guys. His history with Bayard tended to reinforce his suspicions.

Sometimes I played this role of the reassurer. Norman didn't like to schmooze. He is more into explaining things. I am much more into getting into who the person is and maybe stroking their ego a little.

Jim could be a little weird. When asked if he wanted coffee, he'd declare, "I like my coffee the way I like my women, strong and Black." But he was married to a white woman. It makes me laugh to think about it. He also had this big pet snake at his home, so he'd have to get live rats and mice to feed it. I just kept trying to make Jim feel better about what was going on with organizing the Washington march. I didn't know whether it worked or not.

Jim was very nervous when it came to Bayard Rustin, and here we were, Rustinites. I went on with business as usual, working with CORE and putting together demonstrations to integrate the building trades unions in New York. And I looked forward to Norman calling me every night.

*I tried to call Velma before midnight.*

*Yeah, yeah, yeah…but sometimes, Norman, it was one or two in the morning.*

When he made it back home, we'd meet at night and talk about everything. You know, the way you do with your honey. This was our life together. We worked until we got so tired that we couldn't work anymore that day. Then we would come back home, talk a little, get to sleep, get up, and go back to work. We were committed to the movement. It was our life.

Neither of our families thought we were making a good living. We were getting paid, but not that much. Norman and I felt like we were getting paid for doing what we really wanted to do. We would have done it for free, and these organizations were giving us a little money here and there. We were pretty happy.

Although Norman was a program director and I was a field secretary at CORE, we got a chance to do a lot of work together. Sometimes we had the opportunity to work in the same place and on the same projects. Most of the time it was good. Sometimes it wasn't so good. That's honest. I was a troubleshooter and CORE's East Coast field secretary.

At home, I cooked for Norm late at night. But, as I said, I was never a great cook. I'd make little meat loaves. I'd do hamburgers, maybe some kind of little roast. Hot dogs. Beans.

My mother was a feminist before it was fashionable, before it was cool. She didn't raise me to cook and clean house. And Norman knew when he married me that I was no Betty Crocker. We had an agreement, and it may have been unspoken, that whatever Norman wanted to do, I would encourage him to do it. I think that's what kept us together.

I mean, Norman and I never got bored. I think after a while people either get tired of doing the same thing together or they get bored. But we were always bringing things into the relationship, always. That's how you stay together. You have to have fundamental sharing. If you're just there because you love sex together or because of other reasons like that, it is going to be very hard. That's particularly true when you have so many other things in this world pounding at you, and pounding at you as a couple.

There weren't a lot of married couples at CORE. I don't know why. There were Marvin and Evie Rich. And, like Norman and me, they were married a long time till Marvin's recent death. Marvin was in the national office and involved with CORE's public relations and fundraising. Evie was active in New York and Brooklyn CORE. Marvin was white, and Evie is Black. She used to have this oddly genteel approach to direct action. I remember people saying that she'd tell protesters walking CORE picket lines to be on their best Ps and Qs, saying things like, "Now, you can't talk too loud…"

Norman and I lived in a nice little one-bedroom apartment in an elevator building on East 107th Street in Harlem in the early '60s. The place was called Franklin Plaza. And when Norman was traveling, I mostly ate dinner out.

I did worry about Norman on the road. I always thought he was very bright but had no street sense. You know, most Black people are very keenly aware of their environment. Maybe it's a survival technique. But Norm wasn't. So I worried about him being somewhere and somebody coming up on him and beating him up. In that way I always felt maternal about Norman. The years taught me, though, that I didn't have to feel that way because nothing ever happened to him. Me? I always thought God was looking out for me, but then I was the one who always got beat up in the movement.

Still, at times, all the worrying about Norman strained our relationship. I would call CORE people in cities where I knew he was going and ask them to look out for him. And I felt he might have thought that I was checking up on him. I had a big network of friends I could turn to like that. It's the movement and whole family thing. All this made me feel like I was being his momma, and I didn't want to be. And with all that time alone on the road, there was the specter of other women.

I would tell people not to worry about that. Not only did I trust Norman, but I also felt that whatever is going to happen is going to happen. Whatever it is, it is not going to be important to us. I knew where he was, and honestly, I thought he was lucky to get me. But don't get me wrong. I understand the sexual energy that's all wrapped up in being the man out front, the one who makes the speech, who gets the applause. It's the same thing with rock stars. And with Jesse Jackson, by the way. It's power. And it doesn't hurt if the men are cute. Jesse used to be really cute. Norman's okay, too. I've been with Norman when he would make a speech, and he made speeches all the time, and some woman would sit next to him and be rubbing his thigh. That happens sometimes, right?

Years later, I was the assistant to Al Shanker, the United Federation of Teachers president. And he'd make a speech and there would be these women who would come up to me and say, "I'd cut my arm off to sleep with him." And I'd say, "Don't cut your arm off, Hon."

*I didn't mind Velma having her friends look in on me.* She always had a network of friends. I was so busy organizing that I didn't have much time to think about such things. So much of what kept me on the road was happening and happening quite quickly.

There was an outside attempt to separate Bayard from the march. Strom Thurmond, the segregationist senator from South Carolina, went so far as to condemn Bayard in a speech on the Senate floor in which he called him a "communist, draft-dodger and homosexual." He read

Bayard's arrest in 1953 for having oral sex with two white men in Los Angeles into the *Congressional Record*.

Bayard had already survived a much earlier attempt by Roy Wilkins to block him from organizing the march for fear that his background—serving prison time as a conscientious objector during World War II, having been a member of the Young Communist League, and having been arrested on the sex charge in California—would be used by detractors of the scheduled march. But Mr. Randolph never wavered in his support, officially naming Bayard deputy director of the march, while unofficially leaving the organization of the march fully in his charge. This was very much in contrast to Dr. King, who had distanced himself from Bayard in 1960. This occurred when Harlem Congressman Adam Clayton Powell Jr.—at the urging of Wilkins—threatened to spread rumors that Bayard and Dr. King were lovers if Dr. King did not remove Bayard from efforts to organize demonstrations at that year's national party conventions.

In time, however, Wilkins came to appreciate how indispensable Bayard was to the Washington march. Yet Wilkins continued to have a certain kind of way of doing things that we all sort of tolerated.

For example, sometime in early July, Mr. Randolph convened a major meeting of the leaders of the Big Six and their staff at the Roosevelt Hotel in New York. I guess Bayard and I took for granted that we would be there with Mr. Randolph, Dr. King, Whitney Young, John Lewis, James Farmer, and Roy Wilkins. We had reserved a private dining room with a table that would have easily sat a dozen or so people.

But when Wilkins walked in and saw the long table and all its place settings he said, "No, this is leaders only." Then he started pointing and telling each of us who could or could not attend this very important meeting. Bayard and I were tapped to leave, along with men like Fred Shuttlesworth and Cleveland Robinson. There wasn't much for us to do but to stand around and wait to learn what had happened inside and what had been decided without us.

*These were serious times when the March was coming together, but Norman and I remember some fun times too.* Bayard had such a great sense of humor. I remember him telling us a story about how he got on the phone to call Dr. King about something key to the march and decided to conduct the whole call in the voice of Mr. Randolph—because he could. He's talking in that deep, rumbling voice and doing a convincing job of it.

Then Bayard gets off the phone and says, "Ain't this a bitch. That was somebody on the phone imitating King while I was on the phone imitating Randolph." We all just laughed. Bayard never took himself that seriously. I always thought of him as forever young.

As the march began coming into focus, one of the last major elements we saw lock into place was organized labor. Mr. Randolph so badly wanted the trade union movement in the initial coalition for the march. Labor came in late, but then it came in very strong.

*In 1963, Velma and I understood that in a very real sense there were always, at least historically, two labor movements.* This was symbolized by the American Federation of Labor and the Congress of Industrial Organizations that merged in 1955 to become a federation of unions, the AFL-CIO. Today, it represents more than twelve million members, including teachers, doctors, nurses, engineers, miners, plumbers, painters, firefighters, other public workers, and blue- and white-collar workers.

Before the merger, the CIO represented what some considered the more progressive wing of the labor movement, the more industrial part of organized labor, autoworkers and steelworkers, for instance. On the other hand, the AFL's membership was more craft unions, based on particular trades. Sometimes you had to work hard to bring them along to support progressive issues and causes.

In 1963, George Meany, who had fought to create the AFL-CIO, was still its first and only president. Walter P. Reuther, the president of the CIO at the time of the merger, was made one of many vice presidents in the combined federation. He was also the president of the United Auto Workers from 1946 till his death in 1970, and he drew additional clout from his position as the president of the AFL-CIO's Industrial Union Department.

After the merger in '55, Reuther, on more than one occasion, disagreed with Meany on matters that came before the AFL-CIO's governing Executive Council, of which Reuther was a vice president. I used to tell Velma how I would hear Reuther continually say, even after the merger,

"Well, if Meany doesn't like it, or doesn't go along, or doesn't support this, I'm going to do it anyway." That was Walter Reuther.

Reuther, born in West Virginia to a German socialist father, was a model of liberal thinking. And as a progressive, he realized right away the merits of a massive march on Washington that called not only for advances in civil rights for Blacks but also for national concrete economic reforms that could lift the fortunes and create opportunities for millions of Americans.

Bayard agreed. In background papers that seemed to fly out of his Royal manual typewriter, he noted that the "condition of Negro labor is inseparable from that of white labor; the immediate crisis confronting Black labor grows out of the unresolved crisis in the national economy." It was an argument that he had been making for decades.

In 1965, he greatly elaborated on this position in his seminal essay, "From Protest to Politics: The Future of the Civil Rights Movement," published in *Commentary* magazine.

Mr. Randolph appealed to Meany, a tough New Yorker born into the labor movement, to join the coalition backing the march. But Meany was cool to the idea and said no. He thought the march would draw too many people to Washington. He doubted that we could control the crowds, keeping everything peaceful and nonviolent. He said that the last thing he wanted to be associated with was a march that would embarrass the federation he had worked so hard to create.

In attempting to line up major labor support, Mr. Randolph made one tactical mistake. He reached out to Reuther about the march before he spoke about it with Meany. Reuther didn't wait for Meany to move. He said right away that he was on board, adding, "I'm going to support the march no matter what Meany says or does."

In reaction, Meany said, "Well, I'm going to show Reuther who actually runs the AFL-CIO." Before we fully realized it, the Washington march had become a political football—more to the point, a personal, political, and ideological tug-of-war.

Thereafter, Meany's earlier reservations about the march quickly hardened to the point where the AFL-CIO would not endorse the March on Washington for Jobs and Freedom. But many international unions, seventeen or so, did openly support and later participate in the march. Reuther was very, very involved.

*Some march organizers around Mr. Randolph were upset with Meany.* But Norman and I never heard Mr. Randolph say a bad word about him—about anybody, as a matter of fact. After the march, and its stunning success, Meany would come around in ways that seemed unimaginable in the months leading up to the march. He became a lot friendlier.

The march fell on a Wednesday that felt like a Sunday. Right away, we understood what the march meant in terms of Mr. Randolph's principles and vision. For example, his dual approach of melding labor and civil rights had infused the march with demands for civil rights legislation along with a national jobs programs and a national minimum wage of no less than $2 an hour; his insistence on coalition politics had brought a broad range of people to the National Mall that August day. And Mr. Randolph's principles of self-liberation, mass action, and nonviolence were manifested in activists standing up in the South and in the march chanting by the thousands, "Pass the BILL. Pass the BILL. Pass the BILL!"

But when you saw it, all those people, all that was said and done…it didn't dawn on Norman and me just how special the march would be until it was all around us. There was this air of real excitement. People were saying hello to people they didn't know. They were shaking hands and looking for people they did know. It was just wonderful. We were trying to figure out how many different unions were there. So many people wore buttons and paper hats that bore the names in big, bold letters of their unions. Among them were the Service Employees International Union; the Transport Workers Union; the Communications Workers of America; the Retail, Wholesale Department Store Union; the American Federation of State, County, and Municipal Employees; and the American Federation of Teachers.

The unions for the steelworkers, the autoworkers, and the garment workers provided the march's public address system.

I wasn't with Norman at the march, but I saw him and said hello. I had flown in that morning from New York with my brother Wallace and a good friend, Judy Bardacke. I was really excited as we walked to the mall and slowly dissolved into all those people. I couldn't help it. I found myself singing a lot. There was all this anticipation with all the people coming in by trains, coming by bus, by plane. I just broke into song: "Good news, freedom is coming, and I don't want it to leave me behind." Wallace and Judy joined in.

Everyone was told to show up at the Washington Monument by 10 a.m., where signs would be provided. The *New York Times* reported that 40,000 people were on the swell of parkland around the monument at that hour. By 11 a.m., the paper wrote, Washington's police estimated that the crowd had grown to 90,000, "And still they poured in." The *Times* headline Thursday morning was "200,000 March for Civil Rights in Orderly Washington Rally; President Sees Gain for Negro." Another headline read, "Capital Is Occupied by a Gentle Army."

It's funny, looking back on it now, but why would anyone expect that there would have been trouble? Unlike the Million Man March in 1995, this was not just an all-Black affair. It was Black and white, and young and old, and Catholic and Protestant and Jewish; it was like the unity that you wanted for this country. It really was. People were clearly glad to be there in that integrated, intergenerational gathering. And Bayard organized at least 2,000 volunteer marshals, many of them members of the Guardians Association, a Black police officers group from New York, who supplied security throughout the mall.

I later learned that on the day of the march, liquor stores were closed and no alcohol was sold in Washington, for the first time since Prohibition; elective surgery was put off to free medical staff and space for the possibility of emergency care; two Washington Senators' baseball games were rescheduled. I was told that thousands of paratroopers were on standby in the South, and thousands more on alert in Washington's suburbs, and some merchants braced for riots by sending their merchandise elsewhere—just in case.

But it turned out to be such a lovely day. There were no arrests, not even a foul word heard. Nobody was cussing on the stage. It was extraordinary. Unique.

*I could see that Velma had positioned herself near the front of the plat-form that was set up on the base of the Lincoln Memorial.* I was on that platform, at the back of the stage near Bayard, who was a chain-smoking, perpetual-motion machine that day. I had come in on the train the night before from Baltimore, where I was working with a local civil rights activist, doing everything I could to make sure that there was a large Baltimore turnout.

On the platform, I was so close that I did not need the public address system to hear what was being said, and sung, at the podium. It was a tremendously good feeling standing there, being enveloped in a special atmosphere, looking out on all those people swept up in a massive cel-ebration. It was like Velma said, unique, a unique spirit, a unique, great, huge outpouring of humanity.

The march was scheduled to start near the Washington Monument at noon. Somehow it began more than thirty minutes early, moving west for a mile—sometimes without its leaders in front of it—like spilled molasses on a steamy summer afternoon.

Everyone seemed to be there, all of the march's leadership—except for James Farmer, who was locked away in a parish jail in Plaquemine, Loui-siana, after leading demonstrations in that sharply segregated town earlier that year. Floyd McKissick, CORE's national chairman and a colleague of mine, read Jim's speech on his behalf. It said in part, "Our direct-action method is breaking down barriers all over the country in jobs, in housing, in schools, in public places, is giving hope to the world, to people who are weary of warfare."

The day was supposed to begin with the singing of the national anthem led by Marian Anderson, the Black opera star. But she got to the stage too late, so she later sang on the platform "He's Got the Whole World in His Hands." I could see actor Ossie Davis and entertainers who were express-ing their support for the cause, including Harry Belafonte and Sammy Davis Jr., milling about with actors Charlton Heston, Sidney Poitier, Paul Newman, and Marlon Brando in the shadows of Lincoln in his great chair. Lena Horne and Diahann Carroll were there. And there were writers like

James Baldwin and Michael Harrington, whose work highly influenced Kennedy's thinking on American poverty.

Mr. Randolph delivered the first speech that made a simple yet deeply stirring point: "Let the nation know the meaning of our numbers. We are not a pressure group. We are not an organization or a group of organizations. We are not a mob. We are the advance guard of a massive moral revolution for jobs and freedom."

*Norman, I remember those words, and I have used them many times since that day.*

*Mr. Randolph also said: "At the banquet table of nature, there are no reserved seats.* You get what you can take, and you keep what you can hold. If you can't take anything, you won't get anything, and if you can't hold anything, you won't keep anything. And you can't take anything without organization."

*I also remember so much music: Odetta, Bob Dylan, Joan Baez and Peter, Paul and Mary, and the gospel great, Mahalia Jackson.* I can still hear Joan Baez singing "We Shall Overcome" and feel its notes dampen my eyes when I recall how her voice moved me and so many others that day.

Jackie Robinson brought his young son, David. The man who integrated Major League Baseball told marchers that "we cannot be turned back" and I believed him. I also saw Josephine Baker, the famous Black American-born entertainer who was a French citizen, and heard that she had flown in from Paris to be a part of this extraordinary event.

Norman and I came to see the march as part revival and rally, although Malcolm X, who was there and standing under a tree off to the side of the mall, disparagingly called the day a "circus" and ultimately the "Farce on Washington."

I was not surprised. I had come to know Malcolm first from an observable distance. In 1961, he engaged Bayard in a series of debates at Howard University about the civil rights movement and Black liberation. Spike Lee depicted, not very accurately, I might add, these debates in his 1992 movie *Malcolm X*. His depiction of Bayard in the movie cast him as an intellectual lightweight and an apologist for the status quo; both could not be farther from the truth. What Bayard did in those debates was to make Malcolm's call, an appeal to white power, for a separate Black nation within this one, look foolish. I thought Bayard made that whole nationalist notion look a little stupid.

I accompanied Bayard to some of the debates, and I guess Malcolm noticed me. He might have also seen me at a CORE community meeting he once attended. Not long before the Washington march, I was leading a demonstration at Harlem Hospital protesting the lack of Blacks and other minority workers employed in the construction of an addition to the hospital. I could see Malcolm X, planted on the sidewalk like a leafless tree, standing across 135th Street near Lenox Avenue. Without a word, he was taking in the scene.

After a few minutes, one of his lieutenants came up to me—all dark suit and bow tie—and said, "The Minister would like to speak to you."

It was clear that Malcolm wasn't coming to me, so I followed his lieutenant back across the street to him, carrying my picket sign. Malcolm was tall, you know, so if you weren't as tall as he was, and most women weren't—I'm five feet four inches—you couldn't help looking up at him when he spoke to you. He had a real charisma. In his biography of Malcolm, Manning Marable quotes Maya Angelou saying that "his aura was too bright and his masculine force affected me physically" when she met him at a Nation of Islam restaurant in Harlem. Well, I don't know about all that.

I have to say, though, that when I walked up to him that afternoon, he looked right at me. And at that moment, let me tell you, you knew you were looking at a *man*. I knew I disagreed with him, his politics, but you could not deny the magnetism that he had. When he had me summoned, I was thinking, *Okay, whatever he has to say to me is not going to be nice; he's going to say something and I'm going to have to say something back.* But I wasn't intimidated. I really wasn't.

He basically wanted to know why I was out there in the street, leading this demonstration, and not at home, taking care of my house and husband. He obviously thought women were inferior.

I said to him, "Minister Malcolm, if you will take this picket sign and go over there and picket, I will be very happy to stand on this side of the street and support you."

He just smiled this big, open smile and then whispered something to his lieutenant and turned back to me and said, "Velma, we will speak again." But we never did.

I knew Malcolm wasn't much of a fan of marches in general. Yet, even though he was very critical of the Washington march, Norman and I believe he was impressed by it. We also think that Malcolm X respected Mr. Randolph and Bayard. Malcolm and Bayard would run into each other right after the debates and I would hear their conversations; they were friendly, familiar.

At the time of his assassination in 1965, we realized that Malcolm was evolving; he seemed to be moving more toward positions that embraced the types of coalition building and economic reforms long favored by Mr. Randolph and Bayard. There were some in the civil rights movement who were being influenced by the more nationalist and anti-integration-ist rhetoric of the firebrand Malcolm, the one so many want to enshrine despite his political evolution. Stokely Carmichael called the march a "sanitized, middle-class version of the real Black movement."

The closest thing the march had to a genuine crisis came on its eve, when John Lewis was asked to tone down the speech he had planned to give. A number of hands had helped to write it, including our friend Tom Kahn. It has to be said here that John was such a good man, a man who repeatedly put his body where his beliefs were, facing down terrible threats and violence in the name of racial integration and equal rights. But in 1963, he was the leader of SNCC, a group of mostly young people, like Carmichael, who were growing impatient with calls for careful dis-cussions, negotiations, and compromises to bring about change. He and his followers were angry.

Remember, this was the militant wing of the civil rights movement, and John and his organization were very disappointed—to put it mildly—in what they saw as the Kennedy administration's sluggish early support for Black progress, especially in the South. SNCC also felt the civil rights legislation should have been stronger and made the law of the land long ago. They believed they had paid a price in blood for the Kennedys' unfocused attention and weak political will.

In his speech, John had planned to say, "This nation is still a place of cheap political leaders who build their careers on immoral compromises and ally themselves with open forms of political, economic and social exploitation."

Norman and I knew he also wanted to say, "We will march through the South, through the heart of Dixie, the way Sherman did. We shall pursue our own 'scorched earth' policy and burn Jim Crow to the ground—nonviolently."

Learning of John's reference to the Union general who ripped through the South in a campaign of burning and destruction during the Civil War, the Most Reverend Patrick J. O'Boyle, Roman Catholic Archbishop of Washington and a civil rights activist, refused to give the march's invocation the next day. He would do so, he made clear, only if the Sherman reference was removed from the speech. A flurry of backstage appeals that day and the morning of the march by a number of civil rights leaders, including Bayard, moved John to moderate his speech. Even with its changes, it remained one of the most militant, certainly the most controversial, heard that day. It ended with, "We must say: Wake up America. Wake up! For we cannot stop, and we will not be patient."

We think what actually moved John to change his speech that morning was a personal plea from Mr. Randolph, who told a twenty-three-year-old John Lewis to please not mess up the march: "I've waited twenty-two years for this. Would you, young man, please accommodate an old man? Please don't ruin it." Much later, John wrote of the incident, noting, "How could I say no? It would be like saying no to Mother Teresa."

What is often forgotten about the March on Washington for Jobs and Freedom is that it didn't end with Dr. King inviting America to dream with him of a nation in which all of us "will be able to join hands and sing in the words of the old Negro spiritual: 'Free at last! Free at Last! Thank God Almighty, we are free at last!'"

No. Just before Morehouse College president Benjamin E. Mays delivered the benediction, Mr. Randolph again took to the podium, this time to introduce Bayard to read "the demands."

Bayard began, in that punchy style of speaking that he had, telling the audience that the march leaders were scheduled to meet with President Kennedy at 5 p.m. and that they should go with a set of demands from "this revolution" that are endorsed by the march. He went on to read a demand and wait for marchers to affirm it.

"The first demand is that we have effective civil rights legislation—no compromise, no filibuster—and that it includes public accommodations, decent housing, integrated education, FEPC (Fair Employment Practices Commission), and the right to vote. What do you say?"

"YEAH!"

"Number 2: They want that we demand the withholding of federal funds from all programs in which discrimination exists. What do you say?"

"YEAH!"

"We demand that segregation be ended in every school district in the year 1963."

"YEAH!"

"We demand the enforcement of the 14th Amendment, the reducing of congressional representation of states where citizens are disenfranchised."

"YEAH!"

"We demand an executive order banning discrimination in all housing supported by federal funds."

"YEAH!"

"We demand that every person in this nation, Black or white, be given training and work with dignity to defeat unemployment and automation."

"YEAH!"

"We demand that there be an increase in the national minimum wage so that men may live in dignity."

"YEAH!"

"We demand that all the rights given to any citizen be given to Black men, and men of every minority group, including a strong FEPC. We demand."

"YEAH!"

Mr. Randolph, clearly pleased, returned to the microphone and led the audience in a pledge to personally commit to the meaning and mission of the march, to continue to struggle nonviolently for jobs and freedom, to pledge their hearts, minds, and bodies to "the achievement of social peace through social justice."

Norman, who was thirty at the time, and I, twenty-four, could hardly believe what we had just experienced. We realized almost immediately that most of the decisions regarding the march had been the best ones. It was right, for example, to remove civil disobedience and direct action from the march. It had been right to tone down John's speech. It had been right to concentrate the march on domestic matters.

Sometimes movements want to do too much. But there are times when the focus has to be narrower in order for people to come away with what it was all about. Sit-ins, for instance, would have distracted from that.

The movement got a great deal of what it needed that late-summer day in 1963—but not everything.

*There is no doubt that the March on Washington for Jobs and Freedom was a resounding success, despite the fact that no march, no matter how massive, could secure either one of its goals.* We saw the march as an important start, a declaration to action. Mr. Randolph and Bayard certainly felt that the event had exceeded even their considerably high expectations. But in the wake of the march, there was a sense that the real work was about to begin.

Within an hour of the last speech of the day, Mr. Randolph, Wilkins, Young, Lewis, and Dr. King, among other leaders from the march, were ushered into the Cabinet Room. There, they met President Kennedy, flanked by Vice President Johnson. Kennedy, like millions across America, had watched the march live on television. He was duly impressed with Dr. King and his speech, even famously greeting him with "I have a dream" and a kind of good-job nod.

And while Velma and I learned that the meeting was cordial, we know that Mr. Randolph urged Kennedy to press more vigorously to get the civil rights bill through Congress. But Kennedy, facing reelection pressures, soon began supporting a more limited civil rights bill, thinking perhaps that it could find support among powerful elements in Congress that opposed it. By October, a compromise bill was hammered out with House leaders. This bill watered down the public-accommodations clause, exempting retail stores and personal services. Voting rights protections would apply only to federal elections. And the labor provisions, like a Fair Employment Practices Committee, were removed and the proposed Equal Employment Opportunity Commission weakened.

That bill passed the Judiciary Committee on November 20. Two days later, Kennedy was dead.

But strengthened by the march, some of the bill's supporters continued to lobby for a stronger bill. The Leadership Conference on Civil and Human Rights, a coalition of organizations to protect civil and human rights in the United States, had become the main lobbying body pushing for an effective bill. It believed that it was extremely important, for instance, to have civil rights legislation that included a ban on employment discrimination because that was such an essential, important area of life. The Kennedys, both the president and the attorney general, argued against including that ban because they said they would never be able to get the legislation through Congress and overcome a Southern filibuster.

The Leadership Conference—founded in 1950 by Mr. Randolph, Wilkins, and Arnold Aronson, a leader of the National Jewish Community Relations Advisory Council—would not accept this setback. Its leadership, which included the Washington director of the NAACP, Clarence Mitchell Jr.—sometimes known as the "101st senator"—went to George Meany. While Meany had refused to endorse the Washington march, the Leadership Conference appealed to him to help get an amendment to the weakened civil rights legislation that would outlaw employment discrimination.

Meany agreed to do that. He went before Congress and testified that he and the AFL-CIO supported a civil rights bill that included the ban. He went further, saying that the amendment should include not only employers and employment agencies but unions as well. He said there was a need for an "extra stick" to clean up the house of labor.

As a result, Title VII—the section that bans employment discrimination—was added to the civil rights legislation. The Equal Employment Opportunity Commission (EEOC) would enforce the ban.

I think the success of the march had something to do with Meany's evolution. It most likely influenced him to belatedly offer his endorsement to one of the march's central demands.

The march gave energy and focus to the lobbying efforts. Participation in the Leadership Conference was expanded after August 1963, now embracing numerous churches, almost in direct relation to their involvement in the Washington march. In states with low Black populations, white churches pitched in. The National Council of Churches, for instance, made contact through their local churches and branches to their elected officials. But Mitchell and Joe Rauh, a civil rights lawyer and a founder of the Americans for Democratic Action in 1947, directed much of the most successful lobbying for the bill through their stewardship of the Leadership Conference.

On July 2, 1964, President Johnson signed the Civil Rights Act. It was a landmark piece of legislation. The act banned major forms of discrimination against Blacks and women. It set out to end unequal application of voter registration requirements. And it prohibited racial segregation in schools, the workplace, and facilities that served the general public. Over the years, the federal government's capacity to enforce the act grew increasingly stronger.

*But Norman and I think the Washington march could have done so much more for the cause of women.* It bothers me to this day that there was not a major woman speaker during the march. Its leadership had a separate program, a tribute to Black women in the civil rights movement, earlier that day. Yes, their names were called (exactly in this order and in this way)—Daisy Bates, Diane Nash Bevel, Mrs. Medgar Evers, Mrs. Herbert Lee, Rosa Parks, and Gloria Richardson. They each received some applause. But this was done before the march really got started. I mean, come on.

At that time the question of women, women's liberation, was not a big question among most of us. But it would not have in any way taken anything from the march to expand the Big 10 to the Big 11 to include a woman. Dorothy Height, the president of the National Council of Negro Women from 1957 to 1997 and a lifelong civil rights activist, could have spoken. She represented a major organization just like the men who spoke that day. A number of other women pushed to have women among major speakers that day, but in the end, all those calls were rejected, or simply not acted upon.

*I believe Velma is right.* I think that was the one major failing of the march. It could have been done.

But we do not believe that this failure at all tarnishes the overall brilliance of the march's legacy. So much of what was achieved that day is still shaping the best of this nation's possibilities. It has proved, all these decades later, to be precisely what Mr. Randolph described it to be, a "massive, moral revolution for jobs and freedom." President Johnson's War on Poverty, while unfortunately short-lived under the monstrous weight of the Vietnam War, had deep roots in the vision and spirit of the march.

*At the close of that day, Norman and I looked at each other and we knew that the Washington march had crystallized all we had been taught by Mr. Randolph and Bayard—the power of coalition politics, the importance of direct, nonviolent action, and the relevance of combining the struggles for economic justice and racial equality.* These ideas would soon form the foundation for Bayard's essay "From Protest to Politics."

Looking back, we believe that perhaps one of the most remarkable legacies of the march was the success of coalition building, even across lines once thought uncrossable, and helping to create the climate for the passage of the most comprehensive civil rights legislation in our nation's history, the Civil Rights Act of 1964 and later the Voting Rights Act of 1965.

And, of course, all this laid the foundation for the historic election of Barack Obama in 2008. What would Mr. Randolph and Rustin have thought about a Black man as president of the United States, of seeing him taking the oath of office as his eyes looked out on grounds hallowed with the history of the great march on that great day?

*Velma and I think we know, and it makes us smile.*

# CHAPTER 6

# Home, an Anchor in the Storm

Home. We had one, you know. Since the early 1960s, it has been New York, where we first worked for the Congress of Racial Equality. Our commitments to the civil rights movement kept us on the go, especially Norman, who seemed to always be flying somewhere to organize, to protest, to make speeches, the kind of work he did helping to organize the March on Washington for Jobs and Freedom. But we did have a domestic life, although we have to admit it was very different from most people's.

*Velma and I never had a nine-to-five job.* We seldom had full weekends off, either. Saturdays were good demonstration days because that was when people were more available to march or rally. This is still very much the case. Many Americans, if not most, work Monday through Friday. Millions of people still set aside Sunday to attend church or worship in their own ways. That left Saturday to run errands and set themselves to various chores.

*Norman and I have long thought that there are few chores greater than people fighting for, and maintaining, their rights, like working for racial equality and economic justice.* Looking over the state of protest in the early twenty-first century, we know that it was no accident that, for instance, the Women's March on Washington was held on a Saturday. It drew, according to press estimates, three times more people than President Donald Trump's inauguration the day before.

107

*Back in the '60s, Sundays belonged to Velma and me.* This was our day. I'd still get up early, around six or six thirty. I'd exercise, mostly sit-ups and push-ups, some stretching, for a few minutes before I would sit down to breakfast.

It was my routine, and its structure was reaffirming, just like relaxing as the sun rose with the Sunday *New York Times*, swollen with all the news its editors saw fit to print and for me to read. And there would be magazines, like *Dissent* and *Commentary*, to read. We read *The Economist* and books like Max Shachtman's *Theory of Bureaucratic Collectivism*, along with essays by Ralph Ellison, James Baldwin, and Michael Harrington, for example.

*Norman was a morning person, still is.* I never was. Sunday was the only day I could sleep in, so I did. I would stir from my sleep at around nine o'clock. The lengthening morning light at our bedroom window would find me under the covers of our queen-size bed. The glow of our portable black-and-white television would soon add its blue-gray illumination to the room as I watched, and sometimes only lazily listened to, the morning news shows. All these years later, I still do.

I liked the local stuff that dovetailed into our work at CORE, issues like housing desegregation and the terribly low numbers of Black members in the city's building trade unions. And then there were the heavy hitters of national and international news, *Meet the Press* and *Face the Nation*. I soaked it all in from our bed's cushy landscape of covers, blankets, pillows, and scattered sections of partially leafed through pages of the *New York Times*. Today, after a decade of near total blindness, Norm listens for hours to the *New York Times* by way of News Line, a telephone service for the visually impaired.

But back in the 1960s, it might be one in the afternoon on Sundays before I would get out of bed. That was especially true when Norman rejoined me there. We would talk and get playful with each other. Norman said he always liked my skin, soft skin I inherited from my mother.

*Velma's skin is like butter.* As long as I have known her it has been that way, smooth and the color of fine bourbon. On Sunday in bed, our voices would lower as if we were trading secrets.

*Did I tell you that Norman had great legs?* He does, you know. And he was a tender, attentive lover. We were not candles-and-moonlight lovers. We were a couple still in our twenties, and we were so full of love for each other. More important, we *liked* each other. We were good for each other, and we knew it. It shouldn't come as any surprise to anyone that we had our share of silent storms of passion in each other's arms.

I soon realized after Norman and I got married that Mama was wrong about this one thing. Sex wasn't so bad. In fact, it was great. The truth was that making love with Norman was special, very emotional. He knew what he was doing. And I found that sort of strange because Norman told me that he didn't have very much sex before we were married.

I always appreciated how patient Norm was with me. Once, while we were still just going together in Chicago, I decided that I had had enough of my virginity. I wanted him to make love to me. (What a scandal that would have been if my mother had found out. The sexual norms of the early 1960s weren't anything like the era of free love during the closing years of that decade.) We got a place. Once inside, we locked the door, turned off the lights, took off our clothes, and slid into bed.

I screamed.

There was something moving under the sheets. I told Norman that I was sure of it. It was warm and round. I told him that I thought it was a mouse. I could feel him grinning.

Norman assured me that only he and I were in that bed. Then I laughed at myself. I didn't know anything about sex, particularly when it came to the anatomy of an aroused man. Norman ended up holding me all night. I'll never forget that. I always feel closest to Norm when we are in bed, hugging, talking, just being the two interlocking halves of Mr. and Mrs. Hill.

*I always felt the same way about Velma, especially when I would come home from a trip.* It was never just me coming home, but me coming home to Velma. That meant something very special. Even through our ups and downs, that never changed.

*When it came to Norman, since he was away a lot, little things that I would think were so important—stuff around the house, things that needed to be done—were suddenly not as important when I would see him.* I learned that I couldn't even stay mad at Norman when he came home to me.

Just having him home again would melt away lots of the little things that often bedevil couples. Neither one of us knew much about marriage when we started our lives together, but we figured it out, and we are still figuring it out more than sixty years later.

Home life. Yes, even activists had a home life.

But unless your house had been bombed or burned down or something, history has paid little attention to how civil rights workers lived away from the protest lines, the clashes with police and the angry mobs. The truth was that our home lives were essential to our public lives that were pledged to accomplishing nothing less than changing the world. It was our anchor. Home was a place where our batteries got charged and recharged.

One of the essential differences that Norman and I had compared with most other couples in the civil rights movement is that we were *both* activists. That meant there was no one who stayed behind to take care of the important domestic chores, like shopping for groceries, cooking, cleaning house, paying the bills. Even Dr. King, he had Coretta, who would occasionally join a march or stand at his side at a press conference. But they had four children, all very young during the early years of the movement. She principally maintained the household so that he could do his work. The same was true for Andy Young and A. Philip Randolph and for so many others.

But we managed. Norman never cooked and wasn't much for cleaning house either. Sometimes I would ask him to, and he would say, "Yes, dear," but he never did. Still doesn't. But now, I guess, he has an excuse.

Well, he would take out the garbage and help put the dishes away sometimes. But like I said, I couldn't stay angry with him. So I did what I could in those unenlightened domestic days.

*Velma and I did okay.* We realized that our home lives were a part of our foundation. It was our place where we planted our feet at night so that we could stand up the next day.

I joined CORE's national staff as East Coast field secretary, and Velma eventually moved from New York CORE to join me at the national office. Our salaries were always modest but regular. Once, sometime in 1962, CORE couldn't make payroll, so no one got paid.

*Back then, money was so irrelevant to Norman and me.* We didn't do what we did for the money. And we always seemed to find a way to manage.

*For the first few months at CORE, Velma and I lived with my parents, who at the time had a big house in Summit, New Jersey.* I'd wake up there and usually would have a small breakfast. Then I would take a New Jersey Transit train to Hoboken and change there for a PATH train that would travel beneath the Hudson River and into Manhattan. I'd get out at West 33rd Street, near Macy's department store. Then I would catch the subway that carried me southeast to CORE's office at 38 Park Row, which was downtown near the Brooklyn Bridge.

I can't say it wasn't a pleasant way to start the day. In the hour or more I spent on three trains to get to my office, I mostly read the *New York Times*, paying closest attention to the day's offering of national and international news. Then, if I had the time, I would scan the sports section. I was, since the Dodgers left Brooklyn for Los Angeles in 1958, a New York Yankees fan. I still am.

At CORE, I shared an office with Gordon Carey, the program director. I'd usually arrive at 9 a.m. (unless I had attended an evening meeting the night before), always in suit and tie. For me, it was a kind of work uniform. And work began almost immediately. The first thing I would do was write out a list of everything I wanted to address that day.

*While Norman was at the office in those early CORE days, I stayed at home with Norman's mother and grandmother in New Jersey.* And we were joined by a woman who came twice a week to clean the house and do a little cooking.

That seemed to give Norman's mother a lot of time on her hands. With some of that time she turned her attention to me. I don't remember her talking to me very much. She was never impressed by Norman's work and commitment to the civil rights movement, and she seemed even less impressed with me, who was basically unemployed and still recovering from my paralysis.

I was miserable. I felt alone and isolated there in Summit. I did enjoy talking with Norman's maternal grandmother. She was a lovely lady in her seventies then. She had white-gray hair, and its contrast against her brown skin was pleasingly striking.

She was kind to me and liked to tell me stories about Norman, whom she called Sonny and so clearly loved. She would talk about when he was growing up, a sensitive boy who suffered with bouts of asthma.

Norman's mother, Bessie, whose skin was lighter and her features less delicate than her mother's, had a formal streak when it came to me. There were not a lot of, as she would say, Negro women like her in the early 1960s. In a time when most Black people had so little materially, here she was the wife of a successful Black dentist, living in a nice house, and had just about everything she wanted. I'm not saying that she put on airs, but she had this way.

Once, when she called Norman and me down to dinner, she told me I should go and dress for dinner; I didn't change my clothes, but I did make a show by washing my hands before joining everyone at the table.

Don't get me wrong. Bessie was sort of nice. She offered to take me shopping—just out of the blue. She had charge accounts at all the best stores. But I came to realize that she offered to do this only because she didn't think my clothes were up to her standards and taste. I decided that I had to make a stand, a statement.

"No, thank you," I told her firmly. "I want to wait until Norman can buy me those clothes."

It was clear that we needed to find our own place.

Before this move to New Jersey, Norman and I lived in a four-story walk-up in Chicago, in Hyde Park near the University of Chicago. We were newlyweds back then, and you know I'm a Chicago girl. It was nice, comfortable. Hyde Park is a real community, mixed and liberal. Still, when we started looking for our own place in New York I thought, *Hey, we're moving upscale.*

But the first place we looked was in Brooklyn Heights, not far from the East River. A friend of ours was the head of Boss Realty, and I think he was a socialist. He was friendly to us. He showed us an apartment; it was a small one-bedroom—apartments were much bigger in Chicago—but very nice. Yet, I was put off by the neighborhood, even though that part of Brooklyn has been a very good place to live for a long time, the kind of address almost anyone would be proud of.

In fact, in a couple of years, a television sit-com would become very popular featuring an upper-middle-class, teenage girl who lived in Brooklyn Heights with her stay-at-home mother, her New York newspaper editor father, a little brother, and an identical cousin who had traveled the world. It was called *The Patty Duke Show*, and every week its theme song would remind you that, yes, Patty, unlike her urbane cousin, Cathy, had only seen the sights "a girl can see from Brooklyn Heights."

I really didn't know anything about New York. All I knew was that I didn't like all the garbage cans sitting out everywhere on the streets in Brooklyn Heights. In Chicago you didn't see any garbage cans in front of buildings. I didn't realize then that there was a good reason for this, a simple one: Chicago had alleys. New York didn't.

All I could see and smell, standing in front of this apartment building, minutes away from a lovely promenade that looks out on that famous Manhattan skyline, were these garbage cans everywhere.

"Norm," I said, "this is nice and cozy, but let's look around some more."

That was a stupid thing I suggested because I didn't know, first of all, that Brooklyn Heights was a terrific community.

*I listened to Velma, but the garbage cans didn't bother me.* I knew New York didn't have many alleys. I promised her that we would keep looking.

*Briefly, in our search for a New York home, Norman and I lived in an apartment in uptown Manhattan that belonged to this feisty, old Eastern European woman; I think she might have been Russian.* She was something else. She was in her eighties and spoke with a heavy accent, sounding like someone in a faded, old foreign film. I wish we could have had the benefit of subtitles when she spoke. Once a robber tried to snatch her purse when she was in the building's elevator. She viciously beat that guy with her fists and purse and scared him away. She really was something else.

She was also part of a socialist network, a member of the Workers Defense League, which looked out for people like Norman and me. She was sweet and generous with us. I don't remember paying her anything for our room. We all understood that the arrangement was temporary. We were only there for a couple of months.

After that, we moved into a house in Harlem where Hal Jackson, the veteran New York radio broadcaster and personality lived. Back in 1962, Hal was a friend of Gladys Harrington, who was the chair of New York CORE in Harlem. Gladys offered Norman and me a place, and we figured that we'd move there until we could find our own apartment. Hey, it sounded good to me.

Hal was much older than Norman and me. He was born in 1915, grew up in Washington, DC, and had been quite a barrier breaker. He went to Howard University and while there became one of the first African Americans to broadcast sports on the radio. He would do play-by-play announcing of Howard's home baseball games as well as American Negro League baseball games when those teams played in Washington.

On WINX Washington, he shattered the color line in 1939 by hosting a nightly interview show called *The Bronze Review*. He went on to become the first Black broadcaster to host a jazz show on ABC's network, on his way to becoming a broadcasting legend. In 1995 he was inducted into the Radio Hall of Fame. He died in 2012, at age ninety-six.

His brownstone was in the Sugar Hill section of Harlem, around 145th Street and Convent Avenue. We moved in, and Hal was wonderful to us. The only strange thing I remember about the house was that he had hairpieces all over. I didn't know about hairpieces then. I was a little girl from the ghetto. If you lost your hair in the ghetto, you were just bald. Other than wearing a hat, there were no alternatives.

One evening, and I don't really know why I did this, I got out of bed and I snuck over to one of those hairpieces. I was twenty-three years old, and curiosity got the best of me. I just wanted to know what it felt like.

Hal also had a daughter, Jewel Jackson, who would go on to head the One-Hundred Black Women's organization. She also married a prominent doctor and did quite well for herself and her community. Back then, we saw her come and go.

Everyone in the house was so good to us. Gladys, Hal's friend, was very kind to us, too. Norman and I hadn't met Gladys before we reported to New York to work there. She was a social worker. She was a slender, well put together woman; her hair and make-up was always just so. She was attractive and had such a gentle voice and wonderful smile.

I'm sure Gladys was just trying to make sure we were settled in. That's what CORE people did. You came into a city and leadership there always reached a hand out to help you. And later, we did the same thing when we finally got our own apartment in Manhattan.

Somebody's coming in for a meeting or whatever, hey, we'd tell them, you can sleep on our couch, sleep on our floor. Our home was their home. You don't get that anymore. A major part of the difference, you see, is that these were not like people off the street. They were part of the CORE family, the same family we were a part of. In these times we don't have that sense of family anymore; we don't have that sense of a movement, that feeling of moving forward—together.

*In a matter of a few months, Velma and I got our own home, an apartment off East 107th Street, between Second and Third Avenues in Manhattan.*

It was a new, red-brick high-rise near the East River called Franklin Plaza, and it was in a mixed neighborhood that was predominantly Black and Hispanic. It was a one-bedroom apartment on the seventh floor, and yes, we had elevators. There was a good-size living room, and a kitchen big enough for a table and chairs. We furnished it from what we could buy here and there, including a discount mattress from the father of a friend in the Young People's Socialist League. There was a round cocktail table and a brown couch covered in a fake suede, Naugahyde, I think it was.

*Norman and I liked our place.* It felt homey.

This was the late fall of 1961, and New York was beginning to show its wear a little, especially in neighborhoods like this one literally on the edge. The old-money opulence of the Upper East Side was a short walk away, and an even shorter walk would land you in East Harlem, which was richly vibrant but dollar poor. But there was no sense of suffocating crime and peril that came to characterize East Harlem in the decades to come. There were a lot of poor people around, but Norman and I don't remember being conscious of street crime and drugs around where we were living. Franklin Plaza was an environment that I was comfortable with, and I don't recall the neighborhood that surrounded it being bad at all.

Norman and I never, for instance, tripped over junkies or anything like that. It was a big rental apartment complex with lots of buildings with wrap-around windows, and was a quick walk to the Lexington Avenue subway line. Like most New Yorkers, we didn't have a car. And I don't remember being afraid when Norm wasn't there. I'd walk alone, and it was fine. Unlike today, there was nothing like the homeless. There were no people hanging around the subway. I don't even remember panhandlers.

When I walked around the city, anywhere in the city, I smiled, and lots of people smiled at me and said hello. I would say hello back, just like when I was a kid growing up in Chicago. One of my New York friends cautioned me not to do that, but I kept doing it, still do, and it has never gotten me into trouble yet.

When Norman and I moved into Franklin Plaza, no one was swearing on the streets. You didn't hear what you hear today—from kids. Young people were better behaved. Now you get on a subway…well, I don't ride the subway anymore because of my leg. It's hard for me to get up and down all those stairs. But get on a bus, and it's mother-F this and mother-F that. You want to say, "Hey, cool it." But you don't. You might get killed.

People then sort of dressed up before they went out in public. I wore hats sometimes—well, until Bella Abzug, the feminist lawyer who was a New York congresswoman, made hats her trademark. That ruined it for me. She made it seem like theater, a put-on; plus, I didn't like her politics. I was never into big, showy hats. I liked summery hats, a little something with firm brims that would shade your face with a bit of mystery. I also liked tams, and in the wintertime I wore something like a fedora.

Hats or not, it always seemed to take me a long time to get dressed in the morning. I'm much better now. But back then, I was always rushing into that subway. And I don't remember air-conditioning down there, either. I was an anxious rider, worrying whether I had buttoned up everything right, picking at my Afro and knowing I was going to be late to the office.

Some months after Norman started working at CORE's national office downtown, I got a job as executive director of New York CORE, uptown in Harlem on West 125th Street. It was only a few subway stops and a cross-town bus ride from home.

Getting off the bus for work one day, I bumped into Percy E. Sutton. He was a well-dressed, lovely man with such a charming way about him. He became friends with Norman and me. Percy was a lawyer and in 1961 had just been elected president of the New York NAACP and would later become the Manhattan borough president. He also came to represent Malcolm X shortly before Malcolm was assassinated in February 1965.

Sutton was a real political player in New York's Black community, eventually helping to engineer the 1989 election of one of his Democratic Party protégés, David N. Dinkins, as the city's first Black mayor.

In the early 1970s, Sutton would help found and lead the Inner City Broadcasting Corporation, which would operate a number of popular radio stations, including some in New York, Philadelphia, and the San Francisco area. Norman and I approached him about my doing an issues-oriented talk show in New York. He seemed open to the idea but noted that his lineup for the coming year had already been set. He offered to have me come in from time to time as a guest on existing programs. It sounded like a good idea, but I never had a chance to take him up on it.

In the early 1960s, we had a lot of dinner parties in our apartment. On weekends, if somebody in the movement came to town, we'd invite people over and have a little party, singing freedom songs, some gospel, and some Curtis Mayfield, like "People Get Ready."

There was lots of singing. And sometimes dancing, too. It was lots of fun. There would be drinking and there would be people who would pair up, maybe some kissing and hugging, but it was usually pretty innocent.

Sometimes, someone would want to smoke marijuana, and I would always say no, not in my house. That's the last thing a group of activists needed, to get busted by police for smoking grass. No, no, no.

Neither Norman nor I was much into drinking. Norman would occasionally have a little Scotch or a glass of ale, something his father liked to drink. I usually stuck to my glass of sherry or white wine when we went out. It didn't take much alcohol for me to start feeling its effects.

Norman never touched drugs, well, maybe a brush once with a joint— long before I met him.

*It never had an effect on me, Velma.*

*I believe that, Norm, because you are so controlled.* But I also tried marijuana once. It was years later, in 1968, when I was a master's student at Harvard. I went there to get an education and get away from the stress that came with being an activist in the movement. One night, I was at the home of a couple, friends of ours. They were activists like us, outgoing, smart, and urbane.

Another couple came over, and before I realized it, everyone was smoking marijuana like having after-dinner drinks.

This was Cambridge, Massachusetts, in the late 1960s, so marijuana was hardly unknown. But I had never smoked before. I don't know if my friends had either. Remember, I grew up in a strict household. If people smoked marijuana in Chicago, they certainly didn't do it in front of my family and me.

I sat back and watched these two couples lighting up these twisted, little cigarettes, watching the thin, pungent smoke drift over their heads. Then someone handed me this thing and said, "Don't smoke it like a cigarette. You have to suck in the smoke and hold it."

Right then, I decided that I was going to do this. After all, I was with good friends who would look out for my welfare. It was a safe place. I suddenly became determined to smoke marijuana, and everyone started to teach me how.

I had heard that if you smoke pot, it accentuates whatever mood you're in. If you're depressed, it will make you more depressed. If you're happy, it will make you happier, and giddy. If you are paranoid, it will make you more paranoid.

They took the joint and puffed, puffed, puffed, then passed it to me.

Looking back, I remember being a bit reluctant to smoke this stuff even after I decided that I would. I think it wasn't until after the third or fourth time the joint came to me—*What the hell?* I thought—I took my first puff. Then another and another.

I didn't feel anything. I took out my compact and looked at myself in its mirror and asked myself, *Is this changing me at all?* I don't know what I expected to see, maybe my eyes going around in googly circles like they do in cartoons when the mouse hits the cat in the head with a sledgehammer. If I saw that in me, well, that would certainly mean the marijuana was having some effect. Then I started thinking, worrying really, *What if there is something I've been hiding about myself that I didn't know about? A monster lurking somewhere behind my trademark smile?* Norman and I had a friend who really went off the deep end smoking pot.

After some deep draws of marijuana, I sat back on the couch and discovered something. It was a throw pillow. It was furry. And I rubbed that pillow practically all night, and everything was funny to me. I would laugh and rub that pillow. That pillow felt *sooo* good. And I had a warm feeling all through me.

But marijuana didn't do that much for me, not nearly as much as a nice strong drink would. And there was the matter about marijuana being illegal. I felt it wasn't good enough to risk arrest. So, that was that. No more marijuana. I told Norman all about it.

*And I told Velma that I was fine with it so long as she wasn't going to do it again. I wasn't upset.*

*Back in New York with Norman, I especially remember a night at Richard Ravitch's house.* Dick was a native New Yorker who came from money but worked hard for what he had. This was long before he was the chairman of the city's Metropolitan Transportation Authority and long before he was the state's lieutenant governor. Back in the 1960s, when he was developing low- and middle-income housing projects with his family's construction business, he had a big, beautiful apartment.

One night, in his living room, Dick hosted with his wife, Diane, what he called "An Evening with Bayard Rustin." Dick gathered thirty to forty people in his home, hired a renowned pianist, and showcased Bayard, who sang spirituals, civil rights songs, and Elizabethan ballads. It was a concert of the highest order. Bayard was so dapper when he took his place by this gleaming piano. He was terrific, and the night was extraordinary.

Bayard really prepared for the evening, even calling me up that day to sing some of his selections over the phone to see what I thought. "So, what did you think of that, Miss Velma?" he'd ask me in his impish way. I'd just confirm what he already knew. Everything he sang sounded so good, even over a telephone line.

When Norman was out of town, I would go to the movies with friends. Once in the early 1960s, a girlfriend of mine, who was Jewish, and I went to see *Exodus*, which starred Paul Newman and Eva Marie Saint. It was about the founding of Israel.

I was sitting there in the audience, and then during some dramatic point, I think when the Jewish refugees arrived in Israel and were enraptured in song, my friend rose from her seat and started yelling, "These are my people! These are my people!"

I said, "Girl, sit down." But she was a sweetheart.

*Velma and I did so many things together.* One of our favorite times was visiting our friend and mentor Max Shachtman at his home on Long Island. Max was a political theoretician of the Socialist Party USA and later the Social Democrats USA. He was a brilliant writer, thinker, and respected leader of the democratic left. We'd take the Long Island Railroad out to Floral Park and were always so happy to see him and his third wife, Yetta.

Max was older and worldlier than us then and an important mentor to us. He wasn't tall and spoke with a slight accent he carried into English from his native Polish people. He was bald and had a graying goatee, and Velma used to say he reminded her of Lenin or Trotsky. We used to say that he had eyes that sparkled and laughed when he looked at you.

*Norman and I never knew anyone better than Max at carefully listening to you describe a complicated knot of political conditions and conflicts you might be facing and then dispassionately unscrambling the situation and laying out crystal clear options you might best consider.* I learned so much from him. And like Norman, Max was a lover of jazz.

Norman and I loved him and Yetta. Max called me his "Egyptian princess." And I'd say, "Max, how come I can't just be a Black American princess? Why do I have to be something else?" He'd wave me off and just turn up his charm another notch.

The first time I heard him speak, he spoke for four hours. It was incredible. It was a presentation, and he did that all the time. And he would cut down his enemies. *Snap!*—just like that. I saw him debate a communist once and found myself an eyewitness to murder by logic and razor-sharp insight.

Although we talked politics when we got to Max's house, it was a social occasion.

Norman and I would go out there pretty regularly. We would listen to music. He had lots of good music, an enormous collection of jazz records. The kind of jazz that goes *louloulooouloulouloooouloulou.* I thought that was the music of hysterics. They're going all up and down the scale, no melody. Norman had to teach me about jazz and how to listen to it. He introduced me to the music of Horace Silver, and that helped. Norman and I would occasionally go to hear live jazz at places like the Village Vanguard and the Blue Note. In New York, we were comfortable in our skins.

*Velma and I didn't have a second thought about moving in integrated circles or worrying about someone in jazz clubs or restaurants mistreating us or disrespecting us because we were Black.* That was so different from our experiences in the South.

*In New York, Norman and I would just walk into a place—usually white—and feel good about being there, and we would dare anyone to say anything about our Blackness.* Seldom did anyone say a thing.

I did notice that in jazz clubs, there weren't that many Blacks. I struck me sort of odd, given that jazz is largely an invention of African Americans. Then again, maybe the dearth of Black patrons was because these places were relatively expensive. I was into classical music, into folk music, anyway, and into a little blues. None of that *louloulooouloulouloooouloulou* you hear in these jazz places. I thought it was a piece of crap. And at first, I thought Norman was a little weird for liking it.

I also had a kind of sociopolitical bias against it. When I was younger, I thought jazz was a product of middle-class intellectuals, Blacks particularly, who didn't understand rhythm and blues and didn't want to be a part of it. Unlike Norman, who had John Coltrane, Charlie Parker, and Miles Davis, I grew up with the Weavers, Joan Baez, and Odetta; I knew all their songs. Back in Chicago we used to have little parties and we used to play folk music, and Blacks as well as whites used to sing folks songs together.

Some people say Blacks didn't listen to folk music. We did. We sang a lot of folk music when we had parties at our apartment. But along with all the fun, we discussed serious issues that were at the core of racial integration—many are still unresolved to this day. One of them involved dating.

There was a lot of socializing at our apartment, and it usually involved CORE people. And almost without fail, one of the Black girls would say to me, "Look over there. There's Joe Schmoe kissing What's-Her-Name."

I would say, "Right. That's all right as long as they don't go further."

"No, no, no. It's not that," I would hear. "This always happens!"

And that "always" would be a Black man from CORE getting frisky with a white woman from CORE.

By 1962, a group of Black CORE women began visiting me after work hours at the apartment to discuss *the problem*.

I think they came to me because Norman and I were the only Black couple in CORE's national office. We had a natural affinity with these women, and it was obvious that we could move easily in the white world, too. In particular, these Black women wanted my advice and help. They felt rejected, overlooked, as they watched the single Black men in the organization chase after (or be chased by) the white women in CORE.

You have to understand that this was still the early civil rights movement. This was one of the first times that Black people and white people, Black men and white women—the rank and file—could work together on an equal basis. The very ethos of CORE was to promote racial equality.

After all, its cofounder and director, James L. Farmer Jr., was married to a white woman.

I believe the Black guys thought, *Oh boy, woo, woo, woo. All this forbidden fruit and here I am in the orchard. I'm going to pick some of this.*

What ended up happening was that I met privately with these CORE Black women, and then I talked to some of the Black guys too about this issue. I had no hesitation in this. I figured that the worst thing that could happen was that someone would tell me to go and mind my own business. They couldn't hurt me. We were pretty much the same age, and I was in a leadership position.

No one objected. In fact, some like my childhood friend Bobbie, who worked with me at CORE, made a convincing case that I had to do something. She was practically hysterical when it came to this problem.

"I'm sick of this shit," she told me once. "Every time a Black man gets a little money or prestige he goes off and finds somebody white, and it doesn't matter what they look like. They could be ugly. All she just has to have is white skin."

It didn't matter to me who went with whom, who slept with whom. But what mattered to me was the fact that the Black guys seldom paid any attention to the Black girls at CORE. It was unfortunate. I knew there was a hurt there. And as a result, these Black women were angry with the guys. Some of these women were middle class, but a lot of them were working class, and none of them wanted to accept what was happening.

There was an irony that escaped none of them. They worked in an organization dedicated to bringing about equality among the races, yet the very people who made them feel the least equal were their Black brothers who acted as if these women were socially invisible. The problem was very pronounced.

"They don't even ask us out on dates," they would tell me. "They don't go any place with us—lunch, nothing. If we're in a group, they're looking for a white girl."

I'm not going to say that I had all the answers for them. Don't forget that this was before the Black Is Beautiful movement. So, a lot of these women weren't feeling as good about themselves as they should have. But

I asked them what they were doing to attract the attention of the Black men in the organization.

I had noticed that unlike the white girls, most of the Black girls didn't speak up, take the initiative, during CORE meetings. They sat in the back of the room or faded into the background while the white girls were making motions and substitute motions. The white girls gave the impression that they knew what they were doing, and if they knew what they were doing in meetings, maybe, the men thought, they knew what they were doing in other areas, too.

So, I asked the Black girls if they even knew *Robert's Rules of Order*, if they knew parliamentary procedure. Most didn't. I told them that they had to learn if they wanted to compete. So, I started to teach them.

What I was saying to them is that the white girls, unlike them, seemed to have self-assurance and a knowledge that helped them create an impression that they were serious about the movement. They would take organizational positions that indicated that they understood the mission and what was necessary to move things along. The Black girls had to realize why they were in the movement in the first place. They needed to display their commitment, their understanding of the organization. And this was really important; they had to be ready to compete on all kinds of levels. It started with them standing up for themselves as individuals.

I wanted to see them more organizationally sophisticated. Without such sophistication of purpose and performance, no one was going to take them seriously on any level, including romantically. If they asserted themselves more in meetings, for example, I told them that the Black men in CORE would notice them more. But that was just the start in trying to get them to be more assertive. They had been raised by Black families and reinforced in their Black churches to be demure, to wait for the man to make the first move.

The white girls tended to be much more aggressive. They were more sure of themselves socially and sexually. They had been raised to be so, and American culture reaffirmed it in the movies, on television, in advertisements and magazines, almost everywhere they looked, everywhere anybody looked, for that matter. Black women were getting the exact opposite message, and the effects were evident.

The Black guys in the office were not into subtle seduction when these white girls were making the first move, walking up to these young men and saying, "Hey, honey, you want to go out?"

And there was the whispered suggestion that some of the white girls were sexually forward, that some of them were into oral sex. In 1962, oral sex was still quite taboo for most Black women. Black girls were not into that. In fact, most of them thought it was dirty, and some of them told me as clearly as they could that they were not up for much more than standard-issue, missionary-position sex—if any at all.

"We're not going to do it," a group of Black CORE women once told me regarding oral sex—receiving it or giving it.

Part of this sexual conservatism was rooted in the church. The idea that premarital sex was a sin was still very much a part of these women's upbringing. And their mothers'. See, most Black mothers back then didn't talk about sex. I don't know what white mothers did, but I know that when I grew up, Black mothers didn't discuss it with their children, especially not with their daughters.

They might give you a book to read about the basics of sex, but they didn't talk about sex and experimentation and all of that. They talked about having babies. So, what did we grow up with? Sex and procreation—and sex is not for fun.

I think that many Black women in the movement, and outside the movement for that matter, saw themselves as good girls. Anything else was what bad girls did, what whores did.

When we gathered in my apartment, I told the women that they just had to speak up. I told them to know what they wanted and don't be afraid to ask for it. "All you can get is a no," I said. That point is true today. You have to feel good about yourself.

I think Alvin Poussaint, the Black Harvard professor of psychiatry, was right when he said that the Black Is Beautiful movement came about more as a response to Black women than as a political challenge to the status quo. What that meant to me was that reclaiming our appreciation for our unique appearance was to say that our Blackness as women was vitally important: like yourself as a Black woman, and therefore, we can like one another as a Black people.

Then, as it is today, this problem is not entirely Black men's responsibility. Black women have a responsibility, too. And Black women have to develop the attitude, which many of them didn't have in 1962, that a man is a man, whether he is Black or white. Most of these women were afraid to date white guys. We have to foster integration at all levels.

I've said that if Norm had been white, I would have married him anyway. If he was as smart and as sweet and he had my politics and all that other stuff, race would not have mattered. It just wouldn't have. But Norman turned out to have all of that, and he happened to be Black, too.

Norman and I believe that love and work are two of life's essentials. Something magical happens when the two intertwine in such a way that makes them an integral whole, a single, complex weave of enormous strength. That describes our devotion to working for racial equality, and economic and social justice; and that describes our devotion to each other.

That is our love.

Yet, Norm and I understand that there is more at stake in these interactions between Black men and Black women. It is, and has long been, more than just about romance. For example, several years ago, I was told by a friend that Black women students at New York University were feeling much the same way that the Black women at CORE were feeling in the 1960s. But the students were suggesting that there was a deeper dimension to it all. Many of them felt that they, in a larger sense, were being shortchanged by Black men in the collective struggle for equality. So many felt that the struggle had not been reciprocal, that the commitment to overcome Black women's oppression had taken a backseat. That bothers me. That was 2013, and we were still being confronted with this issue, a collision of racial and gender interests. It's what a new generation of scholars and activists call intersectionality.

I am encouraged by what I see among young Black women today. In the office and workplace, they have achieved so much more than Black women were able to in the 1950s and '60s. And they seem to have a much greater confidence, in many cases achieving higher levels of education and salaries than their Black male counterparts.

*Velma and I have also noticed that in a time of scarcities of marriageable Black men, Black women are more open to interracial relationships and marriages.* Perhaps as a consequence of the civil rights movement, as uneven as some of its attention was regarding Black women's issues, Black women today have vastly more options than they did sixty years ago.

*While there is much work still to be done, this makes Norman and me very happy.*

CHAPTER 7

# CORE, Crossroads, and Lightning Rods

In 1965, Curtis Mayfield and the Impressions recorded the song "People Get Ready." It had a gospel feeling to it and was no more than a few minutes long. Almost right away it became a hit and went on to become an enduring anthem of hope and struggle. Decades after its release, "People Get Ready," which was written by Mayfield, was inducted into the Grammy Hall of Fame, and new voices continue to sing it into a kind of everlasting life.

The lyrics feature a haunting call for people, bringing only their faith, to get onboard a train. Everyone knows that the train is en route to freedom for a weary people who had known only a hard life of walking uphill with heavy loads. That train is a lot like the chariot in the old Black spiritual "Swing Low, Sweet Chariot."

No one with ears and a heart has to be told that the chariot isn't swinging by for a joyride. This was serious stuff.

But when "People Get Ready" was being recorded in Chicago, Norman and I knew that lots of people, especially Black people, were not sure what train to board for their freedom, even which track the train might take.

The truth was that the civil rights movement should have been steaming across a transitional bridge, as Bayard Rustin would put it in his 1965 essay "From Protest to Politics." But instead, the movement found itself at a disquieting crossroads. This could not have been more apparent than where Norman and I found ourselves.

We were on the national staff of CORE and based at its New York headquarters as the very fabric of the organization was beginning to fray. Norman and I were right in the middle of what would become a great unraveling of CORE's values and mission.

*Velma and I could see that CORE had, as the mid-1960s approached, declined considerably in terms of its vision and, in some ways, its status.* It was a far cry from CORE at its activist peak, epitomized in its daring days of the Freedom Rides in the spring of 1961, an era that extended to when I joined the organization later that year as its East Coast field secretary and when Velma followed me there a short time later from New York CORE.

By the summer of 1963, James Farmer, CORE's cofounder and director, was beginning to lose control of the organization. Velma and I could see that he was racked with suspicions and visions of office intrigue. There was a very real split developing among CORE's membership along a fault line of what direction the organization should take and who should take it there. The main concern was a lack of leadership.

Velma and I understood that CORE was dedicated to racial integration and the use of direct, nonviolent action to achieve its integrationist goals with a membership that was itself integrated—even its leadership. CORE was also decidedly middle-class, viewing itself as a kind of elite vanguard. When Velma and I joined CORE's national office, the organization was not very interested in an agenda of greater inclusion of the Black working class and poor. But we were.

*By early 1964, Norman, who was then national program director, and I, the East Coast field secretary, could sense the rise of Black nationalism that encouraged Black separatism and a general air of hostility toward whites.* We could practically smell what Norman calls "pseudo-militancy" filtering into the CORE ranks, animating fiery figures like Sonny Carson at Brooklyn CORE and Roy Innis at New York CORE in Harlem. There were meetings when discussions would get heated and a Black CORE member, for example, would shout "shut up" at a white CORE member, then add something like, "Don't forget, this is *our* organization!"

Jim seemed powerless to do much about this. Soon, the idea of an all-inclusive, direct-action movement that embraced nonviolence not only as a moral imperative but also as a tactic seemed outmoded for an increasingly vocal group of CORE members. This was particularly true for some CORE members in Brooklyn and the Bronx; they believed in a kind of mindless radicalism.

This tension between traditional civil rights ideas and impulses and nationalist-inspired ideas was not unique to CORE. Norman and I saw similar issues emerging in other civil rights organizations, like the Student Nonviolent Coordinating Committee, which would in 1966 be led by Stokely Carmichael; he would use SNCC to launch his campaign for "Black Power" and fully denounce nonviolence as a means of achieving equal opportunity and racial justice in America. Stokely helped to popularize the defiant term with the 1967 publication of his book *Black Power: The Politics of Liberation in America*, written with Charles V. Hamilton.

Bayard scoffed at the nationalists, saying that "wearing my hair afro style, calling myself an Afro-American and eating all the chitterlings I can find are not going to affect Congress." Conversely, he often said that if all Black people turned white by noon, by 12:01 they'd still suffer problems of inequality. "The issue was not simply one of race," he said, noting that the problems were not merely racial; they were also economic and social. These required institutional strategies that address both race *and* class.

William Julius Wilson, the Black Harvard scholar, would bear out many of Bayard's conjectures and projections regarding race and class in his own work, including his landmark 1980 book, *The Declining Significance of Race: Blacks and Changing American Institutions*. He dedicated the book to Bayard.

The tilt toward Black nationalism was complete at CORE when Roy Innis took control of the organization in 1968. CORE would become oddly both nationalistic and conservative, aligning itself with the administration of Richard Nixon. Whites fled CORE, especially white women, many of whom went to the peace movement and the women's movement.

Before Innis, CORE's national organizational stance was always pro-Black, but never anti-white.

*All of this—the demise and destruction of the integrationist, activist phase of the civil rights movement—helped Velma and me make our transition from the civil rights movement to the labor movement.* And I'm thinking specifically of CORE first and later SNCC. Bayard seemed to enjoy intellectually challenging a new class of leaders of these organizations who were increasingly embracing the ideas of Frantz Fanon, the Afro-French philosopher who advocated for oppressed peoples to free themselves through violent revolution. Bayard, as only Bayard could in his incisive, penetrating, and thoroughly reasoned way, demonstrated how Fanon's approach was not relevant to successful Black struggle in America.

*I agree with Norman, and yet there was something more: CORE's leadership was ambivalent and lacked clarity when it came to the time to take a leap to programmatically resolve the problems of race and class that beset the Black community.* This was manifested in how its memberships had coalesced into four distinct and opposing tendencies.

One tendency materialized as CORE people who viewed themselves as shock troops for integration. They were both white and Black and were really, in my opinion, a middle-class, elite vanguard. Then there were the pseudo-militants, some of whom were influenced by undemocratic ideologies like those advanced by the Socialist Workers Party and the Communist Party; they were Black and white and characterized by CORE members like Sonny Carson. There were the Black nationalists, personified by Roy Innis, who were primarily separatists who felt that Black America's best hope was to disengage from whites. And then there was us.

We were trying to steer a course that was different from any one of these three tendencies. Norman and I, along with a cadre of CORE members, felt we had to involve the full Black community, of course including its working class and poor. We were dedicated to remaining integrationists and building coalitions, including with labor, liberal and progressive religious groups, to advance a social justice agenda. Linking civil rights and labor was a very important part of our agenda.

*Before we resigned from CORE in the late summer of 1964, Velma was directly involved in the interwoven issues of civil rights and organized labor.* She was working with building trade unions, pressing them to open their ranks to Blacks in substantive and meaningful ways.

She led CORE picket lines and sit-ins at Harlem Hospital, where major reconstruction of the facility was being done without including Black workers. We set up picket lines at New York's luxurious Waldorf Astoria hotel to encourage its management to hire more Blacks and upgrade poorly paid Blacks already working there. We did similar work directed at A&P Stores and the Trailways Bus Company.

*Some of the most interesting work Norman and I did at CORE that combined civil rights and economic justice was when we worked with New York–based Black playwrights and performing artists who noted numerous instances in which stage and screen productions did not include Blacks.*

We learned that a film of the D-Day invasion of Normandy had been shot and did not include a single Black actor in its depiction of this monumental military campaign. That 1962 film was *The Longest Day* and was produced by Darryl F. Zanuck, who was probably best known at the time for his film *All About Eve.*

The World War II film starred John Wayne and Richard Burton. The Black actors we met with were very upset. We pressed Zanuck, and he responded by sending a letter addressed to CORE, promising that all his future productions would be sure to portray a more authentic reality.

We were pleased, but still, at the insistence of the actors, CORE set up informational picket lines at the most prominent New York theater where the movie was playing, which was in Times Square.

In this work, Norman and I got to know Black entertainers like Yaphet Kotto, Godfrey Cambridge, Lou Gossett Jr., Ossie Davis, and Harlem-based activist and dancer Barbara Ann Teer. Her older sister, Fredrica, also an activist, worked for a time with us at National CORE in New York.

At one point, actors came to CORE regarding a Broadway musical called *Subways Are for Sleeping*, produced by David Merrick. It was set in New York but included no Blacks in its cast, not even as extras on its subway set. The musical ran from 1961 to 1962. We understood artistic license, but all-white New York subways? Come on.

Norman and I met with the actors at night, usually at eleven or midnight, because they were working actors and couldn't meet with us during regular working hours. We all agreed that even fictional subway cars should not be segregated. CORE readied for direct action—demonstrations, boycotts, and such. Again, concessions were made and CORE received a promise from the musical's production team that it would make a good-faith effort to place Black actors in its future productions.

Yet at CORE, especially in 1963 and 1964, pressures of mission and means were leading to troubling fractures along an ideological divide. This flared into the open in April 1964 when CORE planned protests aimed at the World's Fair being held at Flushing Meadows in Queens. National CORE correctly pointed out that this sprawling collection of pavilions and attractions was built by very few, if any, Black workers. And Black representation was hardly any better when it came to the fair's jobs, like ticket takers and concession workers.

*Velma and I felt that CORE was rightly pressing for the inclusion of Black workers in this massive project.* The fair, which famously featured a twelve-story, hollow steel globe called the Unisphere, was already completed. But CORE felt strongly that the absence of Black workers should be called to the attention of politicians, policymakers, and the general public across the country.

National CORE had black-and-white buttons made for the protests that showed the Unisphere, which still stands, encircled by the words "CORE Wants a FAIR World." We firmly believed that the correct kind of protests would, with all the tinsel and glitter of the fair, underscore the lack of a meaningful and significant presence of Blacks and other minorities employed there.

But the national office was compelled to oppose dissident CORE chapters, including those in Brooklyn and the Bronx, that threatened to launch their own protest they called a "stall-in" on the fair's opening day, April 22, which was my thirty-first birthday. The centerpiece of the action was to drive some 2,500 cars over the roads and highways leading to the Queens fairgrounds and then have them run out of gasoline en masse, blocking prospective fairgoers. At the same time, hundreds of others would yank the emergency brakes on subway trains in the area while more protesters would block bridges leading to the fairgrounds with their bodies.

There was even talk of a plan to release rats into an audience gathered to hear President Johnson deliver his opening-day speech at the fair, an event the world would likely be tuned in to hear.

*Jim Farmer, Norman, and I realized that this protest, which promised to create chaos in the name of fighting racial discrimination, was anti-worker.* It was self-defeating. Thousands of people who had nothing to do with the composition of the World's Fair workforce would be prevented from going to not only the fair, but also their jobs in the city. This was unacceptable to us.

Farmer, who called the stall-in "harebrained," decided to launch what he termed a "counter demonstration." National CORE, in combination with some local New York groups, planned to mostly block the pedestrian entrance and some pavilions with protesters who would not leave until they were arrested and carried away by police. We thought this was much more effective and would not likely antagonize and alienate workers and the public, who could be our allies.

This is exactly what we did, and the stall-in petered out. Norman and I were happy to learn that no roadways were blocked. And there was certainly no release of rats during Johnson's speech, which had been made an invitation-only affair.

On the other hand, our World's Fair protest was very successful. We even had a song for it: "It happened April 22 of 1964. CORE people came to New York State, from far and distant shores, to march on the World's Fair and do what they must do."

Norman never sang, but I loved to sing back then. CORE had a song for everything. The refrain was "Freedom now...freedom now... freedom now..."

More than 600 people, Blacks and whites, came to block the fair's entrance and targeted pavilions. And lots of people got arrested, among them James Farmer, Bayard Rustin, Rochelle Horowitz, Michael

Harrington, Tom Kahn, and Ernest G. Green, a member of the Little Rock Nine who became the assistant secretary of labor in the Jimmy Carter administration.

But few people outside the demonstration ever knew what mess we had on our hands. We wanted this protest to be an especially well-ordered operation. To that end, CORE got us almost two dozen walkie-talkies. This was 1964, so they weren't cell-phone-size little things. They were huge and heavy and not the easiest to operate.

We assigned each CORE protest marshal a walkie-talkie and a code name. Norman was "King Cobra." I was "Cobra Number One." Even my brother Wallace got a walkie-talkie and a code name. We went to the fairground and practiced; we taught everyone how to announce themselves on the walkie-talkies so that we could smoothly communicate with one another. We practiced for weeks.

The idea was to be able to fully monitor the protest, to know where the police were and what they were doing, to know who was being arrested, how many were being arrested, and where. We wanted a way to know how everything was going.

But when the protest started, our people got very nervous and started shouting all kinds of nonsense over the air.

"Four…Cobra Four, they're taking them!"

"Taking who? Where?"

"They're taking them! They're taking them!"

I'm laughing now, but on that cold, rainy April day in 1964 it wasn't funny. It was terrible.

Reporters noticed that some of us had walkie-talkies and wrote about how CORE ran the protest like a paramilitary operation. I can only shake my head. Those newspaper people didn't know what they were talking about. It was a mess. But to the untrained eye, everything about the protest seemed to go like Swiss clockwork. CORE made its point, and Jim Farmer had dodged, at least in this instance, a big bullet. He had exhibited shrewd and steady leadership.

*But Velma and I remained very frustrated with Farmer and his inability to engage in meaningful programmatic analysis.* I used to discuss this problem a great deal with Velma in the office and at home.

With the passage of the Civil Rights Act of 1964, civil rights organizations needed to fully grasp the impact of its provisions and protections regarding the elimination of de facto segregation. This was a time for organizations like CORE to make a vitally important transition, to move "from protest to politics." And Velma and I realized early that this kind of political pivot would require keen leadership. We looked to Farmer for that, and he just wasn't up to its demands. He made fine speeches; he exhibited great courage going to jail for the movement, putting his body on the line for the cause of freedom; and he was at heart a good man. But in the larger sense, he just couldn't do what needed to be done.

Velma and I knew that it is one thing to use tactics, like staging a sit-in at a lunch counter of a restaurant that refuses to serve Blacks. In the 1950s and '60s, a single direct, nonviolent action could bring about immediate change, to get the restaurant owner, for instance, to take the risk and do the right thing. But when it comes to the economic and social problems, which have a class dimension facing Blacks, no single demonstration or protest can bring about a positive result.

What is needed—and this is part of Bayard's case for political action—is for institutions to change and for organizations to behave differently.

We knew that with more complex, more systemic problems, like Blacks gaining equal access to quality housing and medical care, no single demonstration was going to bring about change. Demonstrations will not end slums; no demonstration could bring about quality, integrated education. A single demonstration could highlight a problem, but not solve it. The problems that disproportionately face Blacks are of a dual nature—race and class. This calls for the labor and civil rights movements to act in concert along with liberal, religious, and other groups to change the nation's institutions so that they better serve all Americans. We knew that fundamental change was called for, not adjustments around the edges.

*Engaging the movement in politics was to Norman and me a natural transition. We wanted to help the Black community be in the position of electing politicians and holding them accountable.* Neither one of us ever wanted to be a politician. We were activists. We thought we made things happen. We thought of politicians as followers. We were wrong.

Probably, more of us should have gone into politics like Julian Bond and John Lewis did, for example. I had a chance once when Al Barkin, the head of AFL-CIO Committee on Political Education (COPE), encouraged me to run for office. He said that he would bring considerable support from labor in a run for Bella Abzug's congressional seat, representing the West Side of Manhattan. I said, "No, no, no. Politicians aren't leaders." That was stupid, by the way. Norman and I instead concentrated more of our attention on the nexus of civil rights and labor. Their DNAs share so many of the same genes.

*Velma and I talked about appealing to the basic common economic interests of whites and Blacks as opposed to their prejudices.* For generations, race had been used to divide Black and white workers. Historically, Southern bosses, for example, told their white employees that they were superior, worth more than their Black counterparts. As a result, they were told, Black workers were paid less than they were paid. They were told that they should not join a union that included Black workers because they would be forced to associate with Blacks, those they perceived as inferiors.

Velma and I believed this sort of unenlightened self-interest could be overcome. That was our analysis, one we shared with Bayard and A. Philip Randolph. But at CORE I could not get Farmer to turn his understanding of this into any meaningful program of action. There were just certain things that he didn't get.

*Norman and I never got an argument from him about any of this.* But you never knew if he agreed with you. He would say things like, "That's interesting," and "I see where you're going." Even if his responses were half full rather than half empty, the result was the same: nothing. Farmer would waffle, embracing the views and thrusts of whoever spoke to him last.

*Velma and I thought he too often tried to be all things to all people.* He seemed to think that this response would somehow keep CORE from splintering and falling apart. Of course, history proved him wrong. On my departure from CORE, I wrote in my resignation letter that the organization suffered from a "calcification of tactical imagination" in dealing with the emerging challenges facing Black and poor people in America. This was the challenge facing the overall civil rights movement at the time.

*Norman and I were far ahead of not just CORE but also the civil rights movement in our thinking.* We could see the strategic limitations of organizations like CORE and the NAACP that, at the time, never got beyond the race question. That was their raison d'être.

It is very difficult for organizations and institutions to overcome their history. Norman, who by this time was thirty-one, and I was twenty-five, came to realize this. These civil rights groups were born in the struggle for Black rights. So, combating racism became the dominant issue. When we introduced the economic or class component of the struggle, many civil rights leaders didn't want to deal with that because they were unable or unwilling to integrate it into their organizations, moving from race to class. Even combining the two issues, which is what we strived to do, was difficult for civil rights leaders programmatically and organizationally.

*At CORE, Velma and I were trying to move the organization into a more grassroots economic and social thrust.* We had weekend regional conferences around the country to advance this new agenda.

Bayard Rustin, one of CORE's founders, joined the effort to offer his whole approach, his perspectives, regarding coalition building, nonviolence, and direct action. We had Blyden Jackson, a CORE activist and New York leader, who was able to talk about grassroots mobilization; Velma was also a major part of these conferences as part of the staff training team. We were really making headway when Farmer stepped in and told us that CORE no longer had the money and resources for that team to go around and do this work of chapter and staff education and motivation.

He specifically said Bayard could no longer be a part of the conferences. Again, Farmer said the reason was financial. But in fact, Farmer was suspicious of Bayard and this new direction. Elements in CORE, in effect, did what they could to stymie this initiative.

Blyden Jackson would later betray us and Bayard and our allies by falsely accusing us of trying to displace Farmer and take over CORE.

This was the beginning of a rift between Farmer and me in terms of support for the organizational perspective that I was trying to carry out as national program director.

There was a feeling at CORE that social democrats like Bayard and Velma and me were trying to take over the organization. This charge even made it into the Black and white press. Julius Hobson, chairman of Washington, DC, CORE before he was expelled, and Scott Smith, a Chicago CORE staff member, were especially outspoken and covered by the press in their charges against us.

*We never knew for sure if this feeling came directly from Jim, but he certainly didn't do anything to discourage these rumors and growing attacks at CORE.* And when Norman moved to bring in a fellow social democrat and brilliant analyst of the movement, Tom Kahn, to help with Norman's work, Farmer moved to block the appointment.

*I wanted to appoint Tom, who at the time was an official of the League for Industrial Democracy, to be my assistant in my work as national program director.* I told Farmer that what we were doing was a major task and I needed help in carrying it forward. I was trying to help CORE chapters organize around political, social, and economic issues in the Black community.

But Farmer saw my move to bring in Tom as another element of a plot to dislodge him from CORE's leadership. This, in his thinking, would open the way for Bayard to take the reins. There was no truth at all in this. I was not being disloyal, and Bayard had absolutely no interest in leading CORE or, at the time, any organization. That was not his nature.

Farmer had forced my hand. I felt I had no choice but to take the unprecedented step of appealing his decision regarding Tom to CORE's National Action Committee, which oversaw CORE policy between the organization's regular conventions. In a decision that sent shock waves throughout CORE, the committee overruled Farmer in a vote of nine to three.

Of course, this was a blow to Farmer. I was granted the authority to hire Tom, but he, understandably, decided not to join an organization in which its leadership made clear that he was not wanted there. This was a turning point in my cooling relationship with Farmer and CORE.

*Looking back, a great deal of good work was accomplished during our tenure at CORE.* One of the initiatives that Norman and I are most proud of was CORE's effort to desegregate the restaurants along US Route 40 between Baltimore and Washington.

As late as the mid-1960s, it was not uncommon for millions of Black motorists to plan business and vacation road trips as carefully as a general might plan a battle. Because of the ever-present specter of segregation that included practically all of the South, as well as unmarked pockets and stretches of roadside restaurants, restrooms, and motels reaching into the West and North, Black travelers were taught not to stop.

In the 1960s, for instance, a Black Army veteran driving the family car packed with his wife and three young sons drove straight from Kentucky to Philadelphia because he couldn't face the shame of being turned away at a motel or restaurant along the segregated way. This was not unusual.

In 1961, Route 40 was a major highway between New York and the nation's capital. But as it wound its way through segregated Maryland, it was a mostly sleepy road—sometimes scenic, sometimes two-lane, sometimes four-lane. The restaurants were ordinary. Nothing fancy. A Howard Johnson, places like that. But if you were a Black traveler, you had a little something extra in store: Jim Crow humiliations were always ready to greet you along the way.

African diplomats were not immune to this. On June 26, 1961, the newly installed ambassador Adam Malick Sow of the Republic of Chad, in north central Africa, was en route to Washington to present his credentials to President Kennedy. When he stopped for a meal at a diner in Edgewood, Maryland, on Route 40, he was denied service. Worse, he was physically assaulted because of his color and audacity for having some expectation that he would be treated decently in his new home, the Land of Freedom.

A newspaper reported at the time that an owner of the offending restaurant said the African ambassador "looked just like a run-of-the-mill ordinary nigra to me."

At one point, J. Millard Tawes, Maryland's governor, apologized for a string of similar incidents but suggested that African diplomats traveling on Route 40 should be more careful in how they selected restaurants, looking for those that would serve Blacks.

All this embarrassed the Kennedy administration, which was busy trying to woo African countries in hopes of keeping the Soviets from aligning Africans with its communist bloc. The White House went as far as to press businesses along Route 40 to at least serve African diplomats, some places to even let the Africans use whites-only restrooms because they were presumably cleaner than the ones set aside for Blacks.

Around this time, Wallace and Juanita Nelson, members of CORE's Baltimore chapter, initiated a sit-in at a Route 40 restaurant for the general desegregation of the highway facilities for everyone—not just African diplomats. Police arrested the Nelsons, who refused to pay a fine for, we guess, loitering or disturbing the peace. The Nelsons served a two-week sentence, even going on a hunger strike while behind bars.

By August, this led Norman at the national office of CORE to organize and coordinate the "Route 40 Project," a series of targeted sit-ins to break the spine of segregation of these facilities. And I assisted.

We also worked with Baltimore's Civic Interest Group, CIG, which was a SNCC-affiliated group of Black students from nearby Morgan State College and other area schools, including Coppin State College, and some white students from Goucher College and Johns Hopkins University. And there was the Nonviolent Action Group, NAG, from Howard University in Washington, which joined us at the demonstrations.

We also had cars of CORE volunteers coming in, like ourselves, from New York; others came from Baltimore, Washington, and Philadelphia.

*Velma and I never packed a lunch.* We ate before we left. We would have at least thirty to forty protesters on any given Saturday. And we all dressed neatly, never in jeans and sneakers, and broke down into integrated teams of four.

*Norman always wore a red tie.*

*Velma and I and our teams would pile into these big American cars—Buicks, Chevrolets, Fords—which we all were driving in those days.* As East Coast field secretary then, I would organize and coordinate the campaigns. We would split up and drive to restaurants that we had targeted, never driving to the same place twice. If a team saw a car from a different team at a restaurant, it would proceed to another restaurant.

Teams would go in and order meals and see if anyone would be served. We never were. Then we would sit in until the restaurant's owner or management summoned the police. When the police came and asked us to leave, we would comply. Our goal was not to court arrest, but to embarrass the restaurant owners while calling national attention to this "Up South" outrage.

*Even though Norman and I were staring into the cold face of segregation, we never experienced any violence, not even from the police when they arrived.* Oh, they would often play the intimidation card, sometimes the whole deck, putting on an icy mask of disgust at our presence, speaking in the sternest, harshest tones and almost always threatening arrest and jail time.

"Get out!" some would shout in our face. "You can't stay here. Get out!"

And sometimes you'd feel a little anxious, nervous, knowing that the police were there because the restaurant owner or manager wanted you out. You never knew what was going to happen. But this was not like the South, where a situation like this would often stir fears among protesters. People have had their brains beaten out for less down there.

Norman and I knew that the police were there to reinforce the policies of the restaurant owners, which were spelled out in signs all along Route 40: "We reserve the right to refuse service to anyone." I remember a policeman reading us the law, stumbling as he read from a card. Bayard was with us that day and started to assist the police with his legal recitation, turning to the officer with a "Let me help you, my good man" in his best affected British accent. Bayard knew the law by heart because he had been arrested almost two dozen times in the movement.

When it really came down to it, even with the White House less than an hour's drive away, what we faced on Route 40 in 1961 was clearly not an issue of geography. For all intents and purposes, we were in the North. You didn't run into this sort of thing in New York, for instance. This was much more a matter of culture. These white business owners operating along Route 40 operated with the same morals as "segregation now, segregation forever" Deep Southerners.

Usually, a full encounter—entering the restaurant, trying to order a meal, waiting for police to arrive, and then leaving—would last less than an hour.

Norman and I continued with the other CORE-led demonstrations into December 1961, when Governor Tawes finally met with and urged white business operators along Route 40 to open their doors to Blacks. Some complained, even noted that integration would drive off their white customers. Nevertheless, integration came to Route 40.

This was one of CORE's finest hours. And it is a shame that CORE gets very little credit for its desegregation work along that highway. CORE would expand its direct desegregation efforts along Route 1 into Florida and Virginia, and then into North Carolina.

Governor Tawes signed a public accommodations bill in March 1963. This made Maryland the first state south of the Mason-Dixon Line to outright ban discrimination against Blacks seeking to dine in restaurants and stay in hotels. Baltimore CORE dispatched members to check and see if this was indeed true. It was.

The following year, Norman and I were demonstrating in Englewood, New Jersey, for public-school desegregation. This was early 1962, eight years after the Supreme Court's *Brown v. Board of Education* decision had outlawed segregation in the nation's public schools "with all deliberate speed." But change was slow in coming. Public schools in Englewood, like those in much of the country, remained de facto segregated.

We were arrested—four Blacks and seven whites—after our group spent the night demonstrating and sitting in at Englewood's City Hall in protest. The city's mayor, M. Leslie Denning, delivered an ultimatum himself that we leave. When we didn't, Norman and I and the whole group were arrested as "disorderly" persons. We declined bail and were detained. Englewood's jail happened to be in the same building.

In all our years of demonstrating and arrests, this was the first time Norman and I were arrested together. The men and women were taken to separate holding cells, the women on one floor and the men just below us.

Of course, I worried about Norm, worried that he might get hurt in jail. I couldn't see him, but I knew he was there and that he could hear me if I called out. I started singing to him.

*I could hear you singing to me, Velma.* You changed the words of some popular R&B song. But that wasn't the only music we had in the men's cell. A fellow demonstrator, Byron Baer, who would go on to become a distinguished New Jersey state senator, smuggled (in a part of his anatomy I care not to mention) a tiny transistor radio into the cell. Byron, a white man, had been arrested a year earlier as a Freedom Rider in the Greyhound bus station in Jackson, Mississippi. Refusing to pay a $200 fine, he instead served forty-five days in the Mississippi State Penitentiary.

Velma and I and the rest of the protesters stayed behind bars only a matter of hours before CORE lawyers secured our release. By the summer of 1964, I was becoming convinced that demonstrations in and of themselves could not accomplish very much regarding the most intractable issues confronting Black people in America. Yet, CORE's leadership was just as committed to protest as its major thrust as before. Some of the absurdity of this was made apparent to me while leading street protests during the Republican National Convention held in San Francisco.

Arizona Senator Barry Goldwater, who had voted against the civil rights bill in Congress and against a weak civil rights plank in his party's platform that year, was one of our targets. Of course, he ultimately became the Republican nominee to unsuccessfully challenge Johnson in his run for his first full term in the White House. In July, I led a group protesting the Republicans, a party that Farmer had just accused of taking a "position of racism and reaction."

The CORE demonstrations at the Cow Palace, the arena where the convention was held, took on a quality of theater. As coordinator of the demonstrations, I had a meeting with the officer in charge of policing the area. He happened to be a member of the American Civil Liberties Union, a rather rare occurrence. The officer, who was white, was very reasonable. He said he understood that we had a right to picket the convention and that he was fully prepared to accept that—if we agreed not to block traffic around the convention center.

I said fine. What I didn't know was that CORE's western regional director, who was part of the demonstrations, had never been arrested for protesting. What I also did not know was that apparently he felt that this was his chance. On the last day of the convention I was walking around the Cow Palace with my bullhorn and ready to resume the demonstrations. But I did not see any protesters.

A short time later, I discovered that the protesters, two dozen or so, were being led by this regional director, and he had directed them to sit in the street and stop traffic. It was not long after that when I heard the officer in charge yell my name.

"Hill, I thought we had an agreement," he said as his patience was clearly dissipating by the second.

I assured him that we did have an agreement and that this breach was a misunderstanding that I would correct. I asked the officer if he could have the traffic redirected around the sitting demonstrations while I moved to get them on their feet and out of the street. He agreed, and I went to work.

When I told the demonstrators that they were wasting their effort because the traffic had been rerouted away from them, they—including the regional director—stood and walked away. I'm fairly certain I saw disappointment in that director's eyes. If only the new direction for CORE and the civil rights movement could have been that straightforward. Velma and I knew the road to freedom that lay ahead would have to wind through terrain less certain, less simple, than motivating people who had been relegated to the back of the bus to stand up and demand the right to sit wherever they wanted.

In mid-August 1964, Velma and I resigned from CORE. News of my departure was covered in two articles published in the September 4 edition of the *New York Times*. The lead story was written by David Halberstam. My five-page resignation letter, which was the product of nights of collaboration with Bayard, Tom Kahn, and Velma, became a precursor to Bayard's "From Protest to Politics" essay that turned into a sort of ideological light illuminating the best path for the struggle for equality and justice in America.

In it, I called for a coalition of civil rights organizations with the "progressive sections of the labor movement, and of the churches, liberals, democratic radicals and intellectuals." I wrote that I could not see how "the broad goals of the Negro community can ultimately be achieved except in a political alliance with these elements. However much we may criticize the inadequacy of their performance and commitment in given instances."

Velma and I had become much more interested in political mobilization and less in protest, especially, as I noted in my resignation letter, the "glorification of demonstrations as ends in themselves." And when it came to the Black community and its involvement in politics, I wrote, "We can no longer stand on the outside crying 'a pox on both your houses.'"

My resignation was also covered in the September 17, 1964, issue of *Jet*, the popular Black news weekly magazine published by John H. Johnson in Chicago. I made page seven, an item just above another about Martin Luther King Jr. The brief article correctly said that I was joining the AFL-CIO. The item ended with a quixotic quote from Farmer noting that CORE "has rather frequent resignations."

They would soon have more departures, including Farmer's. He would resign from CORE in 1966, taking a teaching position at Lincoln University. Later, he joined the Nixon administration. This closed a proud and brave chapter of CORE and started a new one of uncertainty and programmatic confusion within a major civil rights organization that became a shattered mirror of the movement.

*This time was painful for Norman and me.* Years later, we looked back and realized that for most people, the civil rights movement seemed to have had its time, that in the '60s it splintered away and then passed away. That was the end of it—as most people knew it. The truth is that the movement kept evolving. It's still evolving.

We know that the struggle continues because it has to continue. That is one of the primary reasons we wrote this book.

*Velma and I believe that Mr. Randolph said it best:*

Freedom is never granted; it is won. Justice is never given; it is exacted. Freedom and justice must be struggled for by the oppressed of all lands and races. And the struggle must be continuous, for freedom is never a final fact, but a continuing evolving process....

# CHAPTER 8

# Go Tell It on the Mountain— The Paraprofessionals

I don't remember much about my graduation day from Harvard, except that it seemed like it was a long time coming and that my Norman, who was doing important work at the time with the A. Philip Randolph Institute in New York, couldn't be there. And you know what? I didn't worry about that. I didn't much care about ceremony. I had accomplished what I had set out to do—finish my college education and get some time away from the movement, get some time to just breathe. So, I wasn't really bothered when my family back in Chicago couldn't make it to Harvard, either. Besides, my mother, bless her heart, hadn't been feeling very well. It turned out to be the start of the illness that would take her away from this world. Back then, I thought Ruby Murphy would live forever.

So, there I was, left mostly to my own company and witness on graduation day. But I was, after all, graduating—hot dog!—from Harvard.

I was almost thirty years old, yet I sent my diploma to my mother, proof that I—with Norman's help—had finally fulfilled our promise to her to finish school.

Much later, while researching this book, I learned that Dr. King had agreed in March of that year to speak to the campus on our special day. But this was June 1968, two months after an assassin's brutal bullet had stolen from us The Dreamer, The Doer. He had been a man of graceful urgency with whom Norman and I had worked closely during the movement days of the early and mid-1960s. In fact, Norman was in Memphis working with Dr. King when he was killed. After Norman got the terrible news, he rushed to the Lorraine Motel, greeted by the balcony where the great man fell, still stained with his blood that had pooled and run, he told me, like a crimson spring rain.

In his place, Dr. King's widow, Coretta, spoke at Harvard. That was Wednesday, June 13, a week after the assassination of Senator Robert F. Kennedy. I know it rained that day. It rained so much that Mrs. King's address was moved indoors to Sanders Theater. Students, faculty, family, and friends pressed inside that shadowy, old stone castle of a building without me. I can't recall any details of what I did instead. I do know that I felt immensely proud to have received my master's degree in education. In a very real sense, I could feel my mother's smile beaming down on me like the sunshine that eluded Cambridge, Massachusetts, that day.

Most in mind were my thoughts of what next? How could I put to best use this wonderfully exhilarating college experience I had been given?

Yes, there had been some bumps and rocks in the road. I had some trouble writing a few of the assigned papers, but I didn't have any problems with the readings: heavy tomes and tracts by people like sociologist Nathan Glazer and political sociologist Seymour Martin Lipset, future author of the definitive 1996 work *American Exceptionalism: A Double-Edged Sword*.

My friend and mentor at Harvard, Professor David Cohen, introduced me to Carl Gershman, also a student at the time. You could tell that he was on his way to making ripples if not waves in the way people thought about the nation, democracy, and America's future. He became an activist academic and almost twenty years later would form the National Endowment for Democracy. He would also work for a while as a researcher and writer for the A. Philip Randolph Institute. The works and lives of my Harvard friends, colleagues, and professors would crisscross with mine as well as Norman's life for decades.

Harvard introduced me to so much. I enjoyed learning the material and arguing with professors—and some of the students, too. It was such a rich mix of people and I found it easy to talk to them about what I was discovering through the work. Having this exchange of ideas was wondrous. In the civil rights movement it didn't happen—not the way it seemed commonplace on Harvard Yard. In the movement it was different. We were usually trying to persuade people, like people in CORE, that the organization should have a community focus, or that CORE should put much more importance on forming and maintaining coalitions. We might touch on Vietnam, foreign policy, or women's rights, but these things were not central to our discussions.

But at Harvard, there was another level of discussion, something freer, more ranging, challenging. Sometimes it reminded me of the kinds of jousting for the truth we engaged in with New York democratic socialists, like our dear friend Max Shachtman (who did more arguing than listening) and other intellectuals back in New York. At Harvard, you could talk about anything. You could talk about education and educational reform, what it takes for the Black child to learn, whether even if in fact Black children were intellectually inferior. You could talk about that and develop arguments around these kinds of points in a way you couldn't even consider if you were, for instance, trying to integrate a school.

At the Graduate School of Education you could argue all these intellectual subjects and at the same time be forced to look at the practical. I examined how children actually learned and what methods of teaching could best be applied in the classroom. The graduate school also permitted me to take classes in almost any subject anywhere on campus. So, I did, free-ranging every chance I got. It was fantastic.

Maybe it was too fantastic, because in my last days there I was still asking myself a single question: What next?

All around me, the world seemed to wobble on its axis, bombarded by the forces of tremendous change. Lyndon Johnson was still in the White House, although he had announced on the last day of March that he would not seek reelection; despite peace talks beginning in Paris, the US involvement in South Vietnam continued. It was a war costing tragic numbers of Americans their lives, their limbs, or their sanity. The North Vietnamese launched the Tet Offensive that year, and it deepened our doubts that this war could be won. Even Walter Cronkite told his *CBS Evening News* viewers and the nation that we couldn't win. I kept seeing the image in my head of Buddhist monks and their self-immolation, literally burning for democracy. A lot of things struck me about Vietnam, but at the time, my eyes were much more focused on the domestic front, concerned that America not lose the momentum for substantive progress in the lives of the poor and struggling. I wanted to see the economic and political demands we all made in the March on Washington in 1963 come to fruition, see the spirit of the 1965 Freedom Budget influence how America invested in itself and its future; I even prayed that President Johnson's War on Poverty would win some battles against the status quo and business as usual for those who were merely surviving when they could be thriving.

But in 1968, fresh with my Harvard diploma in hand, I could see that America's deepening involvement in Vietnam was costing us more than blood and treasure, as they say. It was tragically changing the political dynamic.

I believe Dr. King was morally challenged by America's involvement in Vietnam, prompting him to famously denounce the war in 1967. He was widely criticized for his position. I remember how deftly Bayard Rustin dealt with that criticism, drawing a line of distinction between Dr. King's position voiced as a Christian minister and as a civil rights leader. That was Bayard, always looking for ways to bring and keep people together rather than have them cast apart.

I certainly did not support the war, but neither did I want to see North Vietnam prevail. It was a dictatorial communist regime making war against the South. Yes, South Vietnam's government was weak and corrupt, and did not include strong democratic institutions, but within the country there was the possibility of the emergence of true democratic forces. For that reason, and being anti-communist ourselves, Norman and I wanted to see America support and defend those democratic elements.

But we certainly did not want this to come at the expense of burying all the important domestic work that needed to be done on the home front.

In June 1968, there was still a civil rights movement, but it seemed that, among other factors, without Dr. King it had lost its beating heart. We had endured long, hot summers of riots, including shockingly violent racial clashes in Detroit and Los Angeles. The incendiary chant of "Black Power" was in the air. The struggle for social and political and economic change had to stay relevant. I was sure about that.

After graduation, I returned to New York. I lived with Norman on the nineteenth floor of a high-rise apartment building in the Chelsea section of Manhattan, a cozy apartment in a co-op. The complex was built with the help and support of the labor movement, specifically the now defunct International Ladies' Garment Workers' Union (ILGW). Norman and I had moved there shortly before I went to Harvard. Once back in the city, I tried to take it a little easier for a time, watching Norman get up early in the morning as he always did and go to his office at the A. Philip Randolph Institute, which he joined in 1967.

There, Norman was right in the middle of the merged interests of the civil rights and labor movements. The institute was, in its words, "an organization of black trade unionists to fight for racial equality and economic justice," and its cofounders included Bayard and, of course, Mr. Randolph.

During those weeks in the summer of '68, I never really took it *that* easy. My head was still busy wrestling with what to do. I had an affinity for education. I liked school, and teachers liked me. But I didn't want to be a teacher. When I was growing up, my mother wanted me to be a doctor when she wasn't consumed with dreams of me becoming the president of the United States. Remember that I had three sisters, and all were nurses. And I got to meet a lot of doctors, Black and white, who all thought my sister Thelma, whom they called "Murph," should have been a doctor.

But I had long ago taken a different path, one that led me to activism, to Rainbow Beach, to Norman, and now after Harvard to a place of decision. I could still hear what Max Shachtman told me in his sage, fatherly way when I first headed off to Harvard: "When you come back, you find your niche and be a leader. You are a leader."

But a leader of what? The civil rights movement as I appreciated it no longer really existed. Sandy Feldman, a close friend who was herself an educator, civil rights activist, and labor leader, had been among the first to urge me to go to Harvard in the first place. Now that I had my degree, she wanted me to join her at the United Federation of Teachers.

My politics and history were pushing me in the direction of labor. My mother was active in her factory's union back in Chicago. I had developed great relationships with labor leaders while working in the movement. Sam Fishman, a leader of the United Auto Workers local and later the president of the Michigan AFL-CIO, and Donny Slaiman, the director of civil rights at the AFL-CIO, supported me. I talked to Norman and Bayard and Mr. Randolph.

I had interviewed for a labor position at District Council 37, New York's largest public employee union, part of the American Federation for State, County and Municipal Employees (AFSCME), which today has more than 1.6 million members nationwide. I was enthusiastic about the job. I met with Victor Gotbaum, the executive director of DC 37; I liked him and knew that he was generally well regarded as a pragmatic leader. I also spoke with Lillian Roberts, his assistant. Now retired, she was the union's executive director, elected in 2002. We walked the streets of New York for a while, and the whole time they tried to convince me to come aboard. But I ended our meeting by not saying yes or no. I told them I would get back to them.

I had someone else to see, someone else in charge of a very powerful labor union. I had to see Albert Shanker.

Al was already the legendary president of the United Federation of Teachers (UFT), after only coming to power in 1964. I knew he was smart, a working-class son of Jewish Russian immigrants, who grew up in Queens. He was said to have read more newspapers in a day as a kid than many adults read in a week. I also knew he was drawn to philosophy and counted among his idols the brilliant lawyer Clarence Darrow, Franklin D. Roosevelt, and Bayard Rustin. That last part sat very well with me.

I had met Al years earlier when I was the field secretary for CORE. The organization was calling for a full-scale boycott of New York City public schools in February 1964 to protest the generally poor quality of many of them and the fact that many remained racially segregated— mostly Black and Puerto Rican—a decade after the Supreme Court called for the desegregation of all public schools. Even Malcolm X, who had long opposed racial integration, spoke in favor of that boycott.

I was the CORE representative to a coalition supporting this action and also a leader of a delegation that went to Al Shanker seeking his union's support of the boycott. He agreed to see us in his office. When we did, he told us that he could not recommend that his union support the boycott. I was a little surprised. Before the meeting, people I trusted, including Bayard, told me that he was a pretty good guy. The hope was that this would translate into his support for our cause. But something else happened around his typically cluttered big desk.

He talked to us, and as he talked, I felt no hostility from him. It became clear that he believed in school integration and that he knew a great deal about education. He explained how magnet schools, educational parks, and school pairings could more readily bring about an integrated school system. I was impressed. And I did feel like we got something from him that day, especially when he said that any of his teachers who decided not to attend school during the boycott would get UFT support. His recommendations that day became the heart of demands that pro-integrationist forces would later use in negotiations with New York's Board of Education.

When I walked back into his office in the early fall of 1968, I was met by the same man, who said he remembered me. Al was tall and gangly. He wore thick, black, oversize eyeglasses like Clark Kent in the Superman comic books, and he often wore them crooked, unselfconsciously askew on the prominent bridge of his generous nose. His hair was full and dark and combed back from his high forehead. He had a way about him that commanded attention; a hint of the aphrodisiac of power clung to him, to which I was totally immune. When he spoke, heads turned to hear what he had to say. I can't say that he was a charismatic speaker, not like what I had grown used to hearing in get-to-your-feet-and-shout speeches delivered by Bayard and Mr. Randolph. But when Al spoke in that measured tone of his, people, particularly educators, seemed to hang on his every insightful word. He never used notes, or if he did, they must have been on a sliver of paper. Anything about education? He knew it. And he knew people and their inner workings, whether they were staff, teachers, students, parents, or politicians. Teachers loved him even though he was a little strange. He seemed to have few social graces, but few seemed to mind. You'd just dismiss whatever lapse or social faux pas with "That's Al." He was cerebral, and his brain seemed to serve him as if it was an over-stocked private library. Maybe because of that I knew better than to walk into his office with no notion of what I wanted to do.

I had visited some elementary schools. One, PS 33, which was in my neighborhood, stood out. It was a pleasant enough brick building, simple and well maintained. I peeked in. I was immediately struck by all the Black and Hispanic teachers I saw there. In 1968, even in a public school, this would have been very unusual. I didn't realize at the time that these women in the classrooms were not teachers. I watched them reading to children, collecting milk money, sweetly shepherding students here and there, cleaning blackboards and erasers, and settling down the children for their afternoon naps. They seemed indistinguishable from elemen-tary-school teachers until you asked about them, as I did. I was told that they were teachers' aides, commonly known as paraprofessionals.

After a little more digging, I learned that they were all welfare eligible and were paid some $2,000 or so a year—about half of what a family of four would get on welfare.

So why were they working in the city's public schools? They, like many mothers, wanted to be close to their young children and wanted a job that would let them be home when their children returned from school, just like moms in television situation comedies did. And they had a powerful work ethic, too, that made them detest being on public assistance.

With a little research I learned that there were more than 15,000 para-professionals, or paras for short, working in New York City schools. Most were Black or Puerto Rican, and their situation was unbelievable, terrible from a labor rights point of view. None of them had health care benefits or vacation time. There was no grievance procedure or job security. A para could be fired at the whim of a principal. And worst of all, there was no clear career ladder in place so that these very dedicated, highly moti-vated women (and some men) could become full-fledged teachers.

The thinking about the paras was that the New York City public school system wanted to relieve teachers of some of their non-teacher tasks, like taking attendance, collecting lunch money, and monitoring hallways. The idea, and a very good one at that, was to employ the paras to free class-room teachers to do what was needed most from them: teach.

The para program had deep roots. In the mid-1950s, the New York Teachers Guild, in which the UFT has its own roots, pushed for a train-ing program for people to help "clerical and monitoring duties in the schools." The first of these aides were hired in the 1957–58 school year. By the early 1960s, when the United Federation of Teachers was repre-senting New York public-school teachers, these aides, by UFT contract, were clearly defined as being outside professional pedagogical staff. And it seemed that this was the way it was to remain.

But in the mid-1960s, when President Johnson began to wage what he came to call the War on Poverty in America, especially in its urban areas, millions of federal dollars began flooding into community-based programs aimed at reducing poverty. Programs aimed at creating jobs and fostering community involvement began to attract not only dollars but also widespread attention.

This shift would help the cause of expanding the use of paraprofes-sionals in the city's public schools. At the same time, there was a teacher shortage in New York. The city's Board of Education was actually going Down South and to Puerto Rico to recruit teachers for the nearly million-student-strong New York public school system. I thought to myself, why go hunting around down there when they've got a group of people in place who know the job and would probably love to be full-time teachers? They are from the community, they know the system, and they understand and cherish the children. And more, they need the opportunity. Paras, with support and training, I thought, could some-day be teachers.

But there was something else that called to me from my years of work-ing in civil rights and organized labor circles. The para program was, at its essence, an anti-poverty program, one quite different from most in 1968. Rather than use the new stream of War on Poverty federal dollars filtering into impoverished and working-class areas, these dollars were not going to pay salaries to middle-class people who would in turn be expected to work on behalf of and advocate for the poor. These funds were going directly to those who most needed a rung up on the economic ladder.

I also quickly realized that there was a trap here. Without union representation, this relatively new group of school workers could become little more than a cheap source of labor ready made for exploitation. I couldn't stand by and watch that happen.

Shortly before I arrived at Al Shanker's office, I had discussed joining the UFT with Norman, Bayard, Mr. Randolph, and Max. They all supported my decision to tackle the task of organizing the paras into a union that could give them at least what their union-represented counterparts, the teachers, had. This, I told myself, was a way for me to make an important difference, especially if I could find a way for any paras who wanted to be teachers to become educators. In any case, a union, especially the United Federation of Teachers, would give them job security and a path to greater self-respect, and build solidarity between the paras and teachers. Additionally, the UFT could represent them as teachers, something DC 37, with its more general membership, couldn't do. I felt confident that I could do this. Organizing the paras would draw on my knowledge and experience from the civil rights movement and my growing knowledge and interests in education and labor.

I will never forget that day I met with Al Shanker in his dimly lit office that was adorned with African art here and there. He was brilliant and terrific. He never engaged in chitchat. Before I knew it, we were talking about my desire to organize the paras. He listened to me closely. Then he said he supported my ideas and intention, but with one condition: "I need you, Velma, to be a para and work right there with them, side by side."

It took me by surprise. I didn't say anything at first and just listened to his reasoning. Al explained that if I was going to be successful, I couldn't approach them as an outsider. I needed to experience what they experienced, feel what they felt, and win their trust.

My immediate reaction was to think *no way*. The idea of getting up early and reporting to a classroom at 8 a.m. had no appeal. Even after my time at Harvard, I managed to avoid early-morning classes. I have never been a morning person, so reporting to work each day would be a trauma five mornings a week. Then there was the matter of me working as a teacher's aide for a teacher who was probably younger and less educated than I was.

It is a good thing that the mind is quicker than the tongue. I ran through all my reasons to say no in a split second; in another I came to know that Al was right. If I was going to succeed in organizing the paras, a group of women who had likely not gone to college and who had probably been abused by the system, I could not approach the challenge as some union official with a master's of education degree from Harvard. They would probably assume I was some sister with her nose up in the air. They wouldn't know that I had been bloodied on Rainbow Beach marching for desegregation or had been a part of the March on Washington for Jobs and Freedom, had traveled Down South training civil rights workers, nor would they know that I worked with Dr. King and other leaders like Bayard Rustin and A. Philip Randolph.

I had to let them know that I was one of them. Harvard hadn't changed me. It didn't take away my sense of being a Black, working-class girl from segregated Chicago. I was still Velma, the young woman who loved to sing spirituals and movement songs. I always sounded more like my mama when I talked than my professors lecturing me in Harvard's great halls and classrooms.

I knew I could do what Al was requesting. I thought back to how my mother had empowered me when I was growing up in Chicago. She survived on factory jobs, but even more on her ability to mold my sisters and brothers and me into a single unit, all pooling our strengths and earnings for the sake of the family. I began thinking that I could bring a similar empowering unity to the paras. I also wanted to give them, like my mother gave me, a tremendous sense of their self-worth.

Within seconds of him asking me to be a para, I agreed. I was on my way to becoming an Afro-wearing, brown-skinned Norma Rae; at least that's what an AFL-CIO leader called me. That day, I could not anticipate what awaited me and how saying "Okay" would bind me to Al Shanker and the teachers' union for more than a decade.

Somehow it was fixed that I was welfare eligible and fully qualified to be a classroom paraprofessional. I didn't lie about anything. It was a don't-ask-and-I-won't-tell situation about my background. Someone in the right place let it be known that there was an opening for a para and that I was a good fit. I just filled out a form; it required my fingerprints and asked if I had an arrest record. I did. All my arrests had come in the service of the civil rights movement. That didn't seem to make a difference to anyone. I was hired for $50 a week and assigned to an elementary school not far from my home. I was a para. I was one of them.

According to a survey conducted by the Institute for Educational Development in school year 1969–70, "55 percent of paras were African-American or Afro Caribbean, 18 percent were of Puerto Rican descent, 7 percent were 'other non-whites' [presumably Asians and other Latinas] and roughly 20 percent were white [many Latinas identified as white on such forms throughout the 1970s]."

From the inside, I realized that I would have an opportunity to write a new chapter in the story of modern union organizing. This was a movement for economic justice, and because so many of the paras were women or members of racial and ethnic minorities, this was also a story of affirmative action—without quotas.

The teacher I worked for was white and young, in her twenties. I think her first name was Nancy. I'm not sure. But I remember my first assignment: reading to the children. There I was, with all this education and experience, reading to children while someone who could have been *my* aide lorded over the classroom. I felt helpless. Then I turned up my humility and remembered why I was there in the first place. I did whatever Nancy asked me to do while concentrating on getting to know the other paras in the school.

I started to go home with some of the paras. Sometimes, this took me to edgy areas like troubled parts of Harlem and Brooklyn's Bedford-Stuyvesant neighborhood. Sometimes just one whiff would send my ghetto past rushing through me. There was the pungent odor of neglect behind those dark and dented doors of public housing projects, of tenements where landlords were as absent as hope. There was the stale, sugary stench of old urine in almost airless hallways and garbage long uncollected mixed with yesterday's allure of cooked cabbage and hard-fried fish.

Yet, no matter where I went, I was met with a reassuring excitement. Sometimes I would find it in the children at the home of a para. You could see that these children had grabbed a broom and pitched in to clean the place in anticipation of my visit. You could hear it in their whispers to one another, *"Mama's going to be a teacher."* No matter where I went, I was always welcomed into a para's home. I remember people hurriedly brushing clothes off the couch or a chair to make room for me to sit down. There was never any hostility from the paras. In fact, my day was often lifted when I'd come across little Black children who had such a way about them. It would show up in the brightness of their smiles, the clear whiteness in their eyes, in the jaunty rhythm in their little bodies, whether they were dancing, playing, prancing, or helping their mothers clean their homes. They were so cute.

Most of the paras were poor, but that didn't mean that they didn't want what most Americans want: a chance to improve their lives and the lives of their children. The school board had offered some after-school workshops here and there, even some college courses provided by the city's central poverty agency. But they were very limited and available to only a fraction of the paras who wanted what amounted to a career ladder to higher aspirations. I told them that they deserved much more.

When I first started working at the school, I thought my fellow paras didn't like me. But fairly soon I began feeling that they picked up on my sincerity, my dynamism. I also grew confident that they were beginning to understand the great depth of my commitment to them and the para program.

Paras would call me up at all hours; I told them they could. One of the things about organizing is that you have to realize that your life is not your own. You have to be prepared for people to call you at any time.

I could see that the para program, once its members were organized, would have such a wonderful impact on individuals and their community. Knowing this gave me much more drive to make sure I didn't fail them; this was especially true during those long days when I was bone tired, working as a para and then working to organize them. Sometimes, though, I would encounter nothing short of supreme inspiration in the most unexpected places. In a house in Brooklyn, I spoke to a para who had a couple of kids. It was clear that the household was struggling financially. But that was not what struck me at first. What did was this para's mother. She was lying on a cot in the living room. The whole time I talked to her daughter about the advantages of organizing the paras and how the United Federation of Teachers could make that happen, the old lady on the cot listened. Occasionally, she would offer up a faint smile.

After some time, I turned to her.

"It must be very difficult," I said.

"No," she said, her eyes doing most of the smiling now. "I just thank God that I can get up in the morning and do some work."

She told me that she was in her seventies and was a domestic. "I look up and see the sun coming up in the sky," she continued. "I see the sky gaining its color, and I know it's time for me to get up. I know I have work to do."

I listened to her and thought about my own work. I looked at her. I looked at me through her. I was still a young woman, and here she was with no youth, no vitality. She would lie on that cot as long as she could to summon the energy she needed to get up and go to work each day.

At the time, I had been a bit depressed. The work was keeping me from seeing Norman, and maybe all this time being around the young children of the paras made me think about the baby I had lost years ago in Chicago. Organizing the paras was very daunting work. Most had never been a part of organized labor.

And here was this old lady on the cot. She seemed so happy to simply be able to climb off that cot and go to work in somebody else's house so that she could help take care of her daughter and grandchildren. This struck me, and her example gave me perspective. Yes, I was organizing the paras, and it was exhaustive work. And if they lived here or there, I told myself that I could definitely visit these places for thirty minutes, for an hour, for whatever it took to get the job done.

That's exactly what I did. I was beginning to forge unity in the paras, starting with my district—District 2, which was the largest in Manhattan and included the Upper West Side, Chelsea, and Greenwich Village. But I visited paras in all of the city's five boroughs.

Part of my efforts to build and maintain solidity among the paras was to take them on educational retreats. In the early 1970s, we'd take a hundred or so paraprofessionals and their leaders to various sites near the city, like Glen Cove, Long Island. But a favorite was Tarrytown in Westchester County.

We'd leave on a Friday and return on Sunday. None of the paras would have to pay a penny. It was good for them to be away from home and family and children. They would be in a nice, middle-class setting, an environment where they could relax and think—and learn. Of course, these weekends gave paras a chance to know one another and become more acquainted with the union and some of its leadership. We would have speakers come out, like Norman and Bayard, who would talk to them about the history of the labor and civil rights movements.

They would also learn more about what a labor contract is, what their rights would be under one, and the procedures to utilize and protect their rights as workers. We also helped them to become advocates for labor, helping them with things like public speaking and community involvement.

There was always so much camaraderie and a grace about these weekends. We'd even sing union and gospel songs.

Then one time, in Tarrytown, we had an incident. The weekend was coming to a close. Everyone was checked out of the conference center, and we were about to leave when we were told by the center's administration that something was missing. It was a radio.

Each room had one, a radio probably not worth more than $50. My first thought was, I don't believe this.

I gave a little talk, reminding everyone why we were there and what we were accomplishing not only for ourselves but also for our union and communities. And Maria Portalatin, vice president of the union's paraprofessional chapter, supported my remarks by indicating that we had learned a lot that weekend as para representatives. But, she added, we had to set good examples for our members and our communities. I then told them that each para should go back inside, back to her room, and come back a little later with their heads held high (and the radio back where it belonged). I promised them that no one would ask any questions. That is exactly what happened. Everything ended well. On the ride back to the city we all sang "Solidarity Forever."

Along the way, Norman's and my apartment became a paras gathering place. It was wonderful. I would invite them over and before long it was like the old civil rights days with all of us singing and eating and talking.

I even had Mr. Randolph come and address them there. Some of the paras didn't know who this great leader was, but they were impressed with his commanding presence and rumbling baritone. He talked about the need for unity among all workers despite their race and ethnicity. He told them that they were part of a universal struggle for economic justice. It was really something. Most of them had never met anyone like Mr. Randolph and Bayard Rustin, who also used to come and speak with them.

I stayed connected with many of the paras, some of whom went on to become teachers and principals and even union leaders. Once I asked Shelvy Young-Abrams, the recently retired chair of the UFT's paraprofessional chapter, if she remembered those days gathered at the feet of Mr. Randolph. She said she did, that she would never forget the experience, but couldn't tell me exactly what he had said.

Shelvy could only say that she knew she was sitting with greatness and that inspired her. I understood what she meant. It didn't feel like it was that long ago when I sat in her place, sitting with greatness and inspired in much the same way.

# CHAPTER 9

# A Triumph of the Paraprofessionals and a Soulful Solidarity

Norman and I were no strangers to hostility in the struggle. You know the type: screaming red faces, balled-up fists, the chest pounding, the marking of territory, telling you in no uncertain terms, *"You've come far enough. Don't dare take another step."* In the civil rights movement, we were accustomed to this sort of display of resistance to progressive change. We saw it in the white-hot rage at Rainbow Beach in 1960 but also in New York, *up North*, during the closing years of the 1960s. Norman could not be at my side as I came face-to-face with a different turn on the twisted notion of resistance in a collision of local misguided self-determination, city politics, race, class, and education. It happened in one of the poorest sections of Brooklyn but was felt far beyond its borders. In time, it would shake the whole of New York City.

I remember all the Black faces screaming nasty words at other Blacks. At me. The hostility was so thick you could almost swim in it. A year later, as a thirty-year-old recent Harvard graduate, working for the United Federation of Teachers as the primary organizer of a mostly Black and Hispanic group of women known as paraprofessionals or paras—teachers' aides—I stepped right into the aftermath of a mess that turned out to be counterproductive to advancing the needs of this community, part of one of the largest Black communities in the nation.

Let me set the stage.

After a number of failed attempts to solve the problem of desegregating New York City public schools, a response fueled by the rising influence of Black nationalist thinking began to find traction in some corners of the city's Black neighborhoods, encompassing areas such as Harlem in upper Manhattan and Brownsville in Brooklyn. This response came to be known as "community control." In my view and in Norman's, too, this was less an intellectual response than one more rooted in frustration. It was almost a surrender to segregation. I say this to mean that many in these areas believed that if, in fact, Black students were to go to mostly Black schools, then some in the Black community should control those schools. With local control, Blacks could set the educational agenda of schools and pick and manage their teachers and administrators.

The first great test of this approach was centered in the Black Brooklyn neighborhoods of Ocean Hill and Brownsville.

Ocean Hill was once mostly a working-class Italian area that was separated from the much larger Stuyvesant Heights. By the late 1960s, Ocean Hill was mostly Black.

The same was true for neighboring Brownsville but much more dramatically so. This part of eastern Brooklyn had been mostly white and Jewish in the 1940s. By 1970, according to Wendell E. Pritchett's book *Brownsville, Brooklyn: Blacks, Jews, and the Changing Face of the Ghetto*, 30,000 of its residents had fled. The 70,000 or so who remained tended to be poor, many living in the area's public housing projects. Also in that period, Pritchett writes, the area shifted from 85 percent white to 75 percent Black and 20 percent Puerto Rican.

I understood this kind of wingless flight. I witnessed it happen on the outskirts of my South Side Chicago neighborhood my mother and sisters moved into when we left the ghetto in the mid-1950s. This didn't happen in our relatively new, up-and-coming neighborhood of Gresham, an area with little previous housing history. But white flight, nevertheless, became a major feature of Chicago's South and West sides throughout the 1960s as Blacks continued to move deeper into once white, working-class neighborhoods that went from white to Black seemingly overnight.

In 1967, the Brownsville section of Brooklyn, already taut with racial tension, exploded in September after a Black New York Police Department detective killed an eleven-year-old boy. He had been suspected in the mugging of a seventy-three-year-old Jewish man. It is widely believed that Sonny Carson (yes, the same Sonny Carson of our shared CORE days, and more on him later) spread rumors that a white policeman killed the boy.

In May of the following year, just as I was about to receive my master's degree in education, the newly formed Community School Board of Ocean Hill-Brownsville transferred out thirteen teachers and six administrators. These transfers, which amounted to nothing less than firings, were heard around the city.

Norman and I recognized this radical action as an expression of Black Power, or at the very least an echo of it, after Stokely Carmichael in 1966 introduced and helped popularize this retreat from racial integration. At the time, Stokely had replaced our friend John Lewis, who had shed his own blood for racial integration, as the head of the Student Nonviolent Coordinating Committee. Black Power called for, among other things, Black parents taking control of their neighborhood schools, their curriculum, and the hiring and firing of educators in these schools.

The first flare-up was in 1966 at Harlem's Intermediate School 201. Black protesters demanded that its principal, Stanley Lisser, who was white and Jewish, be replaced. He agreed to a transfer, but a group of Black and white teachers went on strike to protest the move. Al Shanker backed the teachers, and Lisser was reinstated.

This resolution didn't sit well with advocates of community control of schools, a group being stirred up, if not loosely led, by Sonny Carson, the executive director of Brooklyn CORE. Another indication of just how bad relations were becoming regarding schools and the Black community came in June 1967. Al Shanker agreed to talk with Carson and 300 other Black parents and their supporters who were pushing for community control. But when the meeting started, the gathering at Junior High School 35 in Brooklyn turned ugly. When Al tried to speak, he was repeatedly interrupted, loudly and rudely, by the crowd. Exasperated, he announced that if he was interrupted again, he would leave.

The audience laughed at him.

Later, Carson wrote of the clash, saying that Shanker "shuffled toward the door, but was blocked by two burly brothers who refused to allow him to leave. Shanker said, 'Mr. Carson, you gave me your word.'"

Carson wrote that the audience laughed again at the sight of "this great big honky union chief, standing there, blotchy with apparent fright."

Liberal Republican John Lindsay was mayor at the time. And in an experimental program for decentralizing public schools, he oversaw the transfer of some authority from the Board of Education to select neighborhood districts, most predominantly Black, woefully underperforming and mostly staffed with white teachers and administrators.

In May 1968, a month after the assassination of Martin Luther King Jr., the Ocean Hill-Brownsville's community-centered district office and its superintendent flexed their new authority. It was such a volatile time. Following Dr. King's death, Stokely Carmichael erupted. "When White America killed Dr. King last night, she declared war on us," he was quoted as saying in the April 6 edition of the *Washington Post*. "We have to retaliate for the death of our leaders."

Even before he could utter those words, enraged and emotionally wounded Black people had taken to the streets, some setting off a wave of destruction and social disorder that would engulf more than one hundred American cities.

The district office eliminated selected teachers and administrators. All the transfers were white. Most were Jewish. The teachers were represented by the United Federation of Teachers, headed, of course, by Al Shanker, who would soon hire me to organize the paraprofessionals against this combative backdrop.

The leadership and rank and file of the UFT insisted that shipping the educators to other districts was in violation of union contract rules. And despite Black labor and civil rights giants like A. Philip Randolph and Bayard Rustin supporting Al Shanker and the UFT's action, many in the Black community, especially in Ocean Hill-Brownsville, saw the conflict in stark racial terms. For many, it was a sad but classic example of *us against them*.

*I told Velma, and anyone who would ask me, that I believed Shanker was correct in his stand with the teachers.* At the time, I was associate director of the A. Philip Randolph Institute. We at the institute—along with the Black Trade Union Leadership Committee; the New York City Central Labor Council; and Samuel D. Wright, a New York State assemblyman who was chairman of the Black and Puerto Rican Caucus, a temporary ally—firmly supported Shanker and his United Federation of Teachers. We were then, and are certainly today, totally committed to the trade union movement and the principle of due process.

Additionally, I will never forget Shanker's financial and moral support of Dr. King and the 1963 March on Washington for Jobs and Freedom. At the time of the march, Shanker was treasurer of the UFT, and he helped to persuade the union to endorse the march, even urging it to send people and buses, which it did. And shortly after the inception of the Randolph Institute, Shanker served as its treasurer, a post he held for years.

*But the militants who were fueling the conflict in Brooklyn weren't listening to Norman or Bayard or Mr. Randolph or anyone in the labor movement.* When the transferred teachers tried to return to their jobs, they were physically blocked by Blacks who supported their ouster. Within weeks, 350 of the 556 teachers in the district went on strike in protest.

With the start of the new school year in September, the transferred teachers once again tried to return to their old jobs. Sonny Carson joined a group of angry protesters who again barred the teachers from returning to their former schools. One protester shouted at the teachers, "You're dead. We know your faces. We'll get you, your families, your children." When the teachers were told to report to a meeting, someone killed the lights. Sitting in the dark, the teachers heard shouts of "Jew pigs" and threats like "You're going out of here in pine boxes."

Norman and I watched the situation continue to deteriorate—including more teacher walkouts—until October 14, when Al Shanker called for a citywide strike of all the city's 48,000 public school teachers. Sean

Ahern, in a review of Jerald Podair's book *The Strike That Changed New York: Blacks, Whites, and the Ocean Hill-Brownsville Crisis*, wrote that the labor conflict grew into "the most racially divisive event in the city's history since the Draft Riots of the Civil War." Interesting perspective, but we think it is a bit overstated.

The strike did shut down the city's public schools for thirty-six days. Eventually, the Ocean Hill-Brownsville district teachers and administrators were reinstated. And the city's Board of Education agreed to set up local school boards throughout New York. Nonetheless, tensions remained for years.

Diane Ravitch, a historian of education and former wife of Richard Ravitch, once wrote that in the shadow of the conflicts of Ocean Hill-Brownsville, the United Federation of Teachers' image as an "idealistic and progressive union was tarnished among the liberal intelligentsia and many blacks."

In view of this decentralization crisis, few co-called experts thought the paras would choose the UFT as its union. In fact, some of the same people who had tried to exploit the racial tension in Ocean Hill-Brownsville that year were working to persuade paraprofessionals to reject the UFT. In one instance, a community action group that had the responsibility to refer paras to schools threatened to fire them if they embraced the UFT. And here I was working for the UFT and feeling very strongly that it offered the best course for paraprofessionals. One of the first things I did when I met paras was ask them to sign a UFT union card. I was determined to get them organized for so many reasons, not the least of them for economic justice.

In the late 1960s, I walked around with a halo of hair, unstraightened and decidedly not chemically relaxed. I'll never forget how a woman, clearly an agitated opponent of the UFT of which she knew I was a member, verbally assailed me as I attempted to attend a community meeting.

"You might have natural hair," she spat at me in a Southern drawl, "but you got a processed mind."

I once traveled, with seven paras at my side, to a decentralized district in the Bronx. It had a reputation for corruption. And yes, it too was hostile to the UFT. The district's superintendent and its school board, mostly Black and Hispanic, didn't want me and my party of paras to enter one of its schools where a community-control school board was holding a meeting. I had hoped to address the meeting on behalf of the paras. I was there to advance the cause of paraprofessionals in the district's schools.

Nonetheless, we were greeted in front of the school by an angry group of community people. A push and shove and some words broke out that quickly erupted into a red-hot argument. Before any of us realized it, a woman with a baseball bat stepped out of the crowd and started yelling at me.

"Stay out of our district," she cried. "Don't come in here with that damn UFT!"

In the next instant, she lunged at me with her Louisville Slugger in hand. At that moment, one of my paras from a Harlem school, Margaret Horton, who weighed at least 300 pounds and was not light on courage either, stepped into the woman's path. Standing between me and the bat woman, she spoke slowly and clearly into that woman's face.

"All right," she said, pulling back her shoulders and seeming to stand a few inches taller. "You just c'mon because you gotta bring some to get some!"

The woman melted back into the crowd. Everybody left us alone that night. And yes, I got to speak, and yes, I was persuasive. I had a purpose, and I had a family of paras around me, the union at my side, and I had Norman.

This was the atmosphere in which I worked to organize and advance the paras who were noncombatants in this conflict. So many of them, Black and Hispanic and relatively poor (paraprofessionals still had to be welfare eligible to quality for their jobs), were caught in the middle. They, like anyone else, simply wanted a fair wage, some job security, and a chance to move ahead.

This might be hard to believe today, but back then, paras worked at the whim of their schools' principals. They could not assume that they were entitled to vacations, sick days, medical coverage, or pensions upon retirement. Their work was not considered a profession. And of course, there was no comprehensive career ladder for them to advance, to become, as some dreamed, teachers.

There had been a very limited program for this sort of advancement, but these opportunities were rather arbitrary and strictly at the discretion of various school principals. We at the UFT wanted to provide them a profession with dignity, security, and promise.

It wasn't dignified, for instance, that paraprofessionals were routinely expected to file for unemployment to be paid during the summer break when teachers went on vacation. Teachers and administrators didn't have to do that. I also discovered that paras were essentially locked into a dead-end job.

I never believed that the paras' lack of opportunities was in keeping with the roots of the program, which ran deep into President Johnson's War on Poverty. Weeks after Vice President Johnson because the president in the wake of Kennedy's assassination, he was eager, according to Robert A. Caro's exhaustive examination of Johnson's early years in the White House, *The Passage of Power*, to place his own stamp on his presidency. Part of his solution was to take a little-known initiative that had been contemplated by Kennedy and his advisers.

John F. Kennedy, born to great wealth, had been greatly troubled by the systematic poverty he saw in Appalachia while campaigning for the White House in West Virginia. He was also heavily influenced by socialist Michael Harrington's book on poverty, *The Other America*. But it was Johnson who would transform an embryonic intention into a full-blown national program. Johnson announced his War on Poverty during his first State of the Union address in January 1964, a thrust no doubt influenced as well by initiatives called for during the 1963 March on Washington for Jobs and Freedom.

One of the results of Johnson's program was the passage the following year of the Elementary and Secondary Education Act (ESEA), which today is basically the No Child Left Behind Act of 2001. The paraprofessional program for public schools was created under this legislation.

I knew right away that with union representation, the dead end that paraprofessionals were facing could be blasted open for the thousands of them working in that capacity in New York City public schools.

Yet some in the communities where the paras lived wanted them to choose sides. Some wanted them to act as secret agents, spying on the UFT for which I was recruiting them. This wasn't lost on some of the teachers, who tended not to warm to the idea of having two adults—even other teachers (team teaching had failed in New York schools)—in their classrooms. Following Ocean Hill-Brownsville, the inclusion of paras in their midst only heightened some of their suspicions about them. The radicals saw the paras as a vanguard that could help Black communities gain control of their schools and forge revolutionary approaches to educating kids. Political conservatives tended to view the paras as a generally lazy and unmotivated cheap source of labor who did not deserve a nickel more than they already received.

What Norman and I knew was that the paras were just like any other workers. All they wanted was to improve their lives and be close to their children, and they weren't going to allow themselves to be used for the agendas of other people. They wanted opportunities, and that was exactly what the UFT wanted for them. Yet, in this atmosphere of racial conflict and confrontation, the UFT and anyone who spoke for it became symbols of white oppression. It was a difficult period in New York.

There were times when people, sometimes paras from other school districts, would come and picket our efforts to organize the paras into joining the UFT. There was so much misinformation spread against us, some of it circulated by our rival union, District Council 37 of the American Federation of State, County and Municipal Employees, which was out to capture the hearts and minds of the paras.

A large part of the challenge facing the UFT was to educate paras to realize that the union was a benefit for themselves and their families. The other part of that challenge was to ensure that teachers supported paras, who were in many cases different from them in educational, social, and economic status. What we were saying was that there should be a single community, made such by a common commitment to the education and the welfare of the children. To accomplish this, the UFT—headed by Shanker and Sandy Feldman—launched the most extensive educational campaign in its history. It was carried out through meetings with all levels of teacher and para representatives, and through the union's newspaper, today known as the *New York Teacher*.

For weeks, our work with the paras was featured in the union publication, along with pictures and articles depicting paras and teachers happily working together in the classroom. Among the newspaper's reporting staff was Norman's younger brother, John Hill.

The message against our efforts was almost always the same: Shanker was just using the paras and no good would ever come from their joining the United Federation of Teachers. District Council 37 was interested in the paras as well. Many community-control types also charged that paras joining the UFT would be like an oppressed people joining a "colonial power." Community-control advocates were often quick to remind paras that it was the UFT that had "struck against the Black community" in Ocean Hill-Brownsville.

Convincing paras to join the UFT rather than DC 37 was no easy job. After the teachers' strike a lot of paras simply didn't like teachers. Some of the teachers had never trusted the paras. During the strike, some teachers were convinced that the paras were indeed spies. And there was history of some paras being treated poorly, getting assigned to menial tasks like washing blackboards and windows, and watering plants, instead of working with students.

Some would say to me, "We don't want to be maids in the classroom. We can tutor the kids, help them with their homework…things that are very important for the education of the child."

I understood that some of these kinds of jobs needed to be done to free the teachers to teach. But paras shouldn't have been exclusively tasked with these jobs. In the end, I think that some teachers simply took a while to understand just how much paras could assist them with truly educating children, like leading small group-instruction and reading to them.

There was also a deeply held, psychological factor that worked against some of the paras. Lots of them were intimidated by teachers. Some were convinced that teachers looked down on them because paras seldom went further than high school and did not have the bearing, polish, and experience of educators. Both teachers and paras had to be shown that their interests merged. I began to learn that as paras came to see me, a Black woman, emerging as their leader, the more confidence they gained in their own capacity.

Maggie Martin, who was a para and became a New York public school teacher, told me, "It meant a lot to those of us who were Black to see a Black woman in this position. You had the authority. Even when we didn't always agree with you, we were still proud of you. If we had a problem, you came."

Still, I had my own baggage. As I organized the paras, largely working as a para among them, I had to be sensitive to how I might be perceived by them. Even with a Harvard education, I was still this Black girl from the ghetto. I told a few of the paras that I had worked in the civil rights movement. Some knew, especially those who had been beaten and abused, that I had suffered my own beating. I carried the evidence of this in my slight limp that had followed me from Rainbow Beach almost a decade earlier like a less-than-perfect shadow.

And I wasn't above using a little humor here or there, or a well-timed gospel standard like" I Ain't Gonna Let Nobody Turn Me Around" or as the Bible says, "You take one step and I will take two."

Norman, while not physically with me at these schools, helped me so much during this period. We talked all the time about the importance of my work, and he shared strategies with me, even at night, even when we were in bed.

Nonetheless, my paras watched me lose it on more than one occasion as we pushed our way into respectability and recognition as unionized workers. In one instance during the winter, a para who had aligned herself with DC 37 accused me of having intimate and frequent familiarity with a part of Al Shanker's anatomy I'd rather not mention. I took the insult. But then someone standing near her started talking about my mama, you know in the ghetto tradition of "playing the dozens." I was in no mood to play. This woman didn't know my mother, and my mother was a fine woman.

Something snapped.

The next thing I knew I was tearing off my coat and squaring up to beat this woman into the cold, hard ground.

And this woman was as burly as a mountain bear. My comrades restrained me.

"I never saw Velma act that way," said Jeannette DiLorenzo, who was with me that day. She was a dear friend and colleague who, with her husband, John, led the picketing during the UFT's first strike in Brooklyn. In short, she was a grand old leader of the union.

"Did that woman say anything about her mother, Ruby?" Bobbie asked.

"She sure did," Jeannette replied.

"Then," Bobbie explained without hesitation, "that accounts for it."

There would be so many other insults at this time, some even questioning whether I was "Black enough." Bayard Rustin, no stranger to personal attacks during his long career as an openly gay civil rights and labor activist, helped me deal with that part of my job. He would tell me some of the terrible things that were said to him, and I could see that he never lost a single step over that sort of mess. He told me, in so many words and deeds, to keep going. I did.

In 1969, with Al Shanker's oversight and the help of an interim steering committee of paraprofessionals, I was steadily moving to bring paras into the union. At this time, the UFT, its rank and file still overwhelmingly white and Jewish, fully supported the organization of paras into the union. The paras held meetings among themselves. And any time I requested, Al would come and make a case for paras joining the UFT. Part of the battle cry for getting to paras to join us was "What Shanker did for the teachers, he'll do for you."

I even turned to *Alice in Wonderland* in those heady days to make my point, especially to paras still torn over whether to join us or DC 37. I called on the sage advice of the Cheshire Cat, who once, in so many words, told Alice when she was lost and confused, that if you don't know where you're going, any road will take you there. I added, "We have to have direction. We have to know where we want to go." I made it clear that I wanted an annual salary, health benefits, a raise, and a career ladder. "The only way to get those things was through the UFT," I told them. In gatherings with paras, I would stand before them and ask in a chant:

"What do you want?"
"Annual salary," they'd chant back.
"What do you want?"
"A career ladder..."

I tried to learn exactly what the paras wanted most, so we surveyed them. Their top demands were the same as mine—a career ladder, an annual salary, a raise, and a pension. Directly reaching out to the paras felt like the right thing to do. It was, after all, democratic. It also demonstrated, right off the bat, our commitment to giving them a decision-making role in the union.

In the summer of 1969, in a close election, the classroom para-professionals voted to join the UFT (most of the much smaller group of non-classroom paras chose DC 37). In the meantime, many of the UFT's paras remained distrustful of teachers and took a wait-and-see position, feeling that the union would now have to prove its worth. I felt the pressure.

We had finally reached critical mass of paras joining the union to begin to push for our demands. The stage was set for negotiations for an August contract with the Board of Education.

That's when everything got even harder.

The board appeared uninterested in the paras and any need they had for a contract, making the negotiation process very difficult. For example, when the UFT submitted its proposals in December 1969, it took the board five months before it put one proposal on the table. And the board even dared the UFT to strike over its protracted inaction.

One of the first things the UFT did was to conduct an all-out campaign, this time to push the Board of Education. We all—union officers, staff, and district representatives—fanned out to public schools throughout the city to discuss the possibility of another UFT strike, if it had to come to that. We talked about the basics, if that happened, like respecting picket lines. And that to win, we—teachers and paraprofessionals—had to work together.

At the same time, the union also mobilized support from the labor movement, civil rights organizations, and church, civic, and education groups. We were increasing our pressure on the Board of Education to negotiate with us. At the urging of A. Philip Randolph and Al Shanker, Harry Van Arsdale, president of the New York City Central Labor Council, spoke in support of the paraprofessionals. He said that it was "shameful and hard to believe that the Board of Education would drag its feet" in negotiating a contract for the paras. He noted that this was a group of low-income workers who earned only $1,700 to $2,200 a year.

Al Shanker turned to his teachers. In a speech to the UFT's delegate assembly, he said, "We are at a crossroads for our union. We are living in a city with a rapidly changing population where we must have broad support from all people." In other words, he said, the teachers and the paraprofessionals needed each other. On June 3, 1970, the teachers responded by overwhelmingly voting to support a paras strike if it was necessary to force the board into contract negotiations.

The New York Board of Education didn't want to pay the paras higher salaries or give them medical benefits. And the idea of providing paras a path to work and go to school so that they could one day be teachers seemed to fall not only on deaf ears but also closed minds. Some board members argued that paras wouldn't even want to go to college.

Negotiations dragged on for ten very, very long months.

My routine was to get up early and meet with the negotiations team, which was composed of paraprofessionals and teacher representatives led by Sandy Feldman and Lucille Swain. Sandy was already a dear friend. On the other hand, Lucille and I became good friends, despite our audacious beginnings. She used to tell people to call her Dr. Swain because she had a doctorate. And I told her, okay, if she'd call me Master Hill to honor my master's degree. We both got a good laugh out of that. She was an excellent negotiator.

The talks were tough. And to my surprise I found myself struggling to keep the paras focused and united. The truth was that few of them had any experience with organized labor, contracts, and contract negotiations. Strike talk scared many of them. They were immediately concerned for their jobs. We did, in fact, take a strike vote. I believe we had to because the board had been stonewalling us. Instead of empathy and cooperation, we were given all kinds of arguments explaining why the paras could not have what they needed.

At one negotiation session our team was shocked to learn that a group of paras had taken it upon themselves to undermine our position by writing a letter to the Board of Education. It indicated that the group supported the union but was opposed to any strike. A board negotiator actually read the letter to us at the negotiation table. And there would be more internal fights.

When things get really rough, people get frayed, so the Blacks were fighting the whites, and the whites and the Blacks were fighting the Hispanics, and on it went. A side note: Bilingual education had recently been introduced in New York public schools. Paras who were bilingual, mostly Hispanic ones, felt they deserved more money than paras who were not. Some of the Hispanic paras would meet in small groups and speak only Spanish, causing many of the paras who could not speak Spanish to feel excluded.

I had to go before the paras and insist that this was the time to stick together. This was a time for solidarity. That's what I did. We were newly unionized; we were young and full of vitality, and the process for progress had just started. If this movement of the paras was to survive and succeed, we would all have to look out for one another the way Margaret Horton looked out for me when that woman with the bat tried to turn us away.

But when we didn't get a contract right away, a lot of paras got nervous. They were being pressured by some forces in their communities, too. We had to go to local school boards to make a case that the paras deserved a good contract. We had to remind these board members that the paras were part of the same community that they were a part of. We told these boards that the paras deserved to have raises, that they deserved to be treated fairly.

But the local boards were not interested. They would say that they didn't have money to pay paras—even though they were their neighbors, people who looked just like them. We met with some of the paras who were part of our executive board prior to a meeting of the School Board District 5, one of the community-control districts in Harlem. Its superintendent was Black, and he minced no words in letting us know that he did not want unionized paras in his district.

That's when I reminded the paras that a boss is a boss—whatever color he or she is. In plain talk, I told the paras that his role as a boss was to take as much as he could get, and ours, as workers, was to get as much as we could.

Once, I came home from negotiations at one or two o'clock in the morning. I was so sick and tired of trying to convince the paras that they should be together and tired of trying to convince the board that it should give us what we needed, a good and fair contract. I tried to sleep, but I couldn't. I looked at the ceiling, then the clock and realized that dawn was approaching, as was my meeting with my team; and soon after, I would have to spend many more hours back at the negotiation table.

I finally picked up the telephone and called my mentor.

A. Philip Randolph, all his life an early riser, answered. By this time, he was living three blocks away in my high-rise complex in the Chelsea section of Manhattan. For some reason I don't remember, I was a little surprised when he picked up my call. It was six or seven in the morning. I don't even remember if I said good morning. I do remember, though, telling him that the negotiations were driving me nuts.

"Mr. Randolph," I said, "I just can't do this."

He listened for a while and said, "Velma, you come over here."

We had coffee in his apartment, and he was so sweet. He was a widower and lived alone. I brought the coffee. He just listened to me, and I went through all the steps and all the problems. It was incredible. Mr. Randolph tended to be a formal man. Even when he wasn't feeling well at home, he'd put on his jacket. He sat down, back erect, manner just so.

"Velma," he finally said in that deep, breathy voice of his, "I think you've been doing a good job."

He explained to me that I should expect some dissension. He would ask me if I did this, or that. And I would say, yes, I did that, and that, too. He was really interested and very encouraging. Mr. Randolph was such a good man. And he was such a sure and steady hand at labor negotiations. He never said a bad word about anybody, but he did have people who answered to him and could tear people up if the occasion required it.

*Velma and I remember a point at which Mr. Randolph was in negotiations and he wasn't getting anywhere.* Finally, he turned to one of his vice presidents, C. L. Dullens, and said, "Maybe you can talk to them," because C. L. could be rough and tough. We knew that C. L. would be boom, *boom,* BOOM with them.

*Norman and I knew that Mr. Randolph had a couple of people like that around him.* After I got through telling Mr. Randolph all about my para problems, he said things were really looking promising. Then he said, "Well, Velma, let me tell you this story. It is the story about a stonecutter."

You know what? I didn't know what a stonecutter was. I had seen some movies, *The Ten Commandments*—Joshua…I think he was a stonecutter in that film. I listened to Mr. Randolph, and I didn't dare ask, "What's a stonecutter?"

Mr. Randolph said there was this stonecutter, and he was hammering away at this rock. He said this man was trying to break this rock, and he just didn't seem able to break it. The rock was solid, and it would not budge. This stonecutter pulled back his arm, and he would hit it, and he would hit it again, and he would hit it *again.* Mr. Randolph said the rock wouldn't crack; it wouldn't break. But, Mr. Randolph continued, the stonecutter kept banging away at that big rock. He would hit it again, and he would hit it again, and he would hit it yet again. As I listened, I said to myself, *Hmmm. Okay.*

Mr. Randolph said that stonecutter must have hit that rock at least one hundred times. Well, he told me, the man kept going and was tired and he was sweating, but he knew he couldn't quit. And he lifted his heavy arm and on the 101st blow that rock just split apart.

"You know, Velma," Mr. Randolph said, his voice as smooth as warm cream, "the stonecutter knew that it wasn't that last blow that did it. It was all that went on before."

I looked at him and he looked at me, and we both smiled. I have to tell you that Mr. Randolph made me feel good. And even though he was not a hugger, he gave me a hug. And he said, "Now, Velma, you just let me know what happens and just remember it's going to turn out good."

I thought to myself, *Boy, if I had a daddy, he would have said something like that to me.* I don't know if he told that story to anybody else, but I knew one thing for sure: Mr. Randolph told *me* that story. They were the right words at the right time. I left and went back to the office and started working, refreshed and renewed and feeling as if I was walking in the footsteps of a giant.

In August 1970, after ten hard months of negotiations, the paras got their contract with the New York Board of Education. The agreement almost tripled their salaries, ranging from $5,500 to $7,800 a year. It also guaranteed paraprofessionals four weeks of paid vacation, along with sick leave, and extended health care, which included full dental and optical care for them and their families.

Later that month, the A. Philip Randolph Institute issued a news release written by Bayard Rustin, the institute's executive director. I tingled with pride when I read its title: "The Triumph of the Paraprofessionals."

In it, Bayard detailed the result of our struggle to gain the paras benefits and protections in our new three-year contract with the Board of Education. He noted that the thousands of paraprofessionals, most of whom were Black and Puerto Rican, would now get wage increases and benefits, retroactive to January 1, 1970. This would effectively end paying paras well beneath the government-set poverty level.

Most of all, Bayard noted, there would be a "career ladder" that would enable paras to go to school and become full-fledged teachers. Such an opportunity, he wrote, is "clearly of benefit not only to the paraprofessionals but also the entire society."

When the City University of New York Career Ladder Program first opened its doors in 1971, thousands rushed in to enroll; there were 6,000 in class each semester. This absolutely shocked the board, whose members had long been skeptical that paras would be interested in further education.

I will never, no matter how long I live, forget the first day that paraprofessionals could register for classes at New York's colleges, which included fine institutions like City College and Brooklyn College, Queens College, and the Borough of Manhattan College. A bunch of us crowded into a car that day and drove around to see if paras were taking advantage of this new opportunity to become public school teachers.

My Lord, you wouldn't believe the lines. They were all around the campus at every campus we visited, and we visited them all that nippy fall day. It was amazing. Amazing. Thousands of paras had come to register for college. It was a sight to behold.

No one, not even those of us in the United Federation of Teachers, was fully prepared for such an enthusiastic outpouring by paras stepping up to improve themselves and, by doing so, their communities and their city.

In time, the success of the career ladder helped to effectively integrate the teaching staff of New York's public schools. Before the program, minorities were 7 percent of teachers in the city's schools. Today the percentage is more than 40 percent, and much of the increase is a result of the para program and its career ladder provisions.

By 1997, the year Al Shanker died of cancer, the career ladder program had helped more than 8,000 paras become teachers. This, experts say, made our program one of the largest sources of minority teachers in New York City.

For years, the UFT held an annual ceremony in the spring for paras who completed their college studies. It was a magnificent affair held in a hotel ballroom for members of the union and their families. Each recipient had her or his name called, came up, and received a "certificate of accomplishment" for getting their associate degree or their bachelor's.

Most of these paras were women and belonged to racial or ethnic minorities; they were young, and they were old. And you could see that they were so proud when they walked up there. The smile on their faces just melted my heart. You could feel the love. It was a real occasion. For the people who still like to say that these people are among the takers, among those who are lazy and don't want to advance themselves in society, I say you should have been at one of these beautiful events and let the truth set you right. More recently, the ceremony evolved to include workshops and a luncheon.

The New York para story didn't stop here in New York. Our success in organizing the paras led to a movement spearheaded by the UFT to do much of the same for paras throughout America. I felt blessed to be a part of that. In 1972, I was vice president of the UFT's parent organization, the American Federation of Teachers (AFT) and was also elected to the AFT's national executive council. I was the first para to occupy such a post.

When I was nominated for the post, I spoke to the membership, telling everyone, "Don't vote for me because I'm a woman. Don't vote for me because I'm Black. Vote for me because I'm a damn good trade unionist." The convention erupted in applause.

After I was elected, someone told me that I had garnered more votes than even Al Shanker, who was also joining the executive council that day. I shrugged my shoulders and realized that I would have never had the chance to ascend the union's hierarchy without Al's help and support.

The American Federation of Teachers noted that the number of paraprofessionals who joined it between 1970 and 1985 was essentially equal to the number of teachers who joined from 1910 to 1960. As of 2011, according to Loretta Johnson, a former paraprofessional and AFT secretary treasurer, there were 859,656 paraprofessionals working in the United States.

*As Velma's husband and partner in the civil rights and labor movements, I was very proud of Velma for all her work and accomplishments on behalf of the paras.* I understand why some paras came to regard Al as the "head" and Velma as the "heart" of their great success.

*With Norman at the A. Philip Randolph Institute (he would soon succeed Bayard as the organization's executive director), I stayed with the UFT for years to come.* I continued to fight for my paras and more. It would take another contract negotiation to win a pension plan for them. As our successes mounted, my mind raced back to the night we took the first contract to the paras. But I will never forget that evening at the Marc Ballroom in Manhattan's Union Square. And what I remember most is standing before a sea of uplifted hands voting "YES" to accepting the contract we had negotiated. It was more than wonderful.

There would be so many more such deeply moving demonstrations of unity and recognition. The paraprofessionals had become a progressive force, what workers can be when they unify and stand strong and smart. No, we didn't get everything that we wanted in that first three-year contract. I just remember feeling that for many of these women, it was the first time they stood up together to get what they needed, what they deserved.

I talked at this meeting. Al Shanker talked, too. You could feel the solidarity. It was something. Overwhelmingly something great. I felt the tightly knit garment of history on our shoulders, warming us, encircling us, as photographers' shutters clicked and video cameras preserved the moment.

Bayard's concluding words about the paras contract still ring in my ears:

> The new UFT paraprofessional contract is one of the finest examples of self-determination by the poor, and it is likely to be repeated in other cities as part of a nationwide struggle by low-income workers to achieve equality.

History has proven that Bayard's words were prophetic. Yet challenges to organized labor and the continuing struggle for civil rights and economic justice remain. In response, we have the principles that guided the vision of A. Philip Randolph and Bayard Rustin to illuminate the path ahead.

Posterity must never forget that, as they said, we must all commit to a society in which racial equality and economic justice will prevail, and that the pursuit of racial equality and economic justice must be achieved through a majoritarian strategy involving coalition politics, which forcefully rejects authoritarian and totalitarian approaches to change. At the same time, they said, we must maintain a commitment to self-liberation.

As Mr. Randolph often said, "If you don't fight for yourself, then who will?" They also believed in a commitment to mass action and an unwavering commitment to nonviolence.

*These are the principles that brought Velma and me together and have held us together with a kind of programmatic clarity that saw us through storms of political and philosophical distractions, diversions and frustrating fits when symbols seemed to matter more to many than substance did.*

*Norman knows that without Mr. Randolph's and Bayard's principles and guidance, I could never had achieved what I did with helping to organize the paraprofessionals.* I know both of them would have been pleased, down through the years, with the result.

# CHAPTER 10

# The Next Logical Step— The A. Philip Randolph Institute

I was very pleased to see what Velma was accomplishing, organizing the paraprofessionals in the New York public schools and then expanding her work throughout the United States. This was the type of effort Velma and I talked about during our early years in the civil rights movement.

In the midst of breaking down racial segregation, some of us realized at that time that the movement would have to go beyond solely securing our equal rights. We increasingly had to find more focused means to open and secure equal opportunities for Americans who have had their opportunities systematically denied. It was clear that we were talking about making stronger linkages between civil rights, economic justice, and political action.

This idea crystallized in Bayard Rustin's brilliant 1965 essay "From Protest to Politics." Not only did he make these connections clear, but he also essentially mapped out the immediate future of the civil rights movement. By combining A. Philip Randolph's longtime broad outlook of the Blacks-and-labor alliance with Bayard's strategic mastery of how to bring all these elements of race, labor, and politics together, we could see the underpinning of a new sort of an organization. What emerged in 1965 was the A. Philip Randolph Institute.

It started in earnest with a series of meetings shortly after President Johnson signed the Civil Rights Act on July 2, 1964. Velma and I were deeply involved in those meetings. They were demanding sessions that nevertheless had a casual, relaxed air about them. This was probably because everyone attending them was either a friend or very close associate, or both. We all shared the same politics. There were often Velma and I; Tom Kahn, the director of the League for Industrial Democracy; Don Slaiman, director of the Civil Rights Department of the AFL-CIO; Max Shachtman, leader of the Socialist Party and a noted social democratic writer and theoretician; Rachelle Horowitz, on the staff of the Workers Defense League; and, of course, there was Bayard. Always Bayard.

It was a wonderfully mixed group that revolved mostly around Bayard and Tom; only three of us—Bayard, Velma, and I—were Black. Yet, we had so much in common, among them a great commitment to continue to struggle for economic, social, and always democratic change in America for all Americans. This made for a lively group. Everyone had opinions, and no one was hesitant to voice and defend them.

*I know I wasn't, Norman.* I remember so much electricity in some of those meetings. Yet Bayard had a way of keeping the mood light, like when he once wore bright red shorts and started doing push-ups in the middle of the floor. He could be so funny. His mischievous side could never be fully suppressed even during the most serious of circumstances. He nearly always found a way to put that part of his personality to work for us and the movement. I cannot imagine those sessions without him.

*Velma and I once watched him play devil's advocate, cleverly arguing against his own long-held positions, some concepts that formed the very foundation of "From Protest to Politics."*

*During one of the meetings, Norman and I listened to him say all this nonsense about labor unions, talking them down, being very critical of them.* And Don Slaiman, who was a very smart, well-spoken trade unionist, took the bait. Oh boy. And you have to remember that Don would become one of the institute's greatest advocates. We realized early that Don's role would be vitally important because he would have to be the one to sell the AFL-CIO head, George Meany, on the idea of initially funding the institute we were developing. Our plan sought start-up funding from the AFL-CIO and its Industrial Union Department for a total of $50,000.

But on that evening in Bayard's apartment, Don was unknowingly the mouse in a rhetorical game of cat and mouse played by the Cheshire Cat himself. Before Don realized it, he had been maneuvered into arguing for Bayard's bedrock beliefs about labor and race as Bayard just sat back wearing that big, impish grin of his.

Only Tom Kahn and Max Shachtman approached their roles in the formation of the institute in a bit more sedate manner.

*Velma and I had long realized that Tom was a brilliant writer and was inclined to scribble everything down, to later be reborn as brilliant articles, essays, speeches, and position papers.* It was not a secret that Tom had played a major role in the development of "From Protest to Politics."

*Norman and I thought the world of Max.* We especially enjoyed how he could analyze everyone and everything, and enjoy a good, honest argument. It seemed that his brain was working so hard all the time that you could almost hear it humming.

Most of the early meetings were held at Bayard's New York apartment. And the only thing modest about the place was its size. Bayard was an avid collector, so his living room, where we met, was crammed with African art, eighteenth-century Italian furniture, Russian icons, clocks from various ages and eras. There were even European religious sculptures, including a seven-foot-tall limestone Madonna and Child from the Middle Ages. There was also at least one meeting at Tom's vastly less ornate Manhattan office and another at Max's warm and inviting home in Floral Park, Long Island. We were there for all of them.

*Velma and I understood early that the new organization would be somewhat of a think tank and a platform for Bayard to propagate his strategic thrust for the continuing civil rights movement.* To truly understand who Bayard Rustin was, you had to realize that he was pacifist. He was militantly anti-war in any form or expression anywhere in the world. During World War II, Bayard, who was a Quaker, was a conscientious objector and so would not serve in the armed forces—for which he was imprisoned.

And despite his deep and obvious commitment to the civil rights movement, he never wavered in his commitment to the peace movement.

I thought the formation of a national organization could not only serve as a fertile place for Bayard to explore his evolving ideas regarding the next stages for the civil rights and labor movements; it could, more important, further harness his enormous energy and talents for the good of both of those. Throughout it all, I wanted to keep Bayard engaged in our movements. The last thing I wanted for Bayard was for him to go back to the peace movement.

As a result, during these meetings in his home, I began to argue for him to build on the undeniable success he achieved in the wake of the 1963 March on Washington the previous year. So much of the march's resounding triumph was a result of Bayard's leadership. Deservingly, he achieved national standing by way of the march. No longer did he have to lead from the shadows, from behind the scenes, as he did during the Montgomery bus boycott of 1955 and 1956 in Alabama. Once, during the boycott of a bus system that routinely discriminated against its Black passengers, Bayard had to be rushed out of town. He was about to be attacked by whites. He also began to fear that being a homosexual was becoming a liability to the boycott and to the movement in general.

But by the fall of 1963, Bayard had made the cover of *Life* magazine, posing with Randolph, pictured at the feet of Lincoln seated in his memorial.

My position began to take hold during those meetings, first gaining support among my colleagues. Then, Velma and I did our best to help Bayard refine some of the rougher edges of this own thinking on the matter. We kept hammering at the idea with him that he had achieved a powerful momentum of national civil rights leadership. And there was something else that played to our favor in helping to persuade him that a major new organization must be created and that he must lead it: Velma and I could see that his achievements by way of the March on Washington had made him more open and direct in his manner. We could see that Bayard was, as people like to say, more comfortable in his skin.

In the end, Bayard agreed with us. The new organization would be formed, and he would lead it.

We decided to name the organization after Randolph, particularly because we wanted to project Randolph's ideas and the untarnished reputation he enjoyed in both the civil rights and labor movements. Bayard directly discussed all of this with Randolph, who did not attend these meetings. Randolph was seventy-six years old at the time and still the legendary head of the Brotherhood of Sleeping Car Porters, the first large, successful labor union organized by Blacks. But by the mid-1960s, the union's influence was waning as sleeping cars were fast becoming quaint relics of rail travel.

I wished Velma and I could have been in New York for the final meetings that directly led to the creation of the A. Philip Randolph Institute in 1965. By then, we were living in Washington, DC, and Velma was working with the Office of Economic Opportunity. I was at the Industrial Union Department at the AFL-CIO, serving as its civil rights liaison and legislative representative. It was a post I would keep until 1967. I was, however, kept informed of the institute's early progress. Once the institute was fully established, Randolph was named its chairman and remained in that post until his death in 1979.

It was Bayard, serving as the institute's first president, who actually ran the institute. But this was not assured until Bayard had an audience with Meany, the head of the AFL-CIO, a major supporter of the creation of the institute. Don Slaiman told us that Meany had heard the open secret that Bayard was gay; he also knew that this fact had troubled some in the inner circles of the civil rights movement and Congress. It was widely reported as the March on Washington was being organized. In fact, Bayard was condemned on the floor of Congress when South Carolina Senator Strom Thurmond, a staunch conservative and segregationist, denounced Bayard. He read the details of Bayard's arrest for a homosexual act in 1953 into the *Congressional Record*.

We were never more proud of Randolph when he held a press conference almost right way to publicly voice his unwavering support for

Bayard. He underscored the tremendous work that Bayard was doing on behalf of the Washington March.

Velma and I were very close to Bayard, and we never saw him give in to despair about any of this. He never stopped being Bayard, and somehow the world began to catch up with him. By 1965, he seemed determined to be nothing less than himself.

But before Meany was to give his full blessing to the creation of the institute, especially with Bayard in such a critical leadership position, he wanted his misgivings about having such a high-profile homosexual in charge assuaged in person.

Bayard met with Meany in his office in Washington, which is just in sight of the White House. And Bayard so impressed Meany with his practically preternatural intelligence, astute analytical and psychological insights, and his commitment to civil rights and labor, any resistance Meany may have had evaporated. Early in 1965, the A. Philip Randolph Institute was founded and was housed at first in New York, then later in Washington, DC, as it is today, in the AFL-CIO headquarters at 815 16th Street NW.

Almost right away, the institute began moving to publish pamphlets on major economic and social issues affecting Black people. It also began promoting the unionization of Black workers. At the same time, it started forging stronger ties between the Black community and organized labor. One of the institute's chief objectives was to advance ways for Blacks to benefit from trade union know-how.

For decades, even when Randolph's Brotherhood of Sleeping Car Porters was fighting for better wages and working conditions for Blacks toiling on long-distance and overnight passenger trains, many, if not most, Black workers in America saw unions as troublemakers. Historically, many unions barred Black workers. And some Black workers, especially before World War II, thought their bosses, like Henry Ford, who was rabidly anti-union, had their best interests more at heart than white-led unions.

Velma and I realized that a great deal of education needed to be done, even after most unions lifted their color bars in the 1950s and 1960s.

At the same time, labor had to find ways to transfer and translate its mastery of organization, collective power, and personal dignity to the Black community. Shortly after I began work at the Industrial Union Department of the AFL-CIO in the fall of 1964, I was given a special assignment by Jack Conway, who had hired me. I was asked to consult with Brendan Sexton of the United Auto Workers, who had come up with the idea of "community unions."

The concept applies the principles and techniques used to organize workers to better organize poor Black communities. It was understood as a means to economically and socially uplift Black people. On Chicago's West Side, for example, there was an effort to apply organized labor principles to residents of slum dwellings. Community unions could initiate rent strikes against landlords to protest the living conditions there and press for improvements.

We also thought people in these communities could learn various processes, like how to file a grievance, how to effectively organize their thoughts for public addresses, basically how to challenge the powerful much like labor unions fearlessly did every day.

Velma helped, volunteering to work at my side in Chicago.

*Norman and I always worked well together.* I was assigned to organize the street gangs, and I was happy to help. Listen, this is something we deeply believed in. My first job was to try to get these various gangs to go to community centers in their neighborhoods. The idea was that if they'd go and play basketball and do things like that, they would use up all that excess energy they had for violence and destructive things.

First, we wanted them to stop fighting one another. So, off I went, this Black woman, a native of the Chicago ghetto, to meet these gang leaders. I was still in my mid-twenties and walking around in my mini-skirt outfits. I was a little nervous, but I had the promised protection of the gang warlords to do this work. Around this time, some of the gangs were seemingly inspired by the civil rights movement and were running their own community programs.

Chicago had a long history of gangs. Norman and I were fairly certain that many of the whites who had assaulted us and the other demonstrators at Rainbow Beach in 1960 had belonged to Chicago's white ethnic gangs. But by the 1960s, Black and Latino gangs were coming into prominence, especially on the West and South Sides, where most of the city's racial minorities lived. It seemed that the names of Black gangs like the Black-stone Rangers, the Vice Lords, and the Black Disciples were splayed across the pages of Chicago newspapers, as they were sprayed in graffiti across the crumbling walls and sour-smelling empty lots of Black Chicago.

I guess my work went okay. I'd talk. They'd listen. And some of the gang members started coming to the community centers, but few of them wanted to share the space with an opposing gang. Consequently, success was short-lived. It was just something we couldn't sustain. Old habits and hatreds die hard.

There was also a great deal of chauvinism during this period among the gang members as well as some of the gathering of trade unionists. There were regularly held unions meetings to which the whole Black community was invited. These meetings were part of our attempts to tighten a Blacks-and-labor alliance in Chicago. At one of these meetings, I was supposed to give a report on my work with the gangs. I was not only wearing a mini-skirt, hardly scandalous at the time, but also smoking one of those new feminine cigarettes, a cigarillo.

You would have thought I was breastfeeding a newborn orangutan by the way some of those men carried on when they saw me. One big, Black trade unionist seated next to me interrupted me in the middle of my report with a stage whisper.

"If you don't take that damn, motherfucking cigar out of your mouth," he said, "I'm going to take it out."

At first, I was shocked. This unionist wouldn't have said a thing if it had been a man up there giving a report—and smoking. But no, he could not tolerate seeing a woman addressing a meeting about a serious topic—while smoking.

It took only half a moment for my anger to accompany my shock. At that instant, I found myself glaring at him.

"What did you say?" I asked with the sharpest edge I could work into my voice.

He didn't blink.

"You heard what I said," he boomed back. "Put the cigarette out!"

I looked at Norman.

"Norm, Norm…" I pleaded. "Are you going to let him talk to me like that? Go over there and bop him one."

But Norman, long a devotee of nonviolence, hardly stirred. He just looked back at me and said in a voice as calm as an undisturbed mountain lake, "Put the cigarette out."

I did. And I went on with the report, finding composure in the fact that business at hand was much bigger than my ego. But as soon as the meeting was over, I went looking for that guy. Lucky for him, he had left.

While we were in Chicago, Norman and I lived in a nineteenth-century hotel, the Windermere, built on the city's South Side in Hyde Park for the 1893 World's Columbian Exposition. We worked hard in Chicago. Norman was on the payroll of the IUD, but I wasn't. Still, it was work that we lived for. And we had strong relationships with the people with whom we worked.

For instance, we had known the Sextons for some time and spent time at their home. Brendan and Dr. Patricia Cayo Sexton's son had worked at CORE. His namesake would become New York City's commissioner of sanitation; and his son, Brendan Sexton III, became a successful Hollywood actor, starring in films like 2001's *Black Hawk Down*.

*When Velma and I were at CORE, Jack Conway offered me at job at the AFL-CIO.* It was a position that I turned down but took later when Velma and I felt there was nothing more we could do at CORE, an organization unable to transition to the new demands of the movement.

When our work in Chicago fizzled, Jack reassigned me to Newark, New Jersey, to try to establish community unions there. In the end, this program proved as unsuccessful as it had in Chicago.

A major part of the problem was that it was much more difficult organizing people around a community grievance as opposed to organizing them around work. It is much less straightforward and much more amorphous. Few people would quarrel with Brendan Sexton's fundamental idea that union skills like organizing people, running meetings, solving grievances, speaking in public, and raising money are bedrock skills for community activism. But transmitting these skills to communities by way of unions proved to be extremely problematic.

Nonetheless, the effort had its fervent supporters. Among them was the political activist and eventual California politician, Tom Hayden. He was very pro–community unions, but couldn't get his head out of the past, his years in the Students for Democratic Society, his Port Heron Statement of 1962. His politics were in the orbit of the anti-democratic left. We weren't surprised when we learned that he married Jane Fonda.

Velma and I were frustrated with the lack of our progress in Newark, but we were willing to carry on. I ultimately realized that this type of community organizing appeared to be a dead end. There was a point in the summer of 1967 when Sam Fishman, a political friend and powerful force in the AFL-CIO and the UAW, was gently pressing to halt our work in Newark, saying what we were doing there was akin to "social work."

Not long after that, Bayard Rustin started talking to me about joining him at the A. Philip Randolph Institute. Accepting his offer was not a hard choice.

Bayard and I decided that the best way to handle this would be for me to meet with Jack Conway, telling him of my decision to leave and why. I wanted to make my departure as smooth as possible. I had no interest in burning any bridges.

It was not the best news to get, but Conway understood. He had always been supportive of the Randolph Institute. As executive director of the AFL-CIO's Industrial Union Department, Conway had helped Bayard secure the $25,000 founding grant that helped to launch the Institute. We were all working on the same big picture: expand labor's role and impact in society and strengthen the Blacks-and-labor alliance for economic justice.

Specifically, Bayard told me that he wanted me to concentrate on organizational outreach, to work to cement relations with civil rights groups, labor unions, and their leadership. I would also work directly on Randolph Institute projects and be available for speaking engagements. It was a spectacular offer.

There was not a moment's hesitation. I was ready. With Velma's encouragement, in late 1967, I joined the institute as its associate director. Velma at that time was one of the institute's founding board members. We returned to New York and soon moved into our apartment in Chelsea, where we live today.

*Norman and I talked at home about new discussions that he would have to be a part of, talks that would explore precisely what the institute's role in civil rights and labor might be.* We talked about how the institute should take on a more grassroots approach while it remained a platform for Bayard's positions and strategies. After the 1968 presidential elections, Norman began to aggressively organize local and state institute affiliates.

*With Velma attending Harvard in Cambridge, I found myself on the road a lot.* This gave me a chance to begin to change the nature of the A. Philip Randolph Institute. It felt like laying critically important groundwork for the organization's future. At the institute's peak, we had some 200 affiliates, many of them working across the country on major initiatives that included voter participation drives and various programs that helped to merge the interests of the Black community with organized labor, and vice versa. It felt natural.

Today, the institute has 150 chapters in thirty-six states. Only recently, as president emeritus, did I stop traveling to Washington to assist the institute four days a week.

*And Norman knows I encouraged him to stay in New York a bit more.* I am so pleased that he now works from an office here. But I think he'll always do institute work. He can't help it. The institute is such a part of him. He was its associate director from 1967 to 1975, its executive director from 1975 to 1980, and its president from 1980 to 2004. He's ninety and, despite being legally blind, has the work ethic and constitution of a college activist bent on changing the world. He wakes up before dawn, and the next thing I know he's saying goodbye just before I hear our front door close and lock behind him.

*When Velma was in her last semester at Harvard, one of my early assignments at the institute placed me on a plane heading for Memphis, Tennessee.* A group of local mostly Black workers had been seeking to end years of horrendous and dangerous working conditions. Besides low pay, routinely terrible treatment, and racially tinged discrimination—even two job-related deaths—the workers declared in February 1968 that they had had enough.

On February 11, 1968, the Memphis Sanitation Strike began.

This was a classic nexus of the promise of the civil rights movement and the American labor movement. There was a logical comingling of race and work in the context of a democratic nation. Approximately 1,300 sanitation workers walked off the job, holding demonstrations, boycotts, and protests while proclaiming on placards that are preserved in the Smithsonian Institution, "I AM A MAN."

It was also a good stress test of what APRI could accomplish with its dual consciousness of seeing the world through the promise and power of civil rights and labor activism. I arrived in mid-March in this barely "reconstructed" former Confederate city on the Mississippi River. I was sent to assist the staff of the American Federation of State, County and Municipal Employees, AFSCME, as it tried to organize the beleaguered sanitation workers who sought to join the union. I was also sent to work with Dr. King's organization, the Southern Christian Leadership Conference, to garner support in the Black community for the strikers.

When I arrived, the city's mayor, Henry Loeb, had refused to speak with the workers, calling their strike illegal. In the meantime, thousands of tons of garbage piled up on the streets of Memphis—despite scab workers who crossed the picket lines.

Right away, I felt a real sense of challenge. I was thirty-four years old, and this was the first time I would attempt to do real race work in the South. I had been primarily a civil rights activist in the North; most of my early civil rights experiences were in such places as Chicago, New York, and New Jersey. For a brief time, I did some work in Louisville, Kentucky, a modern, moderate-size city on the Ohio River and a bridge away from Indiana. I was there in 1963 helping to organize a coalition of support for the upcoming March on Washington. Kentucky was a border state during the Civil War and seemed to keep both feet culturally and politically planted in the North and the South.

But in Memphis, there was no such fuzziness.

I got right to work, literally rolling up my sleeves and plunging into the community, knocking on doors, going to barbershops and beauty shops, anywhere I could find Black people. I discovered a sizable Black community in Memphis. I also found it relatively easy to present the plight of the sanitation workers to this community. It knew them as workers who regularly picked up the garbage but also knew them as people—often as uncles and brothers, fathers and friends.

Further, many of the workers were active churchgoers, which meant I could appeal to key Black ministers to hold rallies and other forms of direct support for the workers and their cause. As a relatively young man, I discovered that I could establish a wide range of relationships with the Black community in Memphis, from establishment circles to less formal groups and alliances.

I was not the only outsider there to help the striking workers in those early months of 1968. Bayard Rustin, Roy Wilkins (the executive secretary of the NAACP), and James Lawson Jr., a leading civil rights movement theoretician and tactician, were also there. They were visibly supporting the strikers as the national media swooped in and splashed it all over America's newspapers; the coverage crackled over radio and television everywhere.

And then, on March 18, Martin Luther King Jr., came to Memphis, against the counsel of his inner circle, to support the strikers. He was there to address what turned out to be a gathering of 25,000 supporters of the strike and for a demonstration he would lead ten days later. That demonstration went terribly wrong as some of the protesters turned to violence, smashing store windows and inviting city police to respond with billy clubs and tear gas. A Black sixteen-year-old, Larry Payne, was shot and killed by police during a melee that included looting. Some city officials estimated that more than 20,000 students skipped school that day.

I was there in that march. It started at a back church, the Clayborn Temple at Hernando Street and Pontotoc Avenue. Dr. King was at the head of the march, and I was close behind him. As we marched through the Black community, we could see people lining the streets in support.

The white people we saw seemed neutral to our cause. I can't say I sensed any hostility toward any of us. Then suddenly I smelled the bite of tear gas, then its terrible irritation of my throat and eyes.

I turned quickly and looked back. I could see young Black men throwing stones at storefronts we were passing. Police seemed to focus their attention on the violent youth. In short order, police were spraying tear gas indiscriminately. The gas became suffocating. I could taste it, and with it, I could taste defeat. It was a crushing setback. Dr. King was sped off to a hotel by car. He and other leaders decided to turn the march around and head back to Clayborn Temple. It was the right thing to do. I could see that Dr. King was a much different man from the one I had worked with years earlier and remembered so well. He was visibly upset, distraught and depressed. He seemed so disappointed. Dr. King said he had experienced tear gas before but never as a result of demonstrators losing their resolve and discipline.

Once we returned to the church, Dr. King joined us and fell almost silent. When he did speak it was to urge the protesters to be peaceful, nonviolent. Before very long, he told the demonstrators that the march was over and that everyone should leave quickly and in an orderly fashion.

Some of us, mostly members of AFSCME and staffers from Dr. King's Southern Christian Leadership Conference, stayed. We were urging Dr. King to lead a second march, in early April. We argued that the strike was part of a larger trade union struggle and that national labor leaders could be recruited to help maintain discipline for the second march.

Dr. King was hesitant; you could see it in his eyes and read it in his manner. He wanted to explore other ways to support the sanitation workers, but eventually he came around. He left Memphis. I, along with AFSCME and SCLC staff representatives, including Bill Lucy, Jesse Epps, and P. J. Champa, went to the city's Black ministers to solicit their support for the second march. They embraced it right away and pledged to urge their congregations on Sunday to do the same. We organized an outreach effort, creating and passing out leaflets supporting the new march wherever we knew Black people gathered, like supermarkets. We were also able to enlist the support of the Black members of the Memphis City Council.

On April 3, Dr. King returned to Memphis, and despite not feeling well, he got out of bed to speak to a gathering at Clayborn Temple. And while history remembers well that this would be his last public speech, the one in which he spoke of seeing the mountaintop, he also spoke directly to the striking sanitation workers.

"We've got to give ourselves to this struggle until the end," he said. "Nothing would be more tragic than to stop at this point in Memphis. We've got to see it through."

It was a magnificent moment. It was the old Dr. King again. I had worked with him before, of course, going back to helping Bayard organize the March on Washington in 1963 and meeting with him and other civil rights leaders trying to help Dr. King decide whether to take on segregation in the Midwest in the summer of 1965. And there was his six-city, get-out-the-vote tour in 1964 that I helped to coordinate for him mostly through the Midwest and Northeast when I was with the Industrial Union Department.

I was in Memphis on April 4, about to attend an early-evening meeting of strike supporters when I got word that Dr. King had been fatally cut down by a bullet. I was, like millions around the world who would learn of this searing tragedy, stunned, shocked. That was natural. I rushed by car to the Lorraine Motel, where I knew he and his aides were staying. All I found were police, sobbing and somber pedestrians, and steps where Dr. King's blood trailed from the balcony where the nation's prophet of peace had been slain.

Velma!

I had to talk to my wife. I found a phone and called her. There was no one else in this world I could turn to. I knew she'd help me make sense of this staggering act of horrific violence, of sickening hatred—not simply for one man, but for an entire race.

In less than two weeks the strike was over. The second march, with Bayard playing a role in its coordination, did take place on April 8. In the wake of Dr. King's assassination, the march played a dual role, becoming a memorial to the great man as well as supporting the striking sanitation workers. Some 40,000 people participated, including Dr. King's brave widow, Coretta Scott King. There were no incidents.

While Memphis Mayor Henry Loeb continued to oppose the unionization of the sanitation workers, his opposition was overridden by the City Council, feeling the pressure from its constituencies complaining about tons of reeking garbage piling in their streets.

Success.

With my work done there, I returned home. But I was shaken by the loss of Dr. King. I was full of troubling questions about the future of the civil rights movement that helped to define Velma and me as we had sought to help define it.

# CHAPTER 11

# Yet Another River to Cross

In the immediate aftermath of the 1963 March on Washington for Jobs and Freedom, Norman and I noticed that most Americans were fixated, if they were paying any attention at all to Black people, on integration. It was the kind of desegregation that hit them at home, so to speak. We're talking about the integration of hotels and restaurants, bus stations, colleges, and such, and to some extent, public schools.

*But at the time, we were beginning to direct more of our energies to labor issues, finding ways to bring more Black people into labor unions, such as Velma's later success in unionizing New York's thousands of predominantly Black paraprofessionals.* I was working with Jack Conway at the Industrial Union Department of the AFL-CIO in expanding the use and influence of organized labor in the struggle to opening the nation to its fullest promise to all Americans.

We were never more certain in the months after the March on Washington that much of the work that had to be done to achieve racial equality and economic justice in America would require tackling the nation's economic and political issues. We knew that we would have to begin to move its leadership to deal with the issues that bedeviled the poor and working classes here. We had to get at the roots of these problems.

By the spring of 1965, the A. Philip Randolph Institute was well established, and the components of its Blacks-and-labor coalition were beginning to coalesce under Bayard's leadership. The stage was set, and leave it to Bayard to deliver.

Taking advantage of an overture made by the Johnson administration, Mr. Randolph announced that he would convene a brain trust of civil rights figures and other progressive thinkers, economists, and social scientists to craft a document that would flesh out the fiscal steps the federal government should take to eradicate poverty and joblessness in America. Bayard soon became instrumental in defining and coordinating this effort. It was understood almost right away that this would be the kind of program that raises the tide to lift all boats, including, of course, the leaky boat in which Black Americans found themselves in the mid-1960s.

This document came to be called the Freedom Budget, which carried a subtitle: "Budgeting Our Resources, 1966–75, to Achieve 'Freedom from Want.'" It was a multibillion-dollar corrective prescription for full employment at a living wage, and Velma and I were involved in its early development.

It was printed into an eighty-four-page document and sold for a dollar apiece, half price if you bought one hundred or more. But I don't think there was ever a great distribution of the original budget booklet to the general public, Black or white.

While Bayard had shared the budget with Velma and me and a number of us who had either worked on it or endorsed it, the Freedom Budget's public release was at a press conference on October 27, 1966, at the stately Salem Methodist Church in Harlem. This was shortly before I officially joined the APRI in 1967.

I am among some 200 signatories of the budget, including Bayard, Martin Luther King Jr., Stokely Carmichael, economist John Kenneth Galbraith, United Nations undersecretary Ralph Bunche, Al Shanker, and actor Ossie Davis.

Bayard dedicated the Freedom Budget to the "full goals of the 1963 March." And Velma and I agreed that this dedication was logical. The Freedom Budget was a natural follow-up to the March on Washington. In a sense, it was the laying out of an economic program that addressed the demands for jobs made at the conclusion of the march. It placed jobs in the context of coalition politics, and the unmet social and economic needs of the country. It recognized that these issues were disproportionately experienced by Black people but affected a great majority of the nation. In that way, it was presented as a budget for all Americans.

Measured in 1964 dollars, this ten-year budget would average annually some $18.5 billion above projected federal budgets for that period—once national commitments for defense, space exploration, and international requirements were excluded. In today's dollars that would be much greater, approaching more than $1.4 trillion.

Nevertheless, the budget's proponents, said all of its program would not require any tax hikes to pay for them. Instead, Leon Keyserling, the budget's author, who had been chairman of the Council of Economic Advisers under President Harry Truman, saw a time of great economic growth in the nation's near future. This, which turned out to be overly optimistic, he termed the "growth dividend" and projected that it would be many times more than enough to afford the proposed Freedom Budget.

Keyserling joined Bayard and Mr. Randolph at the press conference to help explain it. At its most basic, it was a proposal of expenditures that should be legislated through Congress and signed into law by the president. Randolph, acting in his capacity as honorary chairman of the White House conference "To Fulfill These Rights" that Johnson had called, said back in the fall of 1965 that once a Freedom Budget was produced, he would submit its recommendations to the president.

The proposal called for the large-scale creation of low- and middle-income housing and improved transportation systems, like better mass transit so that workers could get to their jobs. The budget also called for much greater and smarter investments in quality education, medical care, and public works expansion to achieve cleaner air and water. And it encouraged the nation to better meet the social and economic needs of Americans. It paid sharp attention to not only guaranteed full employment, ensuring that workers would receive no less than a living wage, but also adequate income for those who couldn't or shouldn't work. There were even proposals aimed at reforming the nation's tax and Social Security systems to make them fairer to more Americans.

There had been an attempt to get all the major elements of the coalition to sign on to the budget. While this did not doom its adoption, it was very difficult to hold this broad-based coalition of civil rights leaders, organized labor, academics, religious groups, and even Black militant factions together.

*In fact, Norman and I could sense the coalition coming apart, especially along the strained seam running between the leadership of traditional civil rights groups like the NAACP on one side and groups like CORE and SNCC on the other, which were leaning much more into the camp of Black nationalism.* They argued that whites had little or no role in the struggle.

That schism often erupted into public view, with one leader calling another misguided or wrongheaded. Even Randolph, then seventy-seven years old, found himself drawn into the fray, by joining Bayard and other prominent leaders of the civil rights movement in taking out a major ad in the *New York Times*; it decried militant and separatist tendencies in favor of the movement's goal of an integrated society.

We came to see that neither Mr. Randolph nor Bayard realized at the time, even though they were visionaries—and Bayard a master strategist with keen analytical ability—that the budget lacked a mass base. A strong and broad base was absolutely important to implement the Freedom Budget, to make it a real and moving project rather than only a well-put-together document.

Norman and I knew that what was needed was a true majoritarian coalition, and that's just about everybody who was committed to racial equality and economic justice. The larger question is how do you create such a coalition, and more important, how do to you keep it? We managed to have some support within organized labor, significant support in the religious community, a good part of the intellectual community, and, at least in principle, the civil rights leadership. But what really hurt the budget, we agree, was the fact that we didn't have full support from the AFL-CIO, lacking the endorsements of the federation's president and legislative director. This created a major stumbling block, resulting in a failure to win over the Leadership Conference on Civil and Human Rights. It had been instrumental in helping to shape and shepherd the legislation that eventually became the Civil Rights Act of 1964 and the Voting Rights Act of 1965.

*Velma and I knew that we needed not only the Leadership Conference, and not just its representatives in Washington, but also many of its member organizations around the country.* The absence of the Leadership Conference may have been an early indication that its leadership understood how complicated the budget effort was.

Another difficulty in maintaining the coalition in support of the Freedom Budget was that some members may have viewed it as a challenge to capitalism by way of national economic planning. Its adoption would, after all, mean the federal government having a much bigger footprint in the private sector than previously known or tolerated. The budget could come to be understood by its critics as a blow to capitalism, a giant step, albeit benevolent, toward an American welfare state.

To really understand the Freedom Budget, it has to be seen not only as an economic plan but also as a policy, an approach to allocate monies in a fashion that would bring about more enlightened national policy.

And probably partially because of this, the budget failed. It was as if we were all trying to build a house in which all Americans could live comfortably without first creating a firm foundation.

A great deal of the budget's failure to be adopted could be blamed on the escalation of the Vietnam War, which famously pitted the opposing priorities of guns and butter. Unfortunately, the guns won.

Even President Johnson's own signature program, the War on Poverty, was no match in the end for the war in Southeast Asia. There's a scene in the 2003 Bayard documentary, *Brother Outsider*, in which he sits with a copy of the Freedom Budget at his side while testifying before a Senate hearing in 1967. When asked if he believed the United States could fund anti-poverty programs at home while the Vietnam War raged abroad, he responded without hesitation.

"I do not believe the war in Vietnam is more important than eradicating poverty," he shot back through his ever-present cloud of cigarette smoke, "and I think history will reveal that."

That was Bayard. And history, of course, has proved him correct.

The Freedom Budget was never reintroduced. There are a number of reasons for this, but we believe the devastating one was that the coalition supporting it was too difficult to hold together for another try. Even some civil rights leaders, a major part of that coalition, saw the budget as territory that was foreign or alien to their traditional civil rights thrusts. The fairly representative and wide spectrum of signatories did not necessarily ensure that we had a movement that was committed to press for the budget's implementation.

This initiative was rooted in a much more complex dynamic than what we were largely using at that time in the movement. In that context, we could fairly easily marshal people to protest segregation and discrimination, particularly in the South. We could get people involved to challenge institutions through direct action, get them to press decision makers who were committed to maintaining segregation by law; we could even move people to press for a federal response because so many of us had little faith that these states, left to their own devices, would eliminate legal segregation.

*Norman and I came to realize that the Freedom Budget required much more.* Unlike a march, the Freedom Budget was academic. And it was legislation, and people just don't get excited by legislation, although they should.

*Velma and I knew we were asking people to move from measures of protests to taking on the basic economic and social problems of the nation, problems that were disproportionately affecting Black communities and, in fact, affecting many more whites.* There was no clear enemy or target in this instance. And this task required a major political movement—based on coalition politics—to undergird and sustain it. The budget needed a movement to galvanize and mobilize a grassroots base of constituents who could press elected officials at the national level to take up the budget. The budget also needed to have additional watchdog groups, lobbying groups, like the Leadership Conference when it was at its best, to ensure that congressmen and senators maintained their focus on it as their prime legislative aim.

None of that ever happened. And Congress and the White House all but ignored the Freedom Budget. Again, it was that movement that failed, first by failing to ever materialize, failing to gel. In large part, this happened because its elements were distracted and disrupted by things like the Vietnam War.

*Norman and I understood the budget as a progression of steps.* First, we had to get the budget done, then the next step was to go out and get the people together to write various parts of it into legislative proposals. But the war came and stopped everything.

Even as President Johnson's War on Poverty sputtered ahead in the shadow of the defunct budget, we failed to feel much excitement about that. The War on Poverty made no commitment to full employment. Looking back on the problems that befell the budget, most illustrative is probably the AFL-CIO's lack of enthusiasm for its adoption. That was most evident in how it was viewed by the federation's legislative director, Andrew Biemiller. His attitude was that the Freedom Budget was too big and comprehensive to effectively be put into legislation. But what we were saying was that we, the proponents of the budget, could take care of the projection of its ideas if he could just use the leverage of the AFL-CIO to get it initiated in the appropriate committees in Congress.

That didn't happen. Nothing happened. The A. Philip Randolph Institute had little choice but to move on.

The presidential campaign of 1968 dawned after a long, painful night marked by a blood moon. In early April, Martin Luther King Jr. was taken from us; then, hardly two months later, Robert F. Kennedy was gone, both victims of assassin's bullets to the head. This would also be the campaign forever remembered for the bloody clash of demonstrators and police during the Democratic National Convention in Chicago.

So much was at stake.

Johnson had bowed out of running for a second term under the sheer weight and worry of Vietnam that sat ominously on his shoulders. Former vice president Richard Nixon won the Republican nomination; Hubert Humphrey, the Democratic nomination. And for the first time in more than fifty years, a powerful third-party candidate was in the race, too—Alabama Governor George Wallace, who had ridden to national fame as a rabid champion of racial segregation in the South. We remembered Wallace's hateful pledge he made in 1963 during his first inaugural address on the same spot where Jefferson Davis had been sworn in a century earlier as the president of the Confederate States: "I say segregation now, segregation tomorrow, segregation forever."

*Velma and I were certain that this would be a crucial election, one that had the potential to greatly hasten or retard our civil rights agenda in a country just beginning to live up to its higher ideals.*

It was against this backdrop that Bayard was invited to a meeting of political directors of labor unions. Alexander E. Barkan, the director of the AFL-CIO's Committee on Political Education (COPE), had reached out to Bayard. Al Barkan, affectionately known as "Mr. Politics," was a great admirer of Winston Churchill. He often peppered his speeches with Churchillian wartime calls to never give in, never give up, to always be resolute, especially when the storm is darkest.

Al's trademark rallying call to organized labor—"On to victory"—was heavily influenced by Churchill. Velma and I liked and respected Al a great deal.

In the midst of Al's invitation to Bayard, we could see the political storm gathering over this three-man presidential race. I was glad to learn that Al wanted the APRI to assist Humphrey's run for the White House. For me, as associate director of the institute, it was the sort of political organizing I wanted to do. It was the very kind of work that I had cut my organizing teeth on during my early days in the movement.

Bayard talked to these political directors about coalition politics. He noted that the forces of organized labor and civil rights formed the essence, the core, of a potentially powerful coalition. As a result of that meeting, a decision was made by the political department of the AFL-CIO that Barkan and COPE should work closely with Bayard and the institute. In short order, the institute held a series of APRI conferences of Black trade unionists in Los Angeles, San Francisco, Chicago, Atlanta, and Philadelphia.

All these efforts were supported by the AFL-CIO. Together with Black members of COPE and staff of the AFL-CIO, along with Bayard and me and the institute, we circulated among these five conference cities. The primary result of those meetings was the formation of committees of Black trade unionists who would conduct voter participation drives in the Black communities of thirty to thirty-five key cities.

The A. Philip Randolph Institute was nonpartisan. But we all well knew that if we mobilized the Black vote that it would largely constitute solid support for Humphrey, the Democratic nominee.

The institute was awarded a grant from COPE to finance these voter participation drives. On a cash basis, APRI made grants to these ad hoc committees of Black trade unionists. Despite Nixon's victory over Humphrey and Wallace, our voter drives were very successful. This was so much the case that we at the institute began to raise the questions, "What would the institute do next?" and "What is the relationship of the institute with organized Black labor?"

At this point, the institute decided to hold its first national conference in 1969. I played a major role in organizing it. It was in Nashville at the Albert Pick Hotel. One hundred Black trade unionists gathered there. It was a remarkable meeting.

Bayard and I developed an agenda for the conference and began to develop what we called a policy statement, and an organizational structure for Black trade unionists planning and participating in a series of voter drivers. All this was done in consultation with key Black staff persons at the AFL-CIO, including Walter Davis, William E. Pollard, Fannie Neal, Earl Davis, and later W. C. Young.

In previous national elections, the AFL-CIO had engaged in voter participation drives. But these efforts usually involved the Committee on Political Education, identifying potentially influential Black communities, and then assigning and financing AFL-CIO Black staffers to organize drives in those areas. That often meant finding a minister, a politician, or a community leader in the area; recruiting them; and then supporting them to help turn out the Black vote.

I saw two problems with this approach. One, the effort usually didn't involve Black trade unionists, and two, once the election was over, there was no ongoing presence of organized labor in the Black community. There is nothing like having Black trade unionists serving as community activists knocking on your door and asking you to come out and vote. It tends to build bridges from the community to organized Black labor. It suddenly makes the invisible very visible.

We at the A. Philip Randolph Institute argued there should be a standing presence of Black trade unionists in areas with large concentrations of Blacks. We maintained that Black trade unionists were especially well situated to play a vital role in broadening the reach of and appreciation for organized labor. These Black trade unionists possessed union know-how, could effectively run election drives, could convince Black workers, at the very least by example, that organized labor was good and in their best interests.

We began to organize these Black trade unionists as affiliates. That was the birth of the whole affiliate organizational aspect of the institute. Early on, I believed that the institute could serve an even more effective and enduring purpose if it was structured along the lines of a grassroots organization, much like what Velma and I proposed for CORE.

I went all around the country, living mostly out of a suitcase, organizing these affiliates, taking advantage of the help of national and international union staff of the AFL-CIO where I found it and, later in the effort, some state AFL-CIO Black staff.

We made every effort to organize local affiliates in just about any corner of the country where there was any large Black population and Black union members. We didn't, for instance, have many affiliates in the Rocky Mountain states or in upper New England because Black populations were so small in these areas.

But in practically every other state, we organized. It was a somewhat audacious step, considering that the institute at the time had a staff of only a handful of permanent people. But I was always optimistic.

*Norman and I have always been optimistic—unfortunately.* But what about realism?

Norm was even optimistic about the Randolph Institute when he was going around talking to just ten people. I don't have that same optimism. I used to think we could have socialism in our time. We had this coalition in the 1960s, and I thought it would stay intact.

*Yes, Velma. We were going to change the world.*

*Or some small corner of it.*

*I understand, Velma, but I continue to be optimistic.* I was optimistic that Obama would be reelected.

*Norman and I are so glad that turned out the way it did.*

*And Velma and I are very pleased that the institute did, and continues to do so to this day, commit itself to a strong affiliate structure.*

*So much of that is Norman's legacy.*

*In another institute effort that would have far-reaching implications for organized labor began when Wilbur Hobby, the president of the North Carolina AFL-CIO, became convinced that the Black vote was very important.* He reached out to hire a Black trade unionist who was working in an area pickle plant. His idea was to encourage Black union members to become union leaders.

At the same time, he reached out to the A. Philip Randolph Institute and me with this idea. I was elated by the possibilities. Between the two of us, we scrounged and scraped to raise enough money to keep the first APRI intern aboard.

The first intern was James Andrews, the recently retired president of the North Carolina State AFL-CIO and the first African American to serve as a full-time AFL-CIO state president; he is also the first state president to become a member of the AFL-CIO's Executive Council.

We later developed a full-fledged internship program. Bayard and I took the lead responsibility for securing funds for the program, which eventually were provided by grants from the Carnegie, Ford, and Rockefeller Foundations, and with matching funds from international unions and state federations of the AFL-CIO. The program was supported by foundations for three years and was seen as a way to help break down racial barriers that still existed in some labor organizations. If the intern did well during the yearlong program, every effort was made to find that person a full-time position in the union or state AFL-CIO.

As a result of that program, we developed the first assistant business agents for Operating Engineers locals in North Carolina and Mississippi, and saw the first Black staff persons for the Michigan, Indiana, Georgia, and Illinois AFL-CIO organizations. Eventually other AFL-CIO organizations followed our example, California notable among them, which also hired a full-time Black staffer. I am very proud of the program, which unfortunately ended in the early 1970s.

Another initiative, which started as the joint apprenticeship program of the A. Philip Randolph Educational Fund and the Workers Defense League, ended long before it should have. Shortly after its inception in the early 1970s, it came to be incorporated as the Recruitment and Training Program (RTP), directed by Ernest Green.

*I tell Norman all the time that most people don't know this about the institute, the path it paved for Black leadership in the trade union movement.*

*During my tenure at the Institute, which formally ended when I retired as its president in 2004, a number of projects and initiatives helped us infuse important new voices and experiences of Black Americans into the nation's labor movement.* With the help of funding from the Department of Labor under the administration of President Jimmy Carter, we started a Youth Employment Program. We received a great deal of support from the secretary of labor, Ray Marshall, and the assistant secretary, Ernest Green. The Labor Department also assisted us with a grant.

Chuck Bremer was its director. We hired a full-time staff in about a dozen cities to identify and place high school dropouts in solid jobs. The program encouraged the youths to continue their education through GED programs. At its peak, the program had some forty-four people on its staff. It was managed under the auspices—as was the Intern Program—of the A. Philip Randolph Educational Fund, which was the institute's tax-exempt arm.

Scores of young people directly benefitted. We had a staff that did the recruiting and placement and the follow-up, all the time encouraging the recruits to continue their education. The participants would be placed in permanent jobs. The institute and its affiliates were often helpful in this because the trade unionists who were part of the program would most likely know from their own places of work and contacts whether a plant or a factory or job site was hiring. And they would pass this information on to the Youth Employment Program staff in their area.

Another dimension of our program was the voter participation strategy—created by A. Philip Randolph, Bayard Rustin, Velma, and me— which became a hallmark of the institute. We could not have been more pleased and elated. It was a great achievement. The A. Philip Randolph Institute was the first national Black organization to conduct extensive voter participation drives on a national basis in Black communities. I must congratulate our affiliates for being the only organized group in the Black community that conducted voter participation drives resulting in the election to Congress of Mike Espy and Bennie Thompson in Mississippi, Barbara Jordan in Texas, and Andy Young and John Lewis in Georgia, and the major Black-led organization that conducted drives that resulted in the election of Bill Clinton as president in 1992. There were eight states that provided the margin of victory. In each of those states, the Black vote was the deciding factor. The Randolph Institute conducted drives in major cities with significant Black populations in those states. I believed the institute was doing exactly what we had hoped it could accomplish, becoming a catalyst to meld the best of civil rights and labor movement activism to make a positive difference for people often left out or overlooked in the nation's political and economic matters.

One of my most satisfying memories of the feet-on-the-ground work we did at the institute was of helping to organize a voter participation drive in Louisiana. It was 1991. David Duke, the coolly handsome face of the ideologically ugly Knights of the Ku Klux Klan, of which he was its former grand wizard, and which was linked to various hate groups, including white supremacists and neo-Nazis, was running for governor.

We mobilized people across the state in voter participation drives, organizing people in every major city in Louisiana. Our state president and New Orleans president at the time was Nat LaCour, who would go on to become the secretary-treasurer of the American Federation of

Teachers and the leader of the New Orleans local of the American Federation of Teachers. I went into Louisiana and organized the local affiliates throughout the state, putting together its organization. LaCour and I raised money along the way for the effort.

We had very active voter participation operations in New Orleans, Baton Rouge, Shreveport, Monroe, and Lake Charles. Every place we had an affiliate in Louisiana you could see Black kids running around with APR Institute T-shirts that said GO VOTE. It was incredible.

It was a comprehensive effort. We reached out to Blacks in nursing homes, anywhere where they needed transportation, and formed carpools to get them all to the polls. If there were lines, we provided chairs for the elderly while they waited to cast their votes.

In the end, we broke a record. The percentage of Black voter turnout in Louisiana was greater, for the first time, than the percentage of white voter turnout in the state. Duke, who ran as a Republican, lost to the Democrat, former governor Edwin Edwards, 39 percent to 61 percent. Velma and I could not have been more pleased. I was elated. It was a great, great achievement.

Our work at the institute was in close keeping with our long commitment to organized labor. It is well known that Bayard was a major supporter of workers' rights. He made headlines getting arrested in 1984 as he demonstrated in solidarity with the job action of clerical and technical workers at Yale University. Similarly, he took part in many labor strikes and long pushed for greater Black and brown participation in construction trades.

In that spirit, the institute, nine years before the voter drives in Louisiana, found itself deeply involved in the struggle of mostly overworked, underpaid Black women toiling in a Mississippi catfish plant called Delta Pride.

Apparently, the 1980s was a period of explosive growth in the Deep South of premium, farm-raised catfish and the plants needed to process them. One of the first major processors was Delta Pride, a huge facility that today encompasses some 60,000 acres of catfish ponds in Grenada, Mississippi, near Jackson. On average, according to the company, it delivers about 1.5 million pounds of live catfish every week in a $650 million industry.

In the early 1980s, Delta Pride's workforce consisted mostly of Black women who were overworked and underpaid. They worked under terrible conditions, had no benefits, and were subject to having their hands cut up while cleaning hundreds of catfish a day. Most made no more than minimum wage, were not entitled to breaks, and even had to ask permission to use the plant's ladies' room.

The institute always encouraged its affiliates to support union organizing, especially when Black workers were involved. Charles Hohrn, the Mississippi state president of the institute, contacted the women workers at Delta Pride. We used that contact to set up a ministers' support committee for the workers and then helped them choose a time for the workers to set up a vote on whether to unionize—to the company's dismay.

The employer decided to hold a big party for the workers with live entertainment in hopes of dissuading enough of them from voting for union representation. When Charlie found out about the party, he contacted its musicians, who were Black. He told them if they came and played, two things were going to happen: one, they would have to cross a picket line, and two, the institute would use its influence in the area and would picket them wherever they appeared in Mississippi.

The group refused to come to the party. And in the fall of 1986, the Delta Pride catfish workers voted 489 to 346 to join the United Food and Commercial Workers (UFCW) Local 1529. They also won a contract, even striking in 1990, and they acquired higher wages and better working conditions.

Everything—the institute's formation and organization and mission—seemed bright. And then, darkness.

# CHAPTER 12

# Climbing through Dark Clouds

By the time the new century approached, Norman and I had long settled into a bit of a routine. We had become quite comfortable in our nineteenth-floor apartment with a view of the Chelsea neighborhood and all the way south to the tip of Manhattan, out to the twin titans of the World Trade Centers that stood like gleaming sentinels on the Hudson River side of the island.

I'm not saying that our lives weren't exciting, even challenging. They were. We had been married for four decades and had been, for almost all those years, close partners in the continuing struggle for racial equality and economic justice. Just that fact alone could sweeten your morning coffee and butter your toast. But there was something more that made us feel so special about our relationship. Together, we embraced the realization that we didn't wake up each day simply for each other or just for our families—or just out of habit. We knew we entered each new day for a cause greater than ourselves, and that cause had helped to animate us from the moment we heard its calling in the early days of our youth.

We were then, and still are today, activists.

Norman was firmly in place at the A. Philip Randolph Institute to become its longest-serving president. Some ten years earlier, I had segued from my union work at the United Federation of Teachers, where I had been the first chairwoman of its paraprofessional chapter, to a leadership role in the American Federation of Teachers that included me representing educators and the AFL-CIO nationally.

And after all those years laboring at the UFT and the AFT with their legendary leader, Al Shanker, I was very pleased with what we had accomplished, especially for public school paraprofessionals. But the truth was that as much as I admired Al, whom I had enjoyed serving as his assistant, I had reached a point when I realized that I could no longer work with him. He was a brilliant man. But we clashed on a number of issues, among them strategies to achieve racial equality in public schools. For instance, Al did not support goals and timetables in most affirmative action programs; I also strongly supported busing to achieve racial equality in schools—with all of its attending problems, while Al was much more hesitant.

Shortly after I left the AFT in the early 1980s, I became the first Black director of civil rights and international affairs of the Service Employees International Union (SEIU). I remembered and applied the quote of A. Philip Randolph, the nation's foremost Black labor leader and father of the modern civil rights movement: "The fight for democracy does not stop at the water's edge." SEIU conducted leadership training, grievance processing, and public speaking workshops with Black South African trade union leaders in Lesotho. Later we demonstrated at the South African Embassy in the United States. We applaud the current president of South Africa Cyril Ramaphosa, who was also secretary general of the National Union of Mineworkers.

Eventually, I began to see my own patients as a psychoanalyst. Given my love for and fascination with people, it, too, seemed a natural transition. Plus, I always wanted to improve the state and conditions in which people carved out their lives. And I never forgot all the long hours I had spent with the paraprofessionals helping them understand that they didn't have to make any excuses to anyone for wanting the most out of their lives.

By the late 1990s, after training for years and occasionally working out of a small office in Greenwich Village, I began seeing four to five patients a day, five days a week, in the living room of our apartment. Sometimes my dear cat, Chelsea, would discreetly look on.

It was very satisfying work, particularly because I had a practice that specifically appealed to racial and ethnic minorities, gays, and others who might have felt dispossessed by mainstream American society. And just as important, this was mostly a group that traditionally resisted therapy. I had quite a few patients from the performing arts—musicians, actors, and lots of dancers. And I wanted them to know that in me, they had a safe harbor, deep but welcoming waters, where they could be heard and understood. Where they could be helped to overcome.

In a way, it was a micro movement, an extension of my labor work reaching out to my mostly working-class patients.

I was determined to maintain a life outside my work with patients. For example, I kept my finger in community work, like running for a seat on the community school board and winning. I was also placed on the community board by Carol Greitzer, who was then a member of the New York City Council. I became very involved in our political club, the Chelsea Midtown Democrats, which was led by our dear friend Eugene Glaberman.

I understood why the psychotherapist community believes that psychoanalysts should not have public lives outside of their practices. It's simple, really. If someone is seeing you professionally, you don't want that patient to form a conception of you that is anything other than what they develop during sessions. In other words, you don't want your patients to have any sense of you other than what grows out of the professional relationship on the couch and on the chair.

Even though I was well trained by the National Psychological Association for Psychoanalysis (NPAP) and studied every single school of thought in psychotherapy—from Sigmund Freud to Theodor Reik to Carl Jung—I decided that I could not make my life that vanilla. I had to be me. As a result, I decided to use everything I had in my head, including my experiences as an activist and organizer, to help my patients. I decided that I wanted to continue some level of involvement and activity in the outside world. So I did.

What was most important, as far as I was concerned, was that the people I treated were doing well and approaching life on their terms instead of its terms.

*All of Velma's work made me very proud of her, and it helped me maintain concentration on my work at the Randolph Institute, where I traveled by rail to my office in Washington every week, returning home and to Velma on Thursday evenings for the weekend.* We were, in many ways, accomplishing what our lives of activism in the civil rights and labor movements had prepared us to accomplish. In many ways, we were acting on local and national stages and forging pathways for progressive change.

We lived a rather gratifying life, surrounded by our friends and colleagues in the movements, attending human rights conferences and forums, and traveling the world, spreading the virtues of organized labor in the Caribbean, Europe, the Middle East, Central and South America, and Africa.

Then, in 2002 I found myself dealing quite suddenly with a loss that seemed to materialize from thin air.

Being the son of a dentist, I understood the importance of regular checkups, and this extended beyond my teeth and gums. I had my eyes examined quarterly. The chief reason I had my vision checked so frequently was that glaucoma ran in my family. My mother had it. My brother had it. And I knew it could slowly rob me too of my vision if I was not careful. Glaucoma strikes one in 200 Americans after age fifty. I was sixty-nine. So, although I never had to wear eyeglasses, I was very sensitive to potential problems with my eyes.

During one of my examinations in the fall of 2002, my ophthalmologist discovered that I had a cataract forming in my right eye. He wasted no time in referring me to a doctor in Manhattan who specialized in removing cataracts.

*When Norman went to have his cataract operation, we lived in a complex of co-ops where the average resident was well into retirement age.* All kinds of people we knew there had cataract operations, and they would describe them to us, tell us all about them, how they are a natural part of the aging of the eye, how it is a fogging of the eye's lens—and easily corrected. I assumed, as Norman assumed, that it was a routine thing. Norm got the operation and came home with a patch over his eye. We had a little dinner and went to bed.

*I was never in pain, really, but I told Velma that my right eye felt uncomfortable.* No one told us that after the operation there would be discomfort.

*That's right, Norman.* The thing I remember very well is that sometime that night you started saying that your eye was bothering you. We were in bed, and I heard something. There was this pop!—and I said right then, "We have to go to the doctor." And Norman, as Norman does, said, "It's probably nothing. We'll talk to the doctor tomorrow."

I didn't push it with Norman for some reason. The next day he couldn't see out of his right eye.

*With Velma watching, my doctor examined me and was really at a loss.* She told Velma and me that the cataract operation she had performed had been flawless. She said she couldn't understand why I had lost my vision.

*In the beginning, Norman seemed to take it in stride.* But I was so upset, upset to the point of contacting a lawyer to see if there was any redress we could pursue. Norman didn't understand it, and I didn't understand it. We went to a lawyer, Eric, a son of Sol "Chick" Chaikin, who had worked with us in organized labor. This lawyer, who worked in the Wall Street area, said the case would be very complicated and that he didn't know if there was enough basis to sue the doctor. I was thinking malpractice, negligence. Chaikin agreed to review the paperwork on the operation. That revealed little more than what we had been told: the cataract removal had been without flaw.

But my Norman could not see out of his right eye. And he still had to contend with a cataract on his left eye. That cataract would have to be removed as well.

*I told Velma at the time that I could see very little.* I could make out only the biggest characters on the eye chart. I had enjoyed near perfect vision all my life, and now this. I did not know what to think about what had happened to me. I hadn't anticipated that there would be any problems.

*And there were other things that Norman could not see—but I could.* My training as a psychotherapist helped me to see the anxiety building up

in him stemming from his vision problems. Norman was always intro-
verted, but I could see him drawing even more into himself.

I could sense that he was becoming quite apprehensive about his life
and what he was going to do. I believed that Norman was becoming clini-
cally depressed. Sometimes he stared blankly, unblinking, looking as if he
had served as the model for the African masks on our living room walls.

I knew he worried over this problem with his eye—I did, too. But for
him it was different. He really worried about how his problems with his
eyesight might impede him from being the leader that he could be. You
know his mentors were A. Philip Randolph and Bayard Rustin, mighty
big legacies to fill. If Norman didn't get a little depressed, you would
wonder about that, too.

Nevertheless, I was starting to become deeply concerned, so much so
that I started having problems concentrating on my practice. I had been
so into my patients that I didn't have to take a lot of notes when I had sessions with them; I remembered them all. I was there, present.

But as Norman's troubles worsened, I just couldn't do that anymore.
You have to understand that Norman and I, besides being husband and
wife, are friends. We really are friends. We really care about each other.
There were times when I would look at him and see the darkness closing
in on him. I would just hold him. It was really something. I felt that I had
to be there for Norman. And yes, that made it a lot harder for me to be
there for my patients. I realized that something had to change.

I told my patients that I was going to discontinue my practice. And I
did and never returned to it.

Norman's eye doctor referred us to another doctor, who removed the
cataract from Norm's left eye. Shortly after that operation, the same thing
that had happened to his right eye visited his left. We were dumbfounded
by this. Now Norman could barely see at all. This doctor told him that his
vision might improve in time. It didn't. I thought, *Oh, my God, what is
this going to mean?*

We were referred once again to a new doctor, Milton Behrens at New
York-Presbyterian Hospital. He was terrific. He reviewed everything that
had happened and closely examined Norman's eyes.

Dr. Behrens discovered that Norman had lost his sight to a rare disease called Leber hereditary optic neuropathy, or LHON. We learned that males are much more susceptible to this disease, although it is passed to them by their mothers. And its symptoms—cloudy, blurry vision—usually show up in children or later in adulthood. It affects one in 30,000 to 50,000 people and can be devastating because it starves and then kills the cells of the optic nerve that relays visual information to the brain. We were very surprised to discover that LHON is virtually unheard of in lots of the world's populations, occurring more frequently, for some unknown reason, in areas of Northern England and Finland.

But there it was, a genetic mutation, striking Norman, an African American who was almost seventy years old at the time, working in Washington and living with me in New York.

*Velma knew that I had always been a very independent man.* I was really at a loss about what I was going to do, how I was going to function. We went to Lighthouse International, the group that is expert in helping people overcome vision problems, on East 59th Street, not far from our apartment.

*The people there were wonderful.* They got Norman large-print books with special magnifying glasses to help him read.

*What I miss most is reading.* I call a special service and have the *New York Times* read to me every day. I also have learned to maintain a great deal of my independence. For instance, I continued to use the subway. I would figure out the subway stop nearest to where I was going; the trains announce each stop. When I got off a train, I would ask people for directions to the exit.

Just as my eyesight was failing, I was scheduled to speak at the national convention of the bakery workers union. For major speeches, I was accustomed to speaking from a carefully written text.

*Norman was exceptionally good at this.* He delivered addresses crammed with compelling ideas, political analysis, and the history of mass movements from a detailed text. And he could make it sound so natural. He could speak for an hour and be very good. That's difficult to

223

do, you know? But without his sight, I didn't know how he was going to do this.

*I didn't tell Velma right away what I was planning to do because I wasn't sure myself.* My first instinct was, gee, I should try to get someone to substitute for me. I called around to the other offices of the Randolph Institute, but no one was available.

*Norman, you are being too nice.* No one else wanted to do it. Most people couldn't do what you do. What we ended up doing was to create a way to get Norman's thoughts on a series of note cards with large print. He used key ideas from each card to create a kind of road map in his mind to deliver the speech from memory.

*This helped me tremendously.* But I never made the speech to the baker's union. I was told that time had run out.

But a new challenge was coming soon, one where I could apply a different approach to public speaking. Shortly after Velma and I received medical confirmation regarding the loss of my vision, the A. Philip Randolph Institute's national conference was scheduled to begin in Washington.

As APRI president, I always keynoted that conference, giving the major address to set the tone and provide the framework for the meeting. Before my eyes began failing me, I had already worked on drafts of my address with APRI staff. But with my sight so severely impaired, I was at a loss. I didn't see any way I could give the speech. It was fairly long and complex.

*I suggested to Norman that he give a brief summary of his remarks and that we distribute the full text to the conference attendees.* Part of that summary, I said, should communicate that Norman remained committed to fighting for racial equality and economic justice and was not going to let trouble with his eyes stand in the way of his lifelong commitment to his and APRI's ideals.

It seemed to me that this was a key moment for Norman. We knew some people at the institute had heard that Norman was having problems with his vision. But we also knew that Norman was much beloved at APRI; one reason was that he was the one who went out to all the institute's various groups when they needed him. It seemed that now they would be there for him.

*By the time the APRI's national conference was to be held that summer, I believed I was ready, as the institute's president, to deliver, as was my duty, the evening's keynote address.* The staff made copies of my speech and distributed them to the attendees that night.

*As Norman spoke, I was on stage with him, holding my breath after almost every word.* He got an amazing standing ovation. It was as if he had lost his eyesight but had gained more insight into his own strengths. Soon after that, someone from the audience came up to Norman and congratulated him, telling him that his speech was a tremendous victory over his blindness. I told the man that yes, what Norm did was what the old Negro spiritual "Climbing Up the Rough Side of the Mountain" sings about.

I explained that on the rough side of any mountain, there are places where you can grab ahold. And for Norman, those rough places are the uplifting principles of Rustin and Mr. Randolph. Even with greatly diminished sight, he could see his way to the top. That's my Norm.

*As I've told Velma, you learn how to manage your losses, overcome them when you can, and when you can't, you live with them and look for those things that bring you some happiness.* When I get right up next to Velma, I can still see her face. For me, that is a comfort and a gift.

\* \* \*

*Norman's eyesight wasn't the first major loss we would have to live through, live with.* In the movement, in every mass movement, there are leaders, lions, whose roars of commitment, insight, and courage ignite, guide, and rally his or her followers. But then, inevitably, comes a day when the lions cease to roar.

Although we had worked closely with Martin Luther King Jr., Norman and I cannot say that he was a close friend. We didn't have the sort of relationship, for example, that civil rights activist Andrew Young had with Dr. King. There were times when the two men were almost inseparable,

Dr. King as the teacher and Andy as his acolyte. Yet, when Dr. King was cut down by an assassin in 1968, Norman and I felt a deeper wound than many because we had had the opportunity to know him, to have known him as a living, breathing human being, flesh and blood like us.

I don't know how many of you have had the experience. Imagine knowing someone, drinking iced tea with them, working elbow to elbow, sleeves rolled up one day, and then, in what feels like the very next day, you are staring up thirty feet into their sculptured face memorialized in pale granite. I'm not entirely sure how Norman feels about this, but I still find it hard to see Dr. King standing stock-still as the centerpiece of the Martin Luther King Jr. Memorial overlooking the Tidal Basin in Washington.

Yes, there is a part of me that is proud to see Dr. King honored in that way. But there is another part of me that, when I see him in stone, mourns even more the man we knew. I don't think it looks enough like the Dr. King I knew. He's called "the Dreamer." So much of what people think about him is based on a kind of mythology made of things he'd said near the end of his life. When I look at him, I look at his whole life. And I realize that he was a man, a son, a brother, a father, and a husband to Coretta, who, like my mother, was left to raise her children alone.

When we lose those closest to us, I don't believe we are ever ready. Norman and I certainly weren't ready to lose Dr. King, and so many who would follow. One of those people was Max Shachtman.

Up until we received word, it had been a rather unremarkable autumn day in New York. Norman and I knew that Max had not been particularly well. But this leader of leaders had long suffered with heart trouble. We figured that he would once again bounce back and fully be back as one of the brightest political thinkers and intellectual lights we knew. After all, Max had always proved to be a hardy soul, and he was only sixty-eight years old.

But before the sun would set on November 4, 1972, we'd learn that Max was gone. He had been a lion of the American Trotskyist movement starting back in the 1930s. Born in Warsaw, Poland, Max, who immigrated with his family to New York as an infant, was a man not afraid to evolve. And that he did, breaking with the Communist Party in the 1940s and later the Trotskyist view of the Soviet Union and its revolution. He went on to become a leader of the Socialist Party in America, opening the way for his advocacy of social democratic principles, of broadening and enriching the essential nature of democracy for all.

In that role, Max advised and influenced from behind the scenes during the 1960s, sharing his insights and strategic thinking with the likes of younger intellectuals like Tom Kahn and Michael Harrington and some of the key leaders and staff of the 1963 March on Washington, as well as labor leaders like Don Slaiman and Al Shanker. And, of course, Norman and me.

*By the time he quietly passed away—the cited cause was coronary failure—in Floral Park, on New York's Long Island, where he had lived with his wife, Yetta, he was much beloved and admired by many.* And not so much by others, especially some of his former colleagues, including those in the Communist Party. His death was a tremendous loss to our movement to further democratize America, to help complete the work of having America live up to its ideals of equal rights and opportunities for all its peoples. Max's death was also a tremendous personal loss for Velma and me.

As I have often noted to Velma, Max was a real father figure for me. He was, especially to those with whom he felt a kinship, a person of great warmth. And his analytic powers...extraordinary. To this day, I feel that there is an intellectual vacuum unfulfilled since his death. Of all the people that I knew in and around the movement, Max's intellect was hard to match.

*I can't say for Norman, but I believe that the news sent me into a state of shock.* I remember most that my good friends Judy Bardacke and Sandy Feldman and all kinds of people gathered around me to tell me that Max had passed. I cried and Joan Suall, who held me as I sobbed, would become one of my best friends.

I kept thinking about the day that Max had come to our apartment. It would be the last time I saw him alive. He loved music, especially jazz, the same types of jazz that Norman liked. And Max liked to tinker with things, electronics and things like that. In fact, he made home stereo systems. One day just before he died, he told me that he had finished building a stereo for Norman and me and wanted to come over and set it up.

I was a little reluctant. I didn't want him to make the trip, and Norman was away. But Max sort of insisted, and when Max made his mind up it was very hard to turn him around. So he came to the apartment in Chelsea all the way from Floral Park. And he was hauling this stuff and sounded a little out of breath when I opened the door. But he looked the same, that round face with eyes that always sparkled and a smile that carried something of the mischievous. He was completely bald and stocky and thoroughly huggable. He was fond of slapping men on the back with glee and pinching the faces of women in the most endearing way. Yet, when at the lectern or at a conference table, he was a fierce debater, a speaker and thinker so formidable that he gave his opponents no quarter, only enough space to surrender.

Still, as I stood there looking at him in the doorway, I was even more worried because before he arrived, I got a call from his wife, whom I adored. I could hear the worry in her voice. She told me that she didn't like the way Max looked and tried to talk him out of traveling to Manhattan. I told her I had tried to dissuade him but couldn't. Yetta told me to tell Max when he arrived that he should go back home. Do this stereo stuff another time.

When I saw him at my door, I tried to do just that. But Max wasn't listening. He set up the stereo and left in seemingly good spirits. I was heartsick. He was a friend and mentor who was more like family. He was the kind of mentor who, when I joined the UFT, had me call him every evening and tell him how things were there for me.

So when Max died, I was crushed.

*We both were, Velma.*

*Maybe it is part of getting older.* If you live long enough, you will find yourself reluctantly saying final farewells to those you hold most dear.

In the movement, one of our most difficult farewells was to A. Philip Randolph. This finely composed, dignified man lived alone in Harlem's Dunbar Apartments after his wife, Lucille, died. She had passed just before the start of the 1963 March on Washington for Jobs and Freedom. They had been married for fifty years and yet, in the crushing wake of her death, he went on with the march that he had conceived.

In 1968, when Mr. Randolph was seventy-nine, he was mugged as he was returning from his office to his apartment building. We doubt that the three muggers who followed him into his building had any idea who he was. To them, he was probably just an old man, an easy target. They beat him when they discovered that he wasn't carrying much money on him.

When Norman and I heard about this, we were heartbroken. Mr. Randolph had been roughed up but seemed okay. Nevertheless, we immediately began working with Bayard to find a way Mr. Randolph could live in our cooperative apartment complex in Chelsea. After all, Mr. Randolph was a pioneering union man, and our modern, multibuilding complex was built and owned by the International Ladies Garment Workers Union. It seemed like a logical fit.

Mr. Randolph did manage to move into a fifth-floor apartment at 280 9th Avenue, at 27th Street, just three blocks from our building. It was a great relief to Norman and me that he was there, safe and comfortable, but also nearby and always ready to counsel and advise us as he had done for most of our adult lives.

Then one afternoon, on May 16, 1979, he was gone.

Asa Philip Randolph was ninety years old and had for some time stopped coming out of his apartment much. He had been trying to write, working when he had the strength, on his autobiography and a history of the union he organized in the 1920s and '30s, the International Brotherhood of Sleeping Car Porters. Norman and I knew that he was not well, that he had high blood pressure and had suffered a heart attack. But he had lived with these conditions for years.

We learned from friends that he did not die alone. His longtime housekeeper and friend, Fannie Corner, was at his side.

*Velma and I were so sad to learn of his death.* Bayard Rustin, who was not only one of his closest colleagues but also like the son Mr. Randolph never had, was visibly shaken by the news.

Mr. Randolph's body was cremated on a Sunday after an early-June memorial service at the Metropolitan African Methodist Episcopal Church in Washington. So many dignitaries, including President Jimmy Carter and Supreme Court Justice Thurgood Marshall, attended to pay their respects. President Carter spoke movingly about Mr. Randolph. The Black opera star Leontyne Price sang.

We never really got over losing him. A. Philip Randolph was an incredible man with incredible integrity. I never heard him say a bad word about anybody or even raise his voice in anger. That is probably why he was known as the "gentle warrior."

Bayard was also at the memorial and spoke, as only he could, so eloquently about Mr. Randolph. And then, in less than ten years—on August 24, 1987—Bayard was gone.

Whenever Velma and I are organizing, putting together coalitions as we did for the fiftieth anniversary of the 1960 wade-ins at Rainbow Beach in Chicago, I think of Bayard. He remains a guide, an inspiration for doing something like that. He was the consummate organizer and brilliant strategist. I cannot imagine the 1963 March on Washington happening at all without his intelligence and able hand directing it. I miss Bayard's mind, his wit, and his air of whimsy.

When I give speeches today, he and Mr. Randolph are the two people I most often turn to. I use their thoughts, their points, and their principles because I find them so relevant. There's an eternal value to what they said, wrote, and stood for.

I still recite Mr. Randolph's words from memory. I'd heard them so often and recited them so often that I think I acquired them through osmosis.

*Norman and I used to say that you always knew when Bayard was in the room.* He had such a personality, and that mind of his—always going. There just wasn't anybody like Bayard. He was, like the Joan Baez song says, forever young. He always walked so upright, with a got-to-be-some-where-fast stride. And he had such a generous smile, genuine, charming, and a little bit devilish. As a therapist I told people not to lose their inner child. Bayard never lost his inner child.

*Velma and I are so gratified to see a resurgence of interest in Bayard and his legacy in museum exhibitions, conferences, and tributes.* In August 2013, I participated in a round-table discussion as part of a very good program to honor him in Washington during the fiftieth anniversary of the March on Washington. The 2003 documentary *Brother Outsider: The Life of Bayard Rustin* has been very well received and shown numerous times on television and at Rustin tributes. A year after the one hundredth anniversary of his birth, 2013, President Barack Obama posthumously awarded Bayard the Presidential Medal of Freedom, the highest civilian award given by the president. We were so honored to attend the ceremony.

We are also pleased that Bayard is beginning to receive a much fuller measure of recognition of his many accomplishments. He and his contributions have too long been ignored because he was an openly gay social democrat. He was also stained by once belonging to the Young Communists League during an era not known for its depth of tolerance.

Barely more than a month before Bayard died, he was so full of life. He left in mid-July 1987 on a human rights mission to Haiti with his longtime partner, Walter Naegle. While in Haiti he got sick and thought he had picked up some bug. He steadily got worse, even after he returned to New York. By August 21, his pain, Walter told us, was so bad that he finally went to the hospital. He died three days later after what turned out to be a terrible misdiagnosis. He did not have an intestinal infection, as he was told by a number of doctors, but a perforated appendix.

*Norman knows that I still get emotional when I think about Bayard's passing.* How do you talk about losing someone so dear to you? How do you talk about how it felt when your mother died? To this day when I go to sleep, I see my mother being wheeled into an operating room with all her kids around her. I remember her saying, "Lord, have mercy." The doctors operated on her brain, trying to remove a tumor, but the procedure didn't work. She was on a respirator for weeks and we were told that she would never wake up. Her last words were, "Lord, have mercy."

For me, when Mr. Randolph passed and when Bayard passed, it was like when I said goodbye to Ma. They were like family.

*There have been so many others we've lost over the years.* Velma and I mourn them all.

*Velma as a teenager.*

*Ruby Murphy, Velma's mother.*

*Velma's older brother, Wallace Murphy.*

*Bessie Hill,*
*Norman's mother.*

*Dr. Norman*
*Hill Sr.*

*John Hill, Norman's younger brother.*

*Velma and Norman with Velma's niece and nephew c. 1980s.*

*Velma's brother Wallace taking part in a demonstration to integrate the building trades in New York City.*

*Norman's brother Julian and Betty Hill and family.*

*Civil rights activists Norman Hill (at left), program director for CORE, Bayard Rustin (1912–1987), director of the March on Washington, and Frederick D. Jones, state education director of the NAACP (center).*

*More than 200,000 people participated in the March on Washington for Jobs and Freedom on August 28, 1963.*

*Congress for Racial Equality (CORE) members picket in the shadow of the Unisphere—the symbol of the World's Fair. Hundreds of civil and labor rights demonstrators, led by CORE director James Farmer, gathered in and around the fair.*

*Velma at one of many meetings for the teachers unions.*

*Dr. Martin Luther King Jr. with wife Coretta Scott King, arrives in Montgomery, Alabama, on March 25, 1965, at the end of the Selma to Montgomery March. At far left is labor and civil rights activist A. Philip Randolph, a key architect of the March on Washington for Jobs and Freedom in 1963.*

*Norman and Velma Hill in Israel c. 1967. They traveled there many times sponsored by the Israeli Labor Movement (Histadrut) to observe their practices.*

*A press conference is held outside the Lorraine Motel where Dr. Martin Luther King Jr. was assassinated on April 4, 1968. Norman Hill stands (at left) on the second-floor balcony.*

Three "generations" of activists: Bayard Rustin, A. Philip Randolph, and Norman Hill.

President of the UFT Al Shanker and Mayor Abe Beame congratulate Velma Hill on the successful unionization of the NYC paraprofessionals, 1970s.

*Velma Hill hands a leadership training award to a South African unionist in the 1990s in Lesotho, Africa.*

*Trade unionists picket the South African embassy in protest of apartheid in the 1990s.*

*Mary Ntseke*
photo by Page One

# THE VIEW FROM SOUTH AFRICA

photo by Tannenbaum/Sygma

*As with all black union leaders, South African police follow Ntseke constantly—ready to detain her without notice or cause.*

*"I have never gotten used to it," she says. "But you can't worry about such things."*

Mary Ntseke is a calm, self-assured, witty woman. She never wears an "executive face." And prefers that those around her don't either.

It's difficult to imagine this 63-year-old grandmother as a troublemaker, but she's been jailed twice, in 1956 and again in 1980. Her crime: helping South Africa's deprived blacks form unions.

But in a *Service Employee* interview during her recent week-long visit in Washington, D.C., it was clear that cold, damp South African jails have failed to chill her determination to bring black workers the basic workplace rights they deserve.

She has much to say. But her words are carefully chosen before spoken. Her country not only refuses blacks the right to vote, but charges them with high treason for publicly speaking against the government.

they must catch the train or bus. But the long walk through hostile, all-white streets in the middle of the night is dangerous.

"Our women are often raped—our men are often beaten."

Ntseke says that the wages of blacks—who comprise the great majority of workers in South Africa are so low that most can barely pay the rent on the "matchbox" houses they are forced to live in—much less pay for the education and other basic needs of their families.

But employers have been quick to make examples out of those who complain. And because blacks are refused citizenship in their own country, getting fired means getting deported to barren "homelands."

Yet, despite the low pay, the government has

A page from the Service Employee newspaper reporting on trade unionist Mary Ntseke. Velma and Norman Hill worked with Ntseke, who later became a South African government employee.

*Norman Hill, president of the A. Philip Randolph Institute, meets President Bill Clinton in the Oval Office.*

*Civil rights and union activist Bayard Rustin received the Medal of Freedom in August 2013. From left to right, Bayard Rustin's partner Walter Naegle, President Barack Obama, First Lady Michelle Obama, and Bayard Rustin. Velma and Norman Hill are at right.*

*Norman and Velma pose at the Lincoln Memorial for the 50th anniversary celebration of the March on Washington for Jobs and Freedom in August 2013.*

*Velma Hill, founder of the UFT's Paraprofessionals Chapter and its first chapter leader, speaks at the 38th annual Paraprofessionals Festival and Awards Luncheon at the New York Hilton in 2021.*

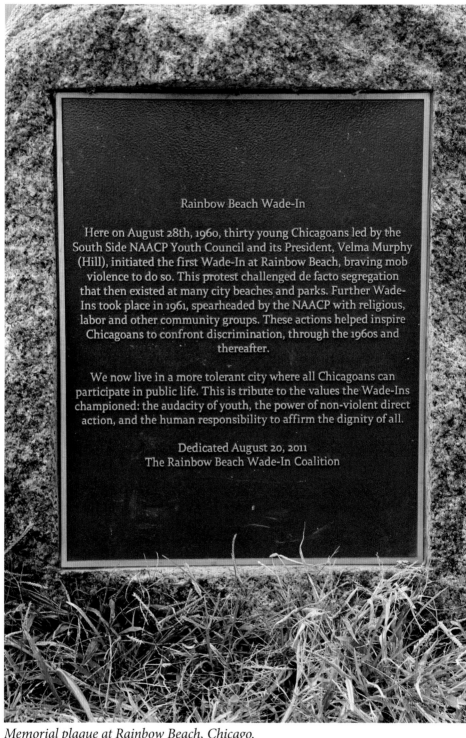

Rainbow Beach Wade-In

Here on August 28th, 1960, thirty young Chicagoans led by the
South Side NAACP Youth Council and its President, Velma Murphy
(Hill), initiated the first Wade-In at Rainbow Beach, braving mob
violence to do so. This protest challenged de facto segregation
that then existed at many city beaches and parks. Further Wade-
Ins took place in 1961, spearheaded by the NAACP with religious,
labor and other community groups. These actions helped inspire
Chicagoans to confront discrimination, through the 1960s and
thereafter.

We now live in a more tolerant city where all Chicagoans can
participate in public life. This is tribute to the values the Wade-Ins
championed: the audacity of youth, the power of non-violent direct
action, and the human responsibility to affirm the dignity of all.

Dedicated August 20, 2011
The Rainbow Beach Wade-In Coalition

*Memorial plaque at Rainbow Beach, Chicago.*

# CHAPTER 13

# Norman Hill Speaks

The request came in a telephone call to my office in downtown Manhattan. There I, with a paid assistant, do my work, Tuesday through Thursday, as president emeritus of the A. Philip Randolph Institute. I can't say that this call in the summer of 2019 came as a surprise.

Shortly after the first of the year, I left my office to attend a meeting of the A. Philip Randolph Institute's board in Washington, DC. I listened to a great deal of discussion regarding the organization's continuing efforts to train and nourish a new generation of labor and civil rights leaders and educate and turn out Black voters throughout the country. And of course, there were discussions and presentations regarding preparations for its upcoming annual National Education Conference to be held just outside Minneapolis in Bloomington, Minnesota, in August of that year. I have a long history of addressing these conferences. In fact, I've spoken at every APRI annual conference, beginning in 1969.

As always, Clayola Brown, APRI's national president who succeeded me in 2004, was enthusiastic and thoughtful in confirming that I would speak, once again, this time to hundreds of members and supporters expected to attend the four-day gathering. She told me that the major speakers for the conference would be Keith Ellison, the attorney general of Minnesota; Tefere Gebre, executive vice president of the AFL-CIO; and broadcast commentators Sheryl Underwood and Joe Madison.

Clayola reminded me that it was especially important that I speak. She said my message would be encouraging because she was confident that whatever I said would be "the real truth."

"I salute you and Velma both for holding the organization together," she added, "and developing a place where we had an opportunity to grow on a good, solid foundation and move forward." I promised right away that I would speak, and speak to a group of 165 young people assembled at the conference.

Later at home, I told Velma of my plans. We agreed that my subject had to be a call to arms to confront the disastrous national and international policies of the Donald Trump White House. We knew that APRI was uniquely situated to make a vital difference in getting out the Black vote in 2020's presidential election, as well as the US Senate races, then controlled by Trump-addled Republicans.

To do this, I firmly believe, the A. Philip Randolph Institute would need to return to its founding principles, ideals, and methods. Ultimately, that is what I said from the podium, and I am told that I received a standing ovation. This is what I said that Friday morning:

> I come to you today offering a simple cornerstone built of four words.
>
> The first two are "thank you." I mean that. These words are not an obligatory expression. I say thank you for giving me this opportunity to speak with you, for permitting me to be your president and then president emeritus for all of these years; thank you for inviting me to stand before you at this year's historic A. Philip Randolph Annual National Education Conference. This is the 50th such conference since my friends and mentors, A. Philip Randolph and Bayard Rustin, founded this vitally important organization in 1965.
>
> The other two words I bring you are equally heartfelt, yet ominous, disturbingly dark, a warning like a "bridge out" sign on a lonely, rain-soaked road in the night. And those words are these: existential threat.
>
> My eyesight isn't at all what it used to be when I stood at a podium like this 25 years ago as APRI president. But I sense you all nodding your heads in recognition of what I mean by those last two words.

Here—51 years after the assassination of Martin Luther King, Jr., years longer since the 1963 March on Washington for Jobs and Freedom, and the passage of the 1964 Civil Rights Act, and the Voting Rights Act the following year—millions of this nation, the United States of America, have fallen under the spell of a severely divisive bigot.

This time, however, the source is not redneck toughs yanking students from lunch-counter sits-ins in 1960, or Deep South sheriffs and governors patrolling the high walls of American segregation as a righteous civil rights movement crashed at its stubborn ramparts. No. This time, one of the greatest threats to this nation living up to its promise as a land of justice, and equality, and democratic governance, sits in the White House.

Let me add here that it is by no means un-American if we deem it necessary to criticize America. That is our democratic right and obligation, and none of us is leaving because we do. James Baldwin, the late writer and activist, probably said it best:

*"I love America more than any other country in this world, and, exactly for this reason, I insist on the right to criticize her perpetually."*

As a consequence of my love for country, I am terribly dismayed by what is happening on our watch. As we meet in this splendid space, the very foundations and best traditions of this great nation are being systematically and grotesquely challenged and dismantled.

I sense you nodding in recognition.

Yes, of course, I am referring to President Donald J. Trump. And before I go on much further, let me make clear that this is not a matter of whether one likes the man—although there are ample reasons not to like a corrupt, racist, liar who is wholly unprepared to hold the highest office in the land.

Exploring that terrain could well be a matter for another speech for another day.

Today, I want to focus on the threat, the existential threat, the Trump presidency represents to America and what we, individually and as a major Black labor and civil rights organization, can do about it.

In the meantime, we cannot hang all our hopes of ending this true American carnage on a Trump impeachment, or on congressional investigations of whether Trump obstructed justice as Special Counsel Mueller probed Russian interference in our democracy. We, as an organization of action, must prepare to take action. This is a call to arms.

First, let's see if we are aligned regarding the Trump threat on this eve of the 2020 presidential and congressional election year.

As *New York Times* columnist Paul Krugman recently pointed out, Trump campaigned for the presidency as a crusader and friend of American workers. But in a clumsy sleight of hand, two and a half years into his administration, it is clear that he has instead championed the causes of the employers at the expense of workers.

This is particularly evident in his administration's resistance to who is afforded minimum wage—nationally a paltry $7.25 an hour—and what and when workers are paid overtime. Despite his frequent promises during his 2016 run for the White House to support a national $10 an hour minimum wage, Trump has neither raised his voice nor lifted a finger to achieve even that. In fact, his administration has been, and continues to be, hostile to American workers and labor unions that advocate for and with them. You can see this spelled out in a whole host of positions—including stripping away regulations and regulators that protect the safety of workers on the job.

In addition, just this spring, the Labor Department, then under now-disgraced Alexander Acosta, ruled in a case with wide and potentially devastating implications for millions of workers. In that instance, the department favored an employer that classified its workers as contractors rather than employees. As many of you know, this is not merely a matter of word play. As contractors, many workers are not entitled to minimum wage, overtime, health insurance or having an employer pay a portion of a worker's Social Security taxes.

And I have not mentioned the Trump administration's appalling support for cases likely heading to the US Supreme Court that would, if the High Court rules in the administration's favor, further set back worker rights and protections, including workers who are members of the lesbian, gay, bisexual and transgender community. By the way, this is the same court on which Neil Gorsuch, Trump's first nominee as justice, cast the deciding vote last year in the case that hamstrung public-sector unions by preventing mandatory collection of fees from workers who decline to join unions—yet reap the benefits of representation.

As I said, existential threat.

And did I mention Trump's assault on affordable health care for the many, Obamacare—as it is commonly referred to—now being challenged in a case also on a collision course with a conservative US Supreme Court, thanks to Trump and Senate Majority Leader Mitch McConnell? Did I fail to mention the Trump administration's assault on women's reproductive health—choice—and its brutal assault on migrants on our southern border?

Let us not forget the $1.5 trillion tax cut enacted last year of which 83 percent of its benefits have gone to the top 8 percent of the country. This comes as the nation's deficit explodes and more than half of Americans live one paycheck away from economic disaster.

Researchers for the Federal Reserve found that 4 in 10 Americans could not afford a $400 emergency, and that about two-thirds of US households making less than $30,000 a year could not manage basic living expenses if they missed more than one paycheck.

Such conditions and circumstances are far from esoteric exercises of statistics. They add up to real human pain. Identifying and helping to alleviate such pain plainly speaks to our organization and its historic mission.

Randolph and Dr. King clearly understood all of this long ago, particularly as it relates to the Black community. They used to point out that, comparatively speaking, few Blacks were millionaires in their day. And not many more owned or managed large businesses. Black people, if they were employed, were employed as workers, laboring for somebody, someone, some firm, some company, some organization, or some institution.

And that, therefore, made them, makes us, the most historically exploited of workers. This gives Black Americans a direct economic, bread-and-butter stake in participating at all levels of the trade union movement. And, in fact, the core, the essence of the coalition, is a partnership between organized labor and the Black community.

In that spirit and insight, I firmly believe that it is appropriate today—right now—that we assess where we are, and what we are about, as an organization in this political climate, in this contentious environment in which we find ourselves. I strongly suggest that we re-examine the A. Philip Randolph Institute's original purpose and thrust.

Of course we all know that we are an organization primarily made up of Black trade unionists, that we welcome anyone who shares our unshakable commitment to racial equality and economic justice. Nevertheless, let's recall that APRI was co-founded by Asa Philip Randolph, the greatest of Black labor leaders and founder of the most significant union of Black workers, the Brotherhood of Sleeping Car Porters. As well, he fathered the modern civil rights movement and the 1963 March on Washington for Jobs and Freedom.

And it was his brilliant colleague, Bayard Rustin, a civil rights leader and master tactician in his own right, who also led in creating APRI in 1965. This was after working shoulder-to-shoulder with Randolph to make the March on Washington an epic and lasting success.

From the start, Randolph, Rustin and I built the Institute on two foundational principles:

First, Randolph was greatly concerned with furthering and strengthening the alliance of organized labor with the Black community and the civil rights movement. This was underscored by his recognition, as I just mentioned, that Black people were among the most exploited classes of workers. As a result, he realized that the trade union movement, much like the civil rights movement, could greatly improve the living conditions of working people, and working Black people.

Secondly, in the wake of the March on Washington, Rustin began exploring the next progressive steps the movement could take from pulling down Jim Crow segregation largely by way of demonstrations in the streets. This was best articulated in his famous 1965 article, "From Protest to Politics."

In it, he wisely wrote about the limits of what came to be called "classic" civil rights work, while pointing out that the problems facing Black America were not merely racial, but economic and social.

For instance, it was not enough to integrate housing, but to eradicate slums, to spur the creation of decent, affordable housing open to Black people. By the same token, it was not sufficient to merely desegregate schools; it was vastly more meaningful to maximize the learning potential of all students, particularly Black students, who face a labor market of rapidly vanishing entry-level jobs, especially those that pay a living wage. This required more than protests. It required sharply focused political action.

This thinking is the very gravity of APRI. I was there in those early meetings with Mr. Randolph, Bayard and my wife, Velma, as a part of those early discussions. The organization began to take shape before I officially joined APRI in 1967 as associate director. Right away, we realized that Black trade unionists were best and ideally suited as a major source to implement APRI's operating premises, which to this day are spelled out in the organization's chief objectives. We also realized that among APRI's objectives was to establish positive human interactions in the Black community as part of our ongoing role in confronting the problems of the community. This thinking informs our ongoing encouragement and expansion of Black political activity at local, state and national levels of government. In fact, I believe we should look upon local and state elections this fall as an opportunity for a trial run of tactics and plans for the crucial contest of 2020, an election in which we must also hold the House and win the Senate.

At the same time, I believe, to be true to our founding principles, we should further increase Black involvement and participation in the labor movement itself. I would like to see more union members encouraging their fellow workers to join unions and further, to encourage them to aspire to union leadership. As leadership, Black trade unionists could be part of the decision-making process, for example, in powerful union endorsements of political candidates.

Such an outcome would not only benefit the Black community, but unions and the larger community in general. I realize that this is hard work. But we must press toward 2020 because the other side—the anti-Black and anti-labor forces—takes no vacation.

Let me correct myself. The occupant of the White House does take vacations—quite a few, in fact. But his mischief and maleficence, however, doesn't as he shakes hands with Kim Jong-un and bear hugs Vladimir Putin, and deflates the free world's confidence in American leadership.

As many of you may already know, my wife, Velma Murphy Hill, who is sorry she could not join us today, and I have recently completed our memoir. It is called *Climbing the Rough Side of the Mountain*, and we are expecting that it will be soon published.

In our book, Velma and I share our lifelong work as civil rights and organized labor activists played out against the backdrop of our nearly 60 years of marriage. There is a fair portion of the book dedicated to Randolph, Rustin and the work of APRI.

One of the stories I tell at some length in the book is an excellent illustration of what APRI uniquely accomplishes in its merging of the needs and resources of the Black community with labor and civil rights in a political context.

Let me share a part of that story with you now.

In the 1991 gubernatorial election in Louisiana, David Duke, the then former Grand Wizard of the Ku Klux Klan and champion of a host of other white supremacist and neo-Nazi groups, had his eyes on the Governor's Mansion. I was helping to direct APRI staff, workers and volunteers to make sure Blacks in that state had a full-throated voice at the ballot box in that race.

Of course, APRI is non-partisan, as it staunchly remains today. So, in our hard work in Louisiana that year we did not advocate how the Black community should vote, only that its members DID vote. To accomplish this, we mounted a massive and sustained voter participation drive. And none of this could have been accomplished, I must add, without the tremendous work of Nat LaCour, national APRI vice president and at the time our Louisiana and New Orleans president, and who I believe is with us here today.

That year, in 1991, APRI had very active voter operations in New Orleans, Baton Rouge, Shreveport, Monroe and Lake Charles. As we write in our book:

*"It was a comprehensive effort. We literally reached out to Blacks in nursing homes, anywhere where they needed transportation, and formed carpools to get them all to the polls. If there were lines, we*

*provided chairs for the elderly while they waited their turns to cast their votes. There is a documentary about what happened that fall."*

In the end, we broke a record. The percentage of Black voter turnout in Louisiana was greater, for the first time, than the percentage of white voter turnout in the state. Duke—a Republican and who today is an outspoken Trump supporter—lost to the Democrat, former governor Edwin Edwards, 39 percent to 61 percent.

We were elated. It was a great, great achievement. The A. Philip Randolph Institute was the first national Black organization to conduct voter participation drives throughout the country. And our affiliates were also active in key congressional elections, including those of Barbara Jordan in Texas, and Andrew Young and John Lewis in Georgia, Mike Espy and Bennie Thompson in Mississippi.

Now I am here to remind you that the stakes are strangely familiar, and yet a great deal larger as 2020 looms ahead.

I do not believe the great American experiment of enlightened self-governance can long endure a second Trump administration. Already, too many American voters are turning disturbingly cynical.

A survey of more than 31,000 Black people drawn from every state in the union found that 52 percent of respondents said politicians did not care about Black people, according to the Black Futures Lab, the group that conducted the survey in 2018. Yet, the same poll confirmed what we already know. Black voters will turn to the ballot box, if nothing else, to effect change. This is most profound during presidential elections.

For instance, in Bill Clinton's run for the White House in 1992, Black voters—and by extension the A. Philip Randolph Institute— made a substantial contribution to his success. Clinton won by a margin of eight states. Each of those states had significant Black voting populations, and in each of those states, we had a strong APRI presence that vigorously drove the Black vote.

Despite Trump's victory, the Black Census Project survey found that almost three in four survey respondents said they voted in the 2016 presidential election. Some 40 percent noted that they helped to register voters, provided transportation to get people to the polls, made campaign donations or handed out campaign materials.

So Black voters are willing to engage. But unlike in 2016, in 2020 the Black community must respond in far greater numbers and at much higher levels of enthusiasm and engagement.

That is our challenge. That is our mandate, a mandate calling out to us from our inspiring history, calling out to our future to further inspire.

We must—all of us—protect and preserve our democracy. As Mr. Randolph reminds us, "There must be no dual standards of justice, no dual rights, privileges, duties, or responsibilities of citizenship. No dual forms of freedom."

We are encouraged and motivated by Mr. Randolph's simple but profound credo:

*"At the banquet table of nature, there are no reserved seats. You get what you can take, and you keep what you can hold. If you can't take anything, you won't get anything, and if you can't hold anything, you won't keep anything. And you can't take anything without organization."*

Now, back to my first words of the day: thank you.

# CHAPTER 14

# The Struggle Doesn't Stop at the Water's Edge

There is a picture, a snapshot really, of Norman and me that I especially like. It's not kept in a frame, although I can't quite say why it isn't. This picture lives in a box with stacks of other photos that are shuffled and reshuffled, from time to time, like cards in a deck of memories.

There are so many pictures of Norman and me that have been taken over the years: black-and-white and color ones; some taken with Polaroid cameras, Kodak Instamatics, and lots more with fine cameras aimed at us by professional photographers, most of them photojournalists eager for an image to go with a headline. There are so many pictures: of us apart and together, standing behind podiums, giving speeches, fielding questions, lecturing and teaching, seated at desks hatching plans and strategies, standing with friends and family, and some pictures that capture all-too-rare moments of sheer relaxation, but so many more of us gathered with the famous and not-so-famous faces of our coalition of civil rights and labor organizations, of churches and centers of learning, of us protesting, of us being arrested for engaging in civil disobedience for a higher purpose.

Some of these pictures are included in this book.

But this one—this snapshot taken some time in the late 1960s—it's different. It is a moment made of only us, husband and wife, lovers and lifelong friends. There we are, pictured side by side, standing on some rather nondescript side street with the sun in our faces—me, with my hair tossed by desert-dry Israeli air, and Norm, his bright, clear eyes slightly squinting in the still young afternoon's glare. He's wearing a dark-green sweatshirt, his head tilted toward mine and his face is a portrait of unconcealed contentment.

I'm wearing earrings long enough to brush the open collar of my black-and-white, polka dot blouse. But what I notice and enjoy most about this picture is what dominates its frame: our matching smiles. They radiate like two heavenly bodies equally drawing light and gravity from the other.

We looked like American tourists despite the fact that we have seldom traveled anywhere as tourists. (Norman doesn't like touring around and doing very much that isn't plugged directly into politics.) But in this moment, we were just an American couple in an exotic place, a couple connected at the heart with invisible yet unbreakable threads.

Thankfully, the decades have not eroded those things most vital in our lives. We still have each other, those matching smiles, our love, those unbreakable threads, and our special and enduring friendship—and yet, always our work. And those years have given us an extraordinary set of common experiences and insights that came into sharpest focus as a result of our years of travels and work outside the United States. It is the backdrop of that photograph, the very reason we were in the Middle East.

As a couple or as individuals, Norman and I have worked with labor activists and leaders in such nations as Israel, France, Germany, Switzerland, Canada, South Africa, Ghana, Nigeria, Senegal, Lesotho, Tunisia, Brazil, El Salvador, Nicaragua, the Bahamas, and Jamaica. During our work in the US, we met with many international defenders of liberty and democracy. Among them was Lech Walesa, the leader of Poland's anti-Soviet trade union, Solidarity, and eventually president of a free Poland; Soviet dissident Aleksandr Solzhenitsyn, and he gave us one of his autographed books. And I will never forget meeting Senegal's president and resident poet-scholar, Léopold Sédar Senghor, in the country's sea-splashed capital of Dakar during one of my many trips to Africa. He had just flown in from France, where he spent most summers. It was one of the most exciting times of my life.

*The one thing that links all the international involvement, work, and exposure that Velma and I have had is the furtherance of democracy.* If you are training trade unionists who will be free and independent, then that work is part of building a free and independent society. If a country has a free and independent labor movement then it has a solid, democratic institution.

The civil rights movement was, in its broadest terms, a movement to extend democracy. Outwardly, the movement was extending the promises and principles of democracy to a discriminated, mistreated group, but always to extend democracy within a democratic framework; that is, one that afforded the opportunity, for example, for anyone to go to the courts and make a case against discrimination.

*That is absolutely the truth, Norman.* Look, I have to be very honest about what I felt when we were doing labor work overseas. Norman tends to be a little purer than me. Yes, I thought that training trade unionists was important for America because it brings workers to a point where they have unions and they can demand higher wages, which does affect American wages here and creates a solidarity with workers in other countries. And I was all for that. I understood the whole global society. I wanted workers in other lands to really be a part of our trade union experience for many reasons and have the capacity to exert more control over their daily lives as a result of their own labor movement experiences.

But I have to tell you that whenever I went to Africa or the Caribbean, starting in the mid-1980s, and I saw these Black people, I felt an extreme connection between their oppression and my oppression. They were like an extension of my family. All the other stuff is true and I really believe it, and I really am a democrat—small "d"—to my core. But the fact that there were Black people who were oppressed was very important to me.

Now, don't get me wrong. I am not a nationalist. I am for workers of every race. I am an integrationist. I am for interracial marriage and interracial struggle. But I do feel a particular something there when I am working to help Black workers organize labor unions abroad.

When I was in Ghana, for instance, I met especially with teachers to talk to them about trade unionism and how it was not simply about jobs but also about democracy and securing more control over their lives. When I spoke about this, I always got a wonderful reception. People would come to me and ask me to come back. When Black Americans would go to other countries, especially African ones, we'd get all these questions about the contradictions, about the struggle of Black Americans to get or keep their equal rights.

I would answer these questions very clearly: Yes, the United States has problems, and some of its problems have a lot to do with race. But it is in America where your rights to organize and confront those problems are protected. We can organize, and we can get a redress of our grievances. In lots of other countries, you can't do that. We have democratic institutions that create environments in which we can solve problems and help remove impediments to freedom. Labor unions are a basic democratic foundation for organizing and protecting the rights of workers, although there are attempts to thwart those efforts.

*Velma and I like to remind people that, of course, a response can sometimes take a long time to work itself through the system.* But eventually, you get a response. It took court case after court case pressed by the NAACP, for example, before it got the 1954 US Supreme Court decision that ruled against racial segregation in the nation's public schools. But we did get a response. This response came about because Black people could engage and confront an independent judiciary, a democratic institution, in this country.

*The first time Norman and I ventured from American shores was to fly, as a couple, to Israel a year after the close of the Six Day War, which began and ended in June 1967.* We weren't especially eager to visit a war zone. But most of the war Israel successfully waged against Syria, Jordan, and Egypt had, in fact, been fought in those Arab nations. That didn't mean that there weren't still rusting relics of the war scattered about the countryside. I have a picture taken that summer of me sitting on a ruined

Arab/Russian tank and waving the blue and white Israeli flag bearing, of course, the Star of David.

At that time, Norman was working in Washington for the Industrial Union Department of the AFL-CIO, and the following year, I had graduated from Harvard and had returned to New York just in time to be confronted with the Ocean Hill-Brownsville public school crisis.

*That first trip for Velma and me was organized by a friend, Greg Bardacke. He was the father of Judy Bardacke, a very close friend of Velma's and a good friend of mine as well.* Greg was the director of the American Trade Union Council for Histadrut. Histadrut is an organization of trade unions that was created for Jewish workers in 1920, some twenty-five years before the official state of Israel was founded in 1947.

It was very natural for us to visit Israel. Velma and I were very interested in the Jewish state and particularly intrigued with seeing how organized labor there worked to advance this evolving and very complicated society. Besides, American Jews had long been close partners in the civil rights movement and a major component of our coalition for progressive change in America. Israel was of paramount interest, concern, and pride for many of our closest friends who were Jewish.

After we returned to the United States, Velma and I began to talk to Black trade unionists about what we saw happening in Israel. And there were Black trade unionists who wanted to go to Israel, too.

I wanted to look at Israel for a number of reasons. One of them had to do with Histadrut. It operated much like the AFL-CIO in America. But in the 1960s, it was not only a federation of trade unions but also owned and operated some Israeli companies (which it doesn't anymore), different from the practices of American trade unions. Velma and I wanted to see how that worked. (Histadrut still exists but in a different form.)

At the time of our first visit to Israel, Velma and I firmly believed that there was solid Black support for Israel, which probably reflected the complex yet generally good relationships most Blacks had with Jews at the time.

Our visit didn't raise the slightest of eyebrows among our other friends and colleagues. Back then, there were not the same fractures that developed in the bond of Blacks and Jews in the United States. There was certainly no pushback regarding our travels to Israel while I was at the A. Philip Randolph Institute. Bayard was quite a vocal and visible supporter of Israel. In fact, he and Mr. Randolph founded the Black Americans in Support of Israel Committee (BASIC) in the fall of 1975 to marshal Black support for the Jewish state. Velma and I also worked very hard and spent a great deal of time to see this effort come to fruition.

*Norman and I were signatories to BASIC, along with dozens of others, including literary giant Ralph Ellison, Harlem Congressman Charles Rangel, legendary Black educator Benjamin E. Mays, and pioneering Black labor leader William (Bill) Lucy.*

In 1991, when David N. Dinkins, serving as New York's first Black mayor, came under fire for his widely assailed handling of a clash between Blacks and Jews in Crown Heights, Brooklyn, he tried to deflect some Jewish heat by citing his early endorsement of BASIC. He was also one of the signatories.

Patricia Jones, a former leader of a chapter of the United Federation of Teachers, who was mentored by me, went on to work closely with Bayard. We played a leading role in a delegation from the United States to Israel when its government was dominated by the Labor Party. At the time, Norman and I wanted to have a first-hand view of what was actually going on there. But with Benjamin Netanyahu's rise to power in 2009, the Labor Party and the labor movement in Israel have been weakened. We, of course, continue to support and to endorse Israel as a Jewish homeland. To be clear, we acknowledge that we have an affinity for Israel because it is a democratic state that has a strong history of trade unions in the midst of Arab states that do not. So, it's also important to defend Israel's democracy, despite its weakening by the current leadership.

*Velma and I believe that a free and independent democracy is the cornerstone of a free and progressive society.* We also support self-determination for Palestinians in the region and encourage a two-state solution regarding the Israeli-Palestinian question. While Israel is not perfect, it remains a democracy, the only one in the Middle East. And with a democracy, like ours in the United States, change is always possible. Velma and I are also encouraged by those among the Palestinians who are attempting to build free institutions, including expanding the rights of women and developing free trade unions.

It was this democratic imperative and its implicit promise of a fair and just society that helped to cement A. Philip Randolph's enthusiastic support of the Jewish state of Israel. During a 1964 address to a Histadrut conference in New York, Randolph noted that Israel was positioned to give rise to a society that gives "materiality to the spiritual and moral values of Judaism, mirroring the justice which the Prophets enjoined, ensuring equality and opportunity for all citizens. In short, a true democracy."

Some fourteen years earlier, in 1950, the seventh biennial convention of Randolph's Brotherhood of Sleeping Car Porters, the nation's largest Black labor union, passed a resolution saluting the Jewish people and the newly formed Jewish homeland.

*After all these years since our direct involvement with Israel, Norman and I have never received any direct criticism for our pro-Israel stance from trade unionists.* As a matter of fact, during that period, one hundred Black trade union, civil rights, and religious leaders voiced support for our position. I think there is a reason for that.

At that time, Israel was considered much more of an underdog than a dominant power in the Middle East, as it is today. Remember, Norman and I started going there after the Six Day War. And believe me, just about everyone understood that Israel was this tiny country—the only democracy in the Middle East, mind you—surrounded by these Arab dictatorships.

Some people, especially the oppressed or formerly oppressed, felt some affinity for the Israelis in that way. Black people tend to readily identify with underdogs, given our history and conditions in this country. I will never forget one evening during a walk in a part of Israel that was hauntingly beautiful, I came across an Ethiopian man who was tall, lean and dressed majestically in robes that seemed at once ancient and timeless. He just stood in the distance. We never talked or acknowledged each other's presence. I later learned that he was an Ethiopian Jew, descendants of the Beta Israel communities in Ethiopia, seen as one of the lost tribes of

Israel. The Israeli government has helped more than 120,000 Ethiopians resettling as citizens in Israel, the last wave coming in 1991. I'm not certain a lot of African Americans know about this, but they should.

As far as trade unionists go, there was a great deal of appreciation for the fact that Israel had a free, independent labor movement. Most Blacks understood that, too, and almost instinctively realized that this was important. Lastly, most Blacks certainly appreciated that they had been historically oppressed and that Jews had been similarly oppressed. Even though there has been this struggle and debate about which group had been the most oppressed, there was an unquestionable common bond of oppression there. And this was openly reflected in the role Jews played in the American civil rights movement.

Norman and I certainly knew that Jews were very, very involved and at all levels. For instance, I cannot imagine that anyone who knows about the three civil rights workers who were slain in Philadelphia, Mississippi, in 1964 would not know that among the dead—James Chaney, Andrew Goodman, and Michael Schwerner—both Goodman and Schwerner were Jewish.

I used to tell Norman that Jews were so involved in the civil rights movement that when I met a white person in the movement, I just sort of assumed that they were Jewish; they weren't always, of course. There was also a kind of general understanding that when Martin Luther King Jr. was raising money for his work in the struggle, two-thirds of the money would come from the Jewish community. And when we got arrested as civil rights activists and needed to call on people to help us with bonds and related matters, it was usually the Jewish community that we turned to. Even in the earliest days of the civil rights movement, like the founding of the NAACP in 1909, the Jewish community was there.

In fact, the highest award one may receive from the NAACP is the Spingarn Medal, established in 1914 and named for Joel Elias Spingarn, the chairman of the organization's board of directors and a Jewish man from a prominent New York City family.

*Of course, Velma and I were well aware of this intertwined history of shared struggle, this natural coalition of Blacks and Jews, when we boarded an airliner in New York's JFK Airport and headed for the Jewish home-land.* We were also aware of a disturbing strain of anti-Semitism that ran through Black America, and we also thought our better understanding of the Jewish state might help us to start mending those wounds.

At its core, we believed that Black anti-Semitism stemmed from a kind of generalized Black reaction to whites. But the whites that many Blacks saw in their severely racially segregated communities were actually Jewish and were even more likely to be authority figures of sorts.

*I agree with Norman.* This Jewish presence tended to be the social worker, the landlord, the store owner, and the teacher. And unfortunately, these individual Jews sometimes became lightning rods for Black resentments of whites, and perhaps even hatred for whites, who either directly discriminated against Blacks or offered indifference or tacit approval of racial segregation, prejudice, and raw discrimination.

Norman and I deeply believe that a lot of the Black anti-Semitism we saw was basically anti-white feelings translated into anti-Semitism. Add the Black community's often prickly relationship with white police, another white authority presence, which has helped to aggravate anti-white feelings for which Jews can often pay a price.

It was, at its root, a kind of throwback to when whites regularly used Jews as scapegoats for all sorts of national ills, including causing world wars in Europe.

We still very much align our position with one expressed decades ago by Bayard Rustin while he was addressing the Anti-Defamation League of B'nai B'rith. He said the issue of hatred is never "simply a problem of Jew and gentile or Black and white. The problem is man's inhumanity to man."

Amen, we say.

When I see even a hint of anti-Semitism, Black or white, I refuse to ignore it. I know a lot of Blacks relate more easily these days to the plight of the Palestinians and see in them something similar to the kind of oppression and landlessness that Black South Africans suffered under apartheid. Muslims, beginning with Elijah Muhammad's Nation of Islam in the 1960s, have done much to sway some Black Americans to see Israel as the aggressor in the Middle East, certainly no longer as the underdog in the region. The Israeli bombardment of the Gaza Strip in the summer of 2014 certainly did little to dissuade many Blacks from viewing Israel as the aggressor. And that is unfortunate. It isn't that simple. Israel is defending against direct attacks on its existence.

Norman and I are especially aware of the tensions in the Middle East regarding Israel and anyone even remotely associated with it and its policies. When I regularly traveled through the region, I got into the habit of having two American passports: one for Israel and one for everywhere else. You think I was being overly cautious? Consider what happened to Norman on his way back to the United States from a meeting in Beirut, Lebanon, in the mid-1970s.

*Velma did not accompany me on this trip.* I had been traveling with Bayard to attend a conference in Beirut. On my return, Bayard decided to stay behind for planning meetings, so I decided to travel back to the US alone. But when I landed in Syria for a scheduled layover, I was detained. There had recently been an unsuccessful attempt to overthrow the government of President Hafez al-Assad, who himself had seized power not long before in a military coup. The Syrian government, which had been badly beaten by the Israelis in the Six Day War, losing both face and territory, was very suspicious of an American, a Black American, with an Israeli stamp in his passport.

Apparently, they thought I could have been some sort of spy. I was questioned and delayed for about an hour. Then I was released to continue my journey home. I really didn't know exactly what had happened. Until I was let go, I kept thinking what posture I should take if my freedom was further denied.

Velma and I understand that the Israeli-Palestinian conflict is extremely complex, but it is a conflict that can be resolved fairly and peaceably. In the meantime, we cannot tolerate intolerance. It is as simple as that.

*Norman and I believe that we must move to stop not only anti-Semitism but also all kinds of bigotry, racism, and prejudice whenever and wherever we find it, even among our own.*

*To be more specific, much of the opposition that Velma and I have toward anti-Semitism flows from our politics.* We are opposed to all forms of discrimination, no matter against whom or for what; not only do we believe that it harms the individual, but we also believe that it weakens the democracy itself.

Whether it's Black anti-Semitism or anti-Semitism practiced by whites, no matter by whom, it's really anti our politics.

*I'm not sure if this was as true for Norman as it was for me, but once I left for distant shores, I wanted to visit so many other places, like Africa.* I most wanted to see if there was anything in my experience as a civil rights and labor movement activist that could be used to help the African continent, the origin of all Black people.

That chance came when I got an invitation to attend a youth convention in Tunis, the capital of the tiny North African nation of Tunisia. Many years later, in December 2010, Tunisia, which is 98 percent Muslim, became ground zero for the Arab Spring, a series of popular uprisings aimed against the region's authoritarian rule.

In the early 1970s, shortly after the Twenty-Sixth Amendment to the US Constitution gave eighteen-year-olds the right to vote, David Dorn approached me. He was a doctoral student from the University of Denver who was working to organize young people in New York.

Norman and I knew him from our time working with Bayard Rustin. We also knew David from our work with Frontlash, a group formed in 1968 to help youth and people of color register to vote and participate in the political process, and it was also supported by the AFL-CIO.

David was smart, energetic, and in his early twenties at the time. Young people were drawn to him. It made perfect sense to me that he might invite me to a world youth conference in North Africa as a delegate representing the United States. This was during some of the chilliest years of the Cold War between the US and the Soviet Union. Despite the Vietnam War still raging and inflaming much of Southeast Asia, the Cold War was less a battle of bullets and bombs, and more of winning hearts and minds.

David knew the youth conference would be stacked with delegates less, shall I say, friendly to America and its international interests. Perhaps an African-American woman with a history of freedom fighting during the civil rights movement might help blunt the simmering resentment in youth mostly from the Soviet Union, its Eastern Bloc satellites, and anti-American leftists from European countries.

At the time, David Dorn was the president of the United States Youth Council, which was being supported by the US State Department to offer a counterargument and presence to Soviet-led romancing of global youth to Communist thinking. When David asked me to join a small delegation of mostly youth activists, four or five people, including a youth delegate representing the NAACP, I literally jumped at the opportunity.

Tunis is a beautiful city overlooking the Mediterranean Sea. You can imagine the sea breezes, the bright sun, and mild temperatures that blessed this former French colony. Once we arrived, we went right to work. The conference was held in a semi-open-air stadium with well-worn bleachers. Nothing fancy. Very Third World. But once the conference got underway, the place was teeming with some 1,000 very politicized young people from seemingly every corner of the earth. And as we expected, Uncle Sam, let me say, was not warmly welcomed to that table of humanity.

David decided to hold a meeting at an exquisite cliffside restaurant on the sea to plot a counterstrategy. It was decided that I should speak, yes, as a young African-American woman in Africa with a background of fighting oppression in the US. But before our delegation could be seated, we were distracted by diners, lots of diners. They all seemed to be looking at me, some even standing and offering me applause as I entered the restaurant.

I looked at David with a question mark practically chiseled into my forehead. Together, we figured it out. The great South African singer and anti-apartheid activist Miriam Makeba was performing in Tunis at the same time we were there. Apparently, these diners had mistaken me for her. (I must admit that, in the right light and at the right angle, I might bear a sisterly resemblance to Makeba.)

"What should I do?" I whispered to David as we tried to make our way to our table.

"Wave," he said without losing a beat.

I did. I gave them the most gracious, queen-of-South-African-civil-and-political-rights wave that I could.

The next day, David attempted to place my name on the list of youth conference speakers. Organizers were resistant. But with the help of a French-speaking professor who was part of our delegation, David prevailed, and I was permitted to speak.

That day, the last of a three-day conference, I decided to wear a stark-white pants suit with my hair wrapped in matching white fabric. There would be little doubt that everyone was going to see me. And with the contrast of that white material against my deep-brown skin, there would be no doubt in anyone's mind that I was an American with prominent African roots.

When my name was called, I had to walk across the row where our delegation was seated and then along a long aisle to the podium. It took some time, and during the first moments there was nothing. No crowd response at all. You could hear a pin drop, roll, and find cover. Then there was this sound of a single person clapping. Later, I learned that it was David Dorn. Soon, his clapping became contagious, and the rest of the delegation began clapping, and then others, many others, hundreds and hundreds of strangers.

By the time I had reached the microphone, the stadium was loud with applause, some of it no doubt simply polite and reflexive.

I launched into my address that we had crafted the night before. I spoke about the universal yearning for freedom and what I had learned about how to wage a peaceful struggle to obtain freedom. I talked about the universality of freedom and that we all are responsible for securing and protecting not only our own freedoms but also those of our brothers and sisters anywhere and everywhere in the world.

All these years later, I don't remember the exact words. But I know I ended with something that amounted to, "In America, as it is all over the world, we cherish our freedoms, the freedom to speak our minds, the freedom of assembly, to organize, the freedom of the press and the freedom of religion. These freedoms are universal; they apply in Mississippi as they must in Moscow; in South Carolina as they have to in South Africa; in Montgomery, Alabama, as they must in Mozambique, Africa…."

When I was bringing my remarks to a close, a suggestion that David and the others had made the night before came to mind. They wanted me to close with a song from the civil rights movement. "We Shall Overcome," I think. I dismissed that then, thinking that it would be pouring it on a little too thick.

But at the moment, hearing ripples and ripples of approving applause, I reared back from the podium and then leaned forward to hear myself say, "You know what? In the civil rights movement we sang songs, songs that encouraged and inspired us.

"Today I want to sing for you, and with you."

The next thing I knew I heard my clear, alto voice soar over the stadium's public address system—and it sounded good. I sang "Everybody Wants Freedom," adding the names of nations locked in a struggle for freedom, like "South Africa wants freedom," "Vietnam wants freedom." The audience started singing along with me. Somebody would yell out more places. Someone yelled out, "Uganda!"

I recall the Soviets walking out, in fact, the whole Soviet bloc.

A short time after my return to America, I ran into Irving Brown. He was a brilliant man and head of the International Affairs Department for the AFL-CIO. He knew Norman, more by reputation as a civil rights and labor activist than personally. He knew even less about me. Trying to figure me out a bit, he asked me a question: "What would you cite as the two most important pieces of literature ever published?"

I thought for a second and just blurted out, "The works of Shakespeare and the Holy Bible."

He looked at me for a moment and then exploded: "I love you!"

I told him that Norman and I had been doing some work overseas, and I mentioned that I always wanted to see Paris.

The next thing I knew, Irving had arranged a speaking engagement for Norman in Paris, and I was to escort Norman there—all expenses paid. It was wonderful. It was my first time in Europe, and Paris didn't disappoint. We stayed at the Hôtel de l'Université Paris in a building dating back to the seventeenth century and located on the picturesque Saint-Germain-des-Prés. I thought of the whole thing as a second honeymoon, especially since Norman and I never really had a first one back in Chicago. I got up in the mornings for long walks and a little sightseeing. But Norman wasn't really into spending time that way.

*While Velma saw a little of Paris, I was concentrating on my speech.* I saw this as a tremendous opportunity, and I wanted to make the best of it.

*Norman's speech was tremendous, and Irving Brown seemed very pleased with his decision to bring us to Paris.* He was there too and took us around. He really enjoyed life, good food and fine wines, festive places, and had a penchant for close-fitting, European-style suits. He acted like a kind of guide for us, taking Norman and me to some nightclub that was a little strange for our taste. It featured women not wearing very much and jumping around a lot. I wish we could have made it to jazz clubs because I know how much Norman loves jazz. Irving and I got along very well.

In recent years, we learned that Irving Brown, who passed away in 1989 in Paris, has been said to have been an agent for the CIA. Norman and I had never heard these rumors. And in our research, we found that he always denied being with the CIA. We take him at his word.

I briefly returned to Paris shortly after being there with Norman, with my friend Judy Bardacke. We thought of it as a kind of extended girls' night in the City of Light, with a nice stopover in London. I truly enjoyed myself in Paris with Judy. We liked so many of the same things. But I missed Norman.

*And I missed Velma, too.* Like periods early in our marriage, our commitment to the struggle for civil rights and racial equality often led us to stage those fights in separate places.

In early 1991, the field director for the American Institute for Free Labor Development—organized labor's Latin American arm—invited me to Brazil, the fifth-largest country in the world and certainly the largest in Latin America. I learned that there were three free trade union federations in Brazil. They all had ideological differences, but apparently each agreed that something significant should be done to address the needs of Black Brazilian workers. In a nation approaching a population of 200 million, only slightly half in Brazil identify themselves as white; most of the remaining population is identified as mixed white and Black. Only about 6 percent of the country's population is seen as Black.

Given the role of the A. Philip Randolph Institute in working with Black trade unionists, and the history of Mr. Randolph himself organizing Black workers, the leadership of the American Institute for Free Labor Development and its Brazilian field director thought it would be helpful if I came, as APRI president, to meet with representatives of the three union federations in Brazil.

I agreed. I had never been to Brazil. Much of the work was centered in São Paulo, which is the largest city in the country. Once there, I quickly learned that Brazil's Black workers had special problems that were part of the legacy of African slavery in South America as well as aftershocks of European colonialism there. No one in Brazil ever mentioned the word "racism." But everyone I met there seemed keen to search for solutions to expand job opportunities for non-white workers there.

Brazilian labor leaders also heavily implied that there was a dearth of Black workers in the leadership of the labor movement in Brazil. I never met any during my first trip to Brazil. In fact, no one whom I could identify as Black attended any of these early meetings, and I noted this to my hosts.

Once I was introduced to the Brazilian leaders of the three trade union federations, I talked at length, through a Portuguese interpreter, about the work of the A. Philip Randolph Institute. I also talked with some depth about how our American experience might provide them with some insights on how to approach their problems regarding Black Brazilian workers. I gave them the history of Mr. Randolph, going back to his success of organizing Black workers with his Brotherhood of Sleeping Car Porters and his ongoing struggle within the trade union movement and its discrimination against Black American workers. I also provided them with a brief overview of the civil rights movement in the United States.

I had been impressed by the fact that these trade union federations, which normally didn't agree on very much, could come together over the issue of widening labor opportunities for Black Brazilians. I could not discern any Brazilian government involvement in this. It all seemed quite organic. And I was made to feel quite welcomed throughout the first series of meetings in São Paulo. As I was about to return to the United States, I was told that the federation representatives wanted to stay in touch with me as they contemplated the next phase of their efforts.

That was encouraging, while I realized that Brazil had special challenges. Its racial history was quite different than our own. There had not been a parallel civil rights movement to pave the way for greater Black participation in a national organized labor movement in that multiracial nation. Unfortunately, there had been no Black Brazilian A. Philip Randolph.

The next phase turned out to be centered on a group of Brazilian labor leaders coming to the US to meet with Black labor leaders. Included among these leaders were Bill Lucy, then the president of the Coalition of Black Trade Unionists; Mary Moore, an organized labor veteran with the United Steelworkers of America; Willie Baker from the United Food and Commercial Workers Union; and the leader of the Coalition of Labor Union Women, Gloria Johnson; and me.

After that conference, I was invited a third time to come and speak, this time at a Brazilian trade union rally near São Paulo. I was asked to bring greetings on behalf of the American labor union movement. My talk was about trade union solidarity. The event, festive yet quite serious, was the Brazilian equivalent of what would be May Day in the United States.

I thought this was a wonderfully perfect chance to make the point that Black workers needed to have a vehicle that was their own and that it could be backed and supported by Brazil's trade union federations. In effect, the solutions to their problems needed to be defined by them. I felt that Black Brazilian workers needed to be encouraged to take the initiative to form and run their own organization to address their special needs.

Partially as a result of those trips to Brazil, the trade union federations came together and backed the founding of what came to be called the Institute on Race, Equality, and Human Rights in Brazil. All this happened in less than two years, and yes, I feel that my efforts helped to make a positive difference for Black Brazilian workers there.

*I realize that Norman might never say it, but I know when he was stand-ing in São Paulo, looking out over all of the faces of Black Brazilian workers listening to him, the eternal words of A. Philip Randolph, who had left this earth more than a decade earlier, had to ring in his ears.* They at least spoke in Norman's subconscious. All these years later, I know Mr. Randolph still speaks to me. Right now, I hear his words he often shared with us: "The struggle for democracy does not stop at the water's edge."

*In that spirit, while I was president of the A. Philip Randolph Institute, the APRI named, for many years, a recipient of our Freedom Award during the organization's national conference.* These were often given to people doing labor organizing and struggling for democracy outside the US, like in Haiti, in Africa.

*One of the international efforts Norman and I are most proud of was made in South Africa in 1987 during the time leading up to the actual dismantling of apartheid throughout the early 1990s.* I had made many trips there, working with Black trade unionists of this rich yet bitterly racially divided nation of some fifty million Black and "Coloured" people controlled by fewer than five million whites. In most trips there, I had worked in Black South African labor centers in the townships, like Johan-nesburg's Soweto, often called the cradle of the anti-apartheid struggle. And this trip in 1987 felt, at first, like it was going to be much like the others. But it wasn't.

Sometimes our work, like running training seminars and workshops for non-white trade unionists, was forbidden by the white-minority gov-ernment. But we managed to do it anyway. In the case of the 1987 work, my visa and all the travel documents of my staff, set to conduct a major workshop in the country, were revoked by the South African govern-ment. We had planned to hold the workshop for Black labor leaders in Johannesburg or Cape Town. But at the time, violent Black resistance to apartheid had sort of knocked the white government back on its heels.

As a consequence, shortly before we were to arrive in South Africa, its government called a state of emergency. And this resulted in the cancel-lation of our visas.

But we would not be stopped. We hastily reorganized and flew to neighboring Maseru, the capital of the Kingdom of Lesotho, a landlocked country that is completely surrounded by South Africa, making it look on a map like the hole in a doughnut. We were able to get a hotel to relocate the labor workshops and seminars, and we also arranged for Black labor leaders from all over South Africa to attend. We called it a South African Union to Union program.

This was my initiative, organized under the auspices of the Service Employees International Union, where I was, at the time, the first Black director of civil and human rights and international affairs. SEIU, which is headquartered in Washington, DC, was perfectly positioned to support these kinds of union-to-union programs. We were also supported by a generous grant from the African-American Labor Center, the African arm of the AFL-CIO. With some two million members, the union represents a diverse group of workers, including janitors, nurses, gravediggers, lab technicians, bus drivers, so many kinds of workers. So if the union wanted to reach out to, say, a union of laundry workers overseas, we would have laundry workers in our union to do this.

That is exactly what we were able to do, reaching out to Black South African labor leaders of all sorts of workers there. And we were grateful that we were able to salvage our program by quickly moving it to Lesotho. But even this move came with its own complications. You see, there had been a military coup in Lesotho the previous year, so the place was under a kind of martial law. Instead of seeing police on corners, for example, you saw military men with big machine guns everywhere. Still, we pressed on.

We were even able to borrow a firefighter's tall ladder and staple almost two dozen Service Employees International Union posters bearing the face of Martin Luther King Jr. across the front of the hotel in Maseru where our workshops were being held. Chalk that up to youthful exuberance, I guess. William Pritchett, then a SEIU official who worked in the union's public affairs and communications department, was part of our teaching team there. And he took pictures of our handiwork across the face of the hotel. It must have worked. Bill and I recently recalled how the signs drew lots of attention and got lots of people asking us all kinds of questions about who we were and what was the work that we were doing there.

Much of our work there was designed to help them to be much more effective labor leaders, which I knew would help drive the anti-apartheid push in South Africa for democracy. We even had sessions on things like being effective public speakers and how best to use the media to get their unions' stories out. We also held major workshops on labor law reform and contract negotiations, even how to set up a union office.

And while the work was so gratifying, it could also be heartbreaking. For example, Bill Pritchett noted that working so closely with these Black South African trade unionists, he could see how they had been hampered by a white-minority government that provided them the barest of education. In many, he said, he could see that they had been educated, even if they had finished high school, to be chauffeurs and dishwashers, housekeepers and cooks—not leaders, not labor leaders in their countries.

Yet, at the same time, your heart could be so lifted when you'd see how these leaders overcame such diminished opportunities. So many of them had a kind of charisma that would steal your breath away. And many of them had knowledge that rank-and-file African trade unionists didn't—a firm interest in and understanding of the provisions of labor contracts, like filing grievances, for example.

And despite this, and maybe a little because of this, these South African labor leaders were so appreciative of what they got out of our work. Sometimes they would be so happy, they would just break into song, often in three- and four-part harmony. Sometimes they would grace us with moving renditions of "Nkosi Sikelel' iAfrika," which would, of course, become the national anthem of a new South Africa once apartheid crumbled.

But from time to time, some Black South African labor activists were reluctant to meet with us, fearing that we might be tools of the CIA, working against their interests. During the Reagan administration of the 1980s, America's official position regarding South Africa was "constructive engagement," which basically meant stay out of it and let the South

Africans solve their own problems. But for trade unionists like us, we believed in active, hands-on engagement.

Norman and I found that a good antidote to those sorts of suspicions of our government and its CIA was the reputation of A. Philip Randolph (once labeled "the most dangerous Negro in America") and the fact that we were very close to the great man. Many Africans knew his name but didn't fully know the depth of his commitment to the worldwide struggle for freedom, his fight against totalitarianism, racism, and discrimination.

*Velma and I also pointed out the example of Mr. Randolph's decades of leadership in the trade union movement and the civil rights movement, and how his support of anti-apartheid struggles went back to the 1950s.* These reminders of Mr. Randolph's credentials as a militant, aggressive, and socialist trade union leader kept opening doors for us.

Sadly, history is too often forgetful of Mr. Randolph's steadfast condemnation of South African apartheid. In the early 1950s, Randolph's Brotherhood of Sleeping Car Porters passed resolutions that roundly criticized "imperialistic colonialism" and "Apartheid of Melanism of South Africa." But Velma and I, we never forgot this, and it served our work well while we were in Africa.

Velma and I were part of a substantive breakthrough when we were permitted to meet with the more radical elements of South Africa's Black trade unionists. Wherever we went, we were interested in making contact with and meeting trade union activists and leaders. We wanted to get a sense of what their labor movement actually was, what its role was in relationship to democratizing the nation's government for all its people, its impact on South African society generally, and its breadth and scope in terms of much of the workforce it represented.

All these points were central to Velma's and my time in South Africa during the late anti-apartheid struggle. And once we were there, we sensed that the country's trade union solidarity was extraordinary.

In South Africa, Blacks and browns used the free trade union movement as a stepping stone to get into politics, creating power bases in labor groups like the Council of Unions of South Africa and the nonracial Federation of Unions of South Africa, and getting exposed to mass organizing.

*Norman and I could see that Blacks learned from South Africa's union movement, even from unions reserved strictly for whites.* They could see how a democratic system of rules works, even if they were excluded from these unions. Much the same could be said about South African courts, too, even when they often ruled in favor of *"Vir Gebruik Deur Blankes"* ("For Use by Whites") apartheid.

The truth was that in apartheid South Africa in general there was democracy—for whites only. But this did not stop Black South Africans from absorbing the lessons of democracy even while they were being excluded from the fruits of a democratic environment.

In addition, the Black trade unions in South Africa were much stronger than in most other African countries. This might have to do with the nature of the work Blacks did in this relatively highly developed country; besides, Black South Africans were a dominant part of the nation's labor pool.

*To a certain extent, Velma and I believed whites there had to accommodate at least some key Black labor needs, including to organize, if they wanted to keep Blacks on the job.* Few really talked about these relationships, but they were meaningful, nonetheless. One of the specific developments, consequences, of our South African work was to open up relations between the American labor movement and the emergence of a strong Black South African labor movement. Shortly after our delegation came back to the US, the African-American Labor Center, which was the African arm of the AFL-CIO, used our time in South Africa, and the contacts that we made on the ground, to organize, along with the APRI, an important international labor conference on the question of South Africa's liberation. And Velma coordinated this historic conference.

In some important ways, the fact that millions of Black workers were organized into unions, democratic institutions, was vitally important. Velma and I realized this early on and knew we had to go to South Africa. An essential element in the maintenance and sustainability of democracy is the existence of a free trade union movement.

*That is absolutely true, Norman.* Our work in South Africa grew directly out of our roles in the United States. Norman was then president of the A. Philip Randolph Institute, and I was in charge of international affairs and civil rights for the Service Employees International Union. It was a good fit.

We could see that oppressive governments were quick to tamp down emerging trade union movements. In the Soviet Union, for example, the government controlled the unions. The same was true for Cuba. In the Middle East, with the exception of Israel, we couldn't find even a facade of a trade union movement. And in China, we knew of only state-controlled labor unions. Although recently, there has been some independent trade union activity.

Norman and I are certain that this is no accident.

*All this sort of global work seemed quite logical to Velma and me.* It was inevitable that our lifelong commitment to the struggle would carry us into an international sphere. It was, as Velma likes to say, a "natural progression."

From the start, our work as activists for progressive change at home had global roots in philosophies of passive resistance and nonviolent protests to the tenets of mass movements in seeking equal opportunities and social justice. You cannot, for instance, speak of Martin Luther King Jr. or Bayard Rustin without speaking, too, of Mahatma Gandhi, whose principles of nonviolent resistance inspired and influenced Bayard, who in turn influenced Dr. King.

Little of any value takes place exclusively in a vacuum. Mr. Randolph and Bayard certainly understood this. Velma and I understood this decades ago, and that understanding was immeasurably deepened when we began to travel and carry our work and commitment to advancing freedom and economic justice—to advancing democracy, really—for people and places far from our native land. Velma and I always knew that all the rights we fought so hard for in America, basic elements of the civil rights and labor movements, were the same rights people needed everywhere.

*Norman and I found this to be true all over.* People craved to live in a system that treated them like human beings while reaffirming their humanity. This meant a number of things, like being able to talk freely among themselves, like organizing freely among themselves. These are basic rights we don't think so much about here. But there is something universal about such things.

In every culture that we visited, we saw the love of parents for their children; we saw one generation's desire to see the next have a fair chance to grow up and be something, to have a better life than those who came before them. That's universal. And the trade union movement offered the world's people a means, and it still does, to have these most important aspects of living, things that represent an essential sense of control over their daily lives. For example, if people got together along common interests, they could negotiate—through unity—with their bosses.

For me, it was like a resounding affirmation of what I had been taught, what I had learned, as a child at the feet of my mother, a union woman at her factory in Chicago. It was really incredible. It was incredible that when we sang freedom songs, whether it was with Africans, Central Americans, or Israelis, or whomever, all could feel the music's universal call and yearning.

We think it's a shame that most people in this country don't understand that the trade union movement offers all this to people. The benefits of being organized transcend the immediate workplace. Organized labor's tenets and tactics of speaking up and being able to risk the consequences—but not alone—are all part of the lessons of organized labor. Being organized helps people everywhere develop their moral muscle to speak up against injustices, to act. Such thinking gave rise to, say, Rosa Parks in the segregated American South. It also informed Nelson Mandela—who passed away at ninety-five while we were completing this section of the book—as he shattered South Africa's system of racial oppression and subjugation with the help of large numbers of Black organized labor.

Most Americans cherish our Bill of Rights. But we also have to cherish the struggle for those very rights for others far from our shores, places where people do not always enjoy these rights protected in our founding documents. Understanding that, Norman and I must say, is so profoundly easier when you are able to stare into the eyes of those denied these rights.

And when we've been able to do this, it has never discouraged us. In fact, facing this challenge overseas has never overwhelmed us or made us feel complacent; quite the opposite—it made us want to struggle even harder, and harder still when we got back here, home.

Sometimes I wonder how to explain this activist imperative to people. Gandhi has a wonderful quotation that is often repeated by President Obama: "You must be the change you want to see in the world."

Václav Havel, the writer and last president of Czechoslovakia and first president of the Czech Republic, also spoke to this activist notion, noting that "vision is not enough; it must be combined with venture. It is not enough to stare up the steps; we must step up the stairs."

In other words, they are saying that we must all act, we must all climb the rough side of the mountain. I know that Norman and I are hardly done in our climb.

Act. Climb. And hold on.

# A Clear View from the Rough Side of the Mountain

August returned to Washington, DC, and with it, like a flock of two, so did Norman and I. It was 2013 and the fiftieth anniversary of the March on Washington for Jobs and Freedom. So much had changed since 1963, when we stood in the heavy, late-summer air with some quarter of a million people gathered on the National Mall. We had been electrified that August 28 by the towering likes of the march's architects, A. Philip Randolph and Bayard Rustin, and its Gabriel, Martin Luther King Jr., whose soaring speech that afternoon trumpeted the undeniable fact that a new day had surely risen for the nation's people, Black and white, rich and poor. He clearly had a dream that day. We all did.

Now, rather than John F. Kennedy occupying the White House, a Black man, Barack Obama, and his lovely family, called 1600 Pennsylvania Avenue home. In fact, President Obama would attend and address one of two major celebrations during the anniversary week of the Great March.

*So much had changed since Velma and I stood on that mall as both observers and participants in the first March on Washington.* We returned to the grassy, tree-lined 150 acres in 2013, amid tens of thousands of others—many of them young people—returning to the march the way some Black people who had never set foot in Africa return to it. There was an understandably strong historic and emotional draw.

*Unfortunately, Norman and I believe, much too much of the march's anniversary was wrapped in nostalgia.* Unlike for the first march, there was no concise, concrete program to find and enact solutions for the nation's contemporary problems. We found this disappointing and a reflection of the general nature of national Black leadership today.

Consider this: the National Association for the Advancement of Colored People, America's largest and oldest civil rights organization, was, during the anniversary of the march, looking for a new national leader.

We do, however, see much promise in the Reverend William J. Barber's continuing demonstrations known as Moral Mondays, aimed at conservative extremism in North Carolina that is, among other threats, restricting voting rights of Blacks and poor people. Reverend Barber, who is a former president of the state chapter of the NAACP, has consistently drawn thousands of protesters in rallies around the state opposing policies arising from the state's Republican-controlled General Assembly and its governor Pat McCrory, also a Republican (succeeded in January 2017 by Roy Cooper III, a Democrat).

Reverend Barber's employment of organized nonviolent tactics such as sit-ins, street marches and demonstrations are clearly recognizable from the civil rights movement of the 1950s and '60s. We also applaud his embrace of the greater lesson of the classic civil rights movement: coalition building.

We strongly believe that a prime example of the best of effective coalition politics at work can be found in an examination of the 1963 March on Washington for Jobs and Freedom. Quite visibly, the diversity of its speakers and thousands of participants illustrated all the elements of the sort of political coalition that march organizers A. Philip Randolph and Bayard Rustin advocated. Perhaps less visible to the eye, but present nonetheless, in that historic march was a combination of race and class that symbolized our point of view on this. The evidence of this powerful coalition was also embodied in the set of demands that grew out of the march itself.

It is clear to us that Reverend Barber's sustained and outstanding work with the Poor People's Campaign (with obvious roots in Dr. King's unfinished work of the late 1960s), for example, along with his Moral Mondays, appear to be living legacies of the best of movement strategies and commitments.

On the other hand, the Student Nonviolent Coordinating Committee, an essential component of the coalition that created the '63 March on Washington, no longer exists. Much the same can be said for the Congress of Racial Equality, our organizational home for years and now little more than a caricature of what it had been during its glory years in the mid-1950s and 1960s. Dr. King's Southern Christian Leadership Conference, an organization cofounded by Bayard, who also wrote its bylaws, is still a vehicle to combat racial discrimination and segregation throughout the South.

Some of the coalition that led the original march is in disarray, and this organizational deficiency has had some debilitating consequences in addressing stubborn old, and new, challenges.

*We must go, as Bayard Rustin advocated decades ago, from protest to politics.* This does not mean curtailing or ending the demonstrations. The pressure on the White House and state and local politicians must continue.

But in the meantime, we must combine the protests with real political action. That means encouraging honest, dedicated Americans committed to a pro-people agenda to run for office. All kinds of offices—school boards, city councils, state legislatures, and congressional seats. Even the White House. And as they run, they must not forget to support the causes of the nation's have-nots and have-littles.

Velma and I suggest a further step. We believe a national clearinghouse must be developed that, turning to the internet, could track nationwide which seats are becoming open when and where. The online clearinghouse could, for example, also instruct people on how to run in targeted cities and help them raise money for campaigns that in the end could change the balance of power across the country—including, of course, in Washington.

*Norman and I also suggest that we establish a summit, bringing veterans of the traditional civil rights movement, like Andrew Young, Jesse Jackson, Eleanor Holmes Norton, and Diane Nash, with the emerging generations of newer movement figures like the Reverend William Barber.* In addition, the summit would include young activists from organizations like Black Lives Matter and groups representing women, gays, and Latinos, for example. We see great value in cross-pollinating the wisdom of the old with the energy of the new, for the struggle is continuous.

*I agree, Velma.* We need today precisely the same sort of coalition of progressive interests that made possible the March on Washington as the foundation of a new, broader coalition including, for example, women, gays and lesbians, and other minorities—particularly Hispanics and Asians—to press government on specific issues.

The summit is one of our goals, to help activists discover and reestablish their footing in this country.

*It was in that spirit that I suggested that the A. Philip Randolph Institute honor Norman with a special dinner marking his eightieth birthday.* I wanted this tribute to coincide with the anniversary of the march that Norman worked so hard on with Bayard and Mr. Randolph to make it the resounding success that it was. The dinner was never meant to simply be a remembrance, but a reminder of what we need to do now. To the institute's credit, its president, Clayola Brown, agreed to hold the gala.

*When that evening arrived, on August 27, 2013, some 700 people filled the banquet hall of the Hyatt Regency on Capitol Hill.* I had actually turned eighty some months earlier, but, along with Velma, I appreciated the occasion to celebrate my life's work thus far.

*I told Norman that there was not a single empty table.* And so many spoke, including the then-outgoing president of the NAACP, Ben Jealous (whom Norman mentored during his early years of activism in Frontlash, a youth group supported by the AFL-CIO); Mary Kay Henry, president of the Service Employees International Union; civil rights activist Jesse Jackson; and Myrlie Evers-Williams, the widow of slain civil rights leader Medgar Evers, who has carried on his work. Also attending was long-time colleague and friend Green Lewis, a vice president of the Office &

Professional Employees International Union, a figure who epitomized the very grass roots of the A. Philip Randolph Institute and the core of affection the organization holds for Norm.

*And as I have told Velma many times, many of the things that were said about me that evening were emotional, even humbling.* But that was not the driving element of the occasion for me, which was masterfully chaired by Clayola. I was gratified to know that my own family, a dear nephew and a niece, along with her husband, were seated among this gathering of my organizational and political family. And I had a feeling that although I didn't specifically touch the life of each person in the audience, a large part of that audience was there as a result of the organizing of the APRI affiliates, a major responsibility that was mine.

It was abundantly clear that night that the great energy, effort, and time that I had expended doing those years of building the organization had been, indeed, worthwhile. In a sense, the evening's outpouring of recognition and appreciation was a vindication of all the hard work, the long days and nights traveling, speaking, and organizing, that helped to give birth to the modern A. Philip Randolph Institute.

Initially, APRI was a platform for the ideas, values, and principles of Mr. Randolph and Bayard. At its founding, there was little thought of using it to develop a base of people participating in and identifying with it organizationally. Obviously, that changed. The fruit of that fundamental rethinking—an infusion of grassroots, working-class energy into a vision of progressive change driven by Mr. Randolph and Bayard—was in great evidence the night of my tribute in Washington. It felt to me that the gathering in that banquet hall was an extension of me, and recognition of what yet could be done to bring about progressive change in this country.

I thought the most impressive presentation that night was made by Carl Gershman, then-president of the National Endowment for Democracy. He had clearly thought a great deal about what he was going to say. As a result, he was clear and analytic, and he really provided a solid political setting to my endeavors. I was moved more intellectually than emotionally.

And there was Velma.

Her words took me back to the important roles we had played in the civil rights movement, like at CORE, integrating restaurants along Route 40 between Baltimore and Washington, helping to lift racial barriers in Broadway theaters and Hollywood, and waging anti-discrimination campaigns against major hotels and retail chains. Velma has a unique way of personalizing me and our relationship, but doing this in a context of how our lives are intertwined in so many of its deepest dimensions, and at the same time clearly projecting what she and I have been all about politically. Much of what we are about is not getting seduced by nostalgia, but about facing the future as activists perpetually ready to meet new challenges.

This ultimate takeaway of my tribute dinner was not its underscoring of the importance of political and organizational achievement, but how those efforts serve as a launching point of what must come next.

*Yes, Norman and I are very conscious of the past and present, but we are very much more concerned about what comes next, where we can go, what we can do.* In fact, I spent some time in my closing remarks talking about issues yet to be adequately addressed in America, such as income inequality, the whole notion of social and economic mobility.

*At the close of the event, a number of people came up to Velma and me, asking if I would sign their program books.* I did, adding to my signature, the phrase "Keep on keeping on." I did this because I wanted to convey the idea that the night was certainly a highlight event, but I also wanted to underscore the fact that this was not an end, that I would find a way, that Velma and I would find a way, to keep on making a contribution politically and organizationally.

In that way, the tribute was a very, very special night.

*Sitting there next to Norman, watching all the people taking their turn to give him his due, I found myself flashing back.* There had been other tributes for Norman; a major one was held in Atlanta for the sixtieth anniversary of his birth. Back then, participants of the event were presented with a journal that bore a picture of Norman's face framed with images of a telephone and an airplane—symbolizing major tools of his work as a lifelong organizer. But this one in Washington was different.

Maybe because Norm had gotten a little older. And maybe because there remains so much work to do.

Norman and I believe the number one issue today is the class question. Long before Occupy Wall Street helped to heighten America's attention to its gross and growing income disparity, we were not only sensitive to the problem but also organizing to address it. We still are.

We are exploring ways that we can more fully reengage the issue of income disparity and broaden the dialogue around the threat it poses to a healthy, fully functioning democracy. Part of our plans include conducting seminars on college campuses to better marry the history of the civil rights and labor movements to the future of those movements.

With this book, Norman and I also hope to further enlarge the debate around this and related issues of class, race, and labor in a series of guided talks across the country. And in doing this, we hope to reach out to the next generation of committed, dedicated, and involved activists. One of the things that we are most concerned about is the very future of the movement. I don't think that young people today are the same as the young people involved in the movement during the '60s, particularly not like the young activists in the South then, those you would likely find, for instance, in the Student Nonviolent Coordinating Committee or Congress of Racial Equality. They had courage, dedication, commitment, and perseverance. They went headfirst into some of the most superheated cauldrons of racism in the Deep South.

In no way is this a criticism of today's young people. In fact, so many young people today have in their hearts a burning desire to improve the world. I was deeply moved when a young girl from Mississippi, Deborah Franklin, took the stage at Norman's tribute and sang that old Mahalia Jackson spiritual, "If I Can Help Somebody." But the times are so much more complicated than our early days of activism. A good heart is not enough.

Racial segregation was more blatant, more overt, generations ago. And this reality brought out a different kind of character than we see today. Norman and I believe that activists have to be smarter now because they have to understand the social and economic and political nuances and challenges before them. We didn't have to know so much of that in the 1960s to break down blatant barriers. Today's Bull Connors and others spewing obstacles to an inclusive America are likely to wear tailored suits and nice smiles and hire public relations experts.

*I agree with Velma.* An effective activist today has to have some political savvy to understand how one generates and develops political leverage, influence, and impact. Effective activists today have to have some economic understanding about how and why, for example, this country, with all its wealth, still has a significant number of people in poverty, a disproportionate number of them Black. This generation of activists has to possess some organizational building skills to hold and sustain an organization that is not just geared to desegregate a lunch counter, for instance, but geared to have a sustained impact on the political, economic, and social climate of the country. This also requires considerable analytic capacities.

*I would add to Norman's view that today's activists must also possess the ability to feel something for the masses, including the ever-widening group of dispossessed and disaffected being cast out of mainstream American society at alarming rates.* Some of our most able potential leaders are likely to come, but not exclusively, from middle-class homes. And while many of these potential leaders might well identify with the music and some of the other cultural markers of the masses, many may not personally identify with such people, young or otherwise, working, for instance, for far less than a living wage.

This perspective is another reason that A. Philip Randolph and his point of view are so important today. He said that leadership, the kind that builds mass movements, was not going to be exclusive to only the talented tenth, as W. E. B. Du Bois talked about. He said this kind of effective leadership was going to include the workers, some of them like health care workers, home care workers, paraprofessionals, janitors, and the workers at McDonald's and Walmart, the kind of workers who have been loudly calling for a living wage.

*Similarly, Velma and I listened to Bayard say many times that no one should expect the Black middle class to behave unlike the white middle class.*

At the same time, intelligent leadership has to be cultivated and oriented to lead—including taking full advantage of the organizing power of social media and other digital tools. In short, making maximum use of opportunities whenever and wherever they are found. This is what Velma and I want to do next.

We realize how difficult the challenges are today. This is partly true because problems are not clearly just racial, although there remains a racial component to some of the most persistent. Therefore, the response requires not just the single demonstration, for example, but a sort of involvement that can, in fact, change institutions and bring about a societal response.

That is what Velma and I are committed to help foster in a new generation of activism. That doesn't mean that we are looking for a new Mr. Randolph or Bayard, a new King or Mandela on the horizon of change. Velma and I realize that no one can truly sense their coming until they, or events, announce their own arrival. What we want to do is to help create the conditions for the formation of these leaders in the making. We take some comfort in realizing that such leaders are likely walking among us today. We are simply not yet aware of them. And conditions and circumstances may force them to step forward at any time.

*Let us be clear, our sentiments also do not mean that we have a messiah complex.* Quite the opposite is true. Norman and I are not invested in the emergence of a single leader, but instead an emerging class of leaders, leaders with the characteristics we have discussed throughout this book. We see one of our primary jobs as fostering an environment that can give rise to this leadership, and then nourishing it to grow. We certainly benefited from similar such environments and figures within both the civil rights and labor movements in which our politics, our activism, and our leadership were mentored.

We realize to play these roles, Norman and I must be more directly involved, to be more, if you will, out there doing the work. In the meantime, we are also committed to creating coalitions that would include like-minded intellectuals, religious figures, organized labor, civil and human rights groups, and academics to form an independent, organizational leverage to press the White House and Congress to enact programs and policies that address our greatest challenges, such as income inequality and joblessness.

A major part of our efforts is being directed at the unfinished business of the demands of the 1963 March. Among them are:

- A national, federal jobs program aimed at training and employing all willing and able to work. In addition, we call on the federal government to provide additional monies to state and local governments to increase the ranks of public employees, which would include teachers and police.

- An American trade policy that no longer places manufacturing workers at a competitive disadvantage in the global economy. The US must end trade, dollar, and tax policies that encourage outsourcing and hasten the deindustrialization of our social and economic fabric. The nation must ensure that its manufacturing sector is once again robust; this is paramount to fueling research and development, spurring innovation in a highly competitive global marketplace. In addition, respecting the fundamental legal rights of all workers must be an essential component of American trade policy, one that must empower all workers to organize and act collectively to ensure that workers are safe, secure, and fairly paid.

- A living wage for workers. President Obama's executive order that increased the national minimum wage to $10.10 for new federal contract workers is a good start to reestablishing ready avenues and ladders to the American middle class.

- A quality education for all. The American education system must work harder to maximize the learning potential of every student, particularly much too often underserved poor whites and racial and ethnic minority students. We must challenge the continuing de facto segregation that appears to be structurally entrenched in our national public education system. We call for more programs targeted to educate and prepare students for the current and projected needs of an American society firmly situated in a global economy. At the same time, we encourage the creation and adoption of free, national pre-kindergarten for all young children, as well as a holistic approach to education, one that includes wrap-around, school-based programs that provide social services and health care to students in need. In addition, in instances in which charter schools are established, we strongly support that such initiatives include unionization of its faculty and staff.

- Universal, quality health care. Despite attempts to dismantle it, we still fully support and endorse President Obama's Affordable Health Care Act, widely known as Obamacare. This, we believe, is a major step in the right direction. Ideally, we ultimately support a single-payer approach much like this country's existing and expanding Medicare, and much like how Canada and a number of European nations provide no-cost health care.

- America's prison-industrial complex. US prisons and jails imprison more people than any other in the Western world. We support a rededication of America's prison system to fairness, rehabilitation, and successfully reintegrating former inmates into mainstream society, meaning restoring their rights to vote, work, and live in decent housing. This especially pertains to the mass incarceration of young Black and brown people who are often jailed under questionable circumstances.

- Protection of our natural environment. We stand in firm support of all efforts to combat the ravages of climate change, including, of course, a national effort to reduce America's ozone-eroding carbon emissions. We also support a national movement to further clean and protect the nation's air, water, and food.

*Along the way, Velma and I will continue to write columns and commentary for various publications.*

*Unlike Norman, however, there are moments when I feel a little downhearted.* The only thing that keeps me going is the idea that if I stop, nothing may happen. I cannot hope to help bring about change without being a part of that change.

*I certainly understand the way Velma feels.* But for me, I am motivated, continually motivated, by the legacy of Bayard Rustin and A. Philip Randolph.

Mr. Randolph often said, "Justice is never given; it is exacted and the struggle must be continuous, for freedom is never a final fact, but a continuing evolving process to higher and higher levels of human, social, economic, political and religious relationship."

When one looks at the world in which we live right now, this moment, those words could not be more strikingly true.

*You're right, Norman.* You're so right.

Together, as we continue our quest as activists into a sixth decade, we have never been more dedicated to see our country known and admired in the world for how it treats its young and old, how it treats its lost and least, how it keeps its founding promises and new ones, to truly be a nation of fairness, justice, and opportunity for all.

# APPENDIX

# The Paraprofessionals

Only heaven knew—certainly not Norman and I—that a path awaited my return to New York in 1968 upon completing my studies at Harvard. That path was rocky and uphill but carried me directly into the heart of helping to set right a terrible wrong that had, for years, befallen thousands of mostly poor women of color who toiled in New York's public schools as lowly paid and generally lowly regarded teachers' aides. More precisely, as paraprofessionals.

Chapters 9 and 10 of this book recount the struggles and triumphs I helped to wage to get the paras organized, to bring job security to their work and to create a career ladder that enabled many to go to college and become teachers and make more of themselves.

It was a journey that combined the best of what the civil rights and organized labor movements taught me over the years. But I don't believe their story would be complete without hearing their own voices and insights.

In that regard, we offer this addendum.

## Maggie Martin: From Paraprofessional to Teacher

Being a paraprofessional really changed my life. First, being a para gave me the chance to get my college degree. I was the first in my family to complete college. My mother was so proud of me. And because of the para program, I was able to go on and earn my master's degree and eventually became a teacher.

I was born and raised on the Eastern Shore of Virginia. I had gone to Norfolk State University and had completed a year there before I moved in 1966 with my husband, James, to New York City. He had gotten a job there. But once we got there, we realized that he wasn't making any real money, and I didn't have a job. One day, I was walking our son to elementary school, PS 50, in Jamaica, Queens. This lady came up to me and said that there was a new position as a teacher's assistant, a paraprofessional. She told me where to go to sign up, and I did. That was 1968.

It seemed to me that the extra money would be good. I thought that it would help us live a little better, and it did. But the job itself turned out to be very interesting. It wasn't all honey and sunshine, though. At first, when we paras went into the schools, some of the teachers didn't really want us there. We lived in the community, and some of the teachers thought of us as spies. In my case, I had a Black first-grade teacher, and she was an excellent teacher. But it was clear that she just didn't want me in her classroom. She even complained to the principal. I never forgot that lady.

Now, it wasn't overnight, but in time this teacher and I became good friends.

The next big challenge came when we learned that paraprofessionals were being organized and that we had to decide which union to join—DC 37 or the United Federation of Teachers. There was a man who was a para at our school who held these meetings in a bar to help us make up our minds. We, about twenty to thirty paras, chose the UFT, the teachers union. I thought, why be in a school with teachers and you are in another union?

Around this time, I met Velma Hill and served on a contract negotiating team with her. After securing contracts, I was eventually able to use their career ladder and go back to school. I got my associate degree from Queensborough Community College in 1973, then my bachelor's degree in 1976 from Queens College, both in education.

I received my master's degree in education from Adelphi University in 1986 and went on to do some postgraduate work there, too.

I stayed a para for a long time. For years, I was active in the UFT as a para chapter leader for Queens. But I just didn't seem to want to make that step to become a full-fledged teacher. Apparently, I needed a nudge. Another teacher with me when I was a para at PS 140 in Queens said, "Maggie, you do everything a teacher does, and you do it well. Why not be a teacher? You have the degree. Maggie, you can do it."

The following year, I went to the Board of Education, took and passed the examination, and became a teacher in South Jamaica, Queens.

My husband was always so supportive of me, and I tell other people don't tell me what you can't do.

I retired as a teacher in 2008 but continue to work closely with the UFT and American Federation of Teachers and serve as a delegate to the New York State United Teachers, the state education organization.

## Shelvy Young-Abrams: From Paraprofessional to Union Leader

First of all, becoming a paraprofessional helped me to understand the American labor movement. I grew up on a farm. I knew nothing about unions. I started to learn about organized labor, though, when I came to New York and started working in a chemical plant in Queens. After thirty days on the job, I found myself asking, "Where's my union? I want to sign a union card."

But it wasn't until I began working in schools as a paraprofessional that I was introduced to the finer points and issues of labor. When paras were working to join a union, one of the major organizers of that effort, Velma Hill, called a meeting of the paras' leadership. It was at her home with her husband. Velma and Norman had a great deal of experience working in the civil rights and labor movements. At the Hills' home in Manhattan, I was introduced to Black labor legend A. Philip Randolph. This is when I truly started to learn the history of labor, how important it was to be a member of a union. Then, I really, really got involved. I got right in.

I had started as a volunteer in the school system. One day the principal of PS 19 on Manhattan's Lower East Side, District 1, told me that there was a full-time job working as a classroom para that I might be interested in taking. That was 1968, and at the time, I had two young children going to that school. It felt like a good fit: I could work and be home when they got out of school and during the summers.

Soon after I took that job, the United Federation of Teachers started organizing paraprofessionals. I quickly understood how vital the union was to protecting our jobs, to getting us health care benefits, to giving us a chance to get a college education and advance. I got very active in my school. In 1970, I was elected the union's paraprofessional representative; then some years later, I was elected the Manhattan Borough coordinator for the paras.

Before all that, I had gotten involved in the Ocean Hill-Brownsville school strike, escorting kids to various buildings but never crossing the picket line. Later, during the 1970s, I remember going to City Hall as a para and sitting across from Mayor Ed Koch in City Hall. He saw paras as temporary workers and thought we didn't need protecting, that we should be on welfare, so I asked him, "Mr. Mayor, why do you hate us?" I still have the newspaper article about that.

As a para, with newly won UFT contract guarantees, I was able to go to school. I went to Touro College in New York at night and got my associate degree in education. Then I got two job offers, but the one that attracted me was a post with the New York Board of Education. I took that job, and it led to so many opportunities. It gave me a career. I also eventually became very active with the A. Philip Randolph Institute in New York.

In the late 1990s, I started working full-time for the UFT. I never wanted to be a teacher. I believed that being a para and a community person gave me more freedom as an outsider to fight for the things that I wanted. My overall experience as a paraprofessional had helped me learn to be more understanding and to relate to *all* my members that I represented. I understand what they are going through.

In 1998, I was elected the first vice chairperson of the UFT's Paraprofessional Chapter. In 2006, I was elected its chair. I was the third person to hold that post. I am also a vice president of the American Federation of Teachers.

Today, I remain very involved. As chapter chairperson, I represent all 24,000 paraprofessionals in New York City in collective bargaining, for example. I try to help everyone I can.

## Lorretta Johnson: From Paraprofessional to National Union Leader

I started in 1965 as a volunteer at my son's school in Baltimore, Maryland. He was in kindergarten, and I had two other children in elementary school. I was working in the school library; then the principal there asked me if I wanted to become a teacher's assistant. It paid $2.25 an hour and didn't include any benefits.

Schools were having large class sizes at that time. The teachers had their hands full, so we were needed. I took a test and was interviewed and was hired. And I wanted that job so I could work and be home when my children got out of school.

Some teachers wanted us, and some teachers didn't. I had a teacher who trained me as a teacher's assistant, and that made me very effective. I understood the need. But some teachers saw this as an imposition. We already had problems in the classroom, some seemed to think, so why send in a person who is untrained?

This is one of the things—knowing how to best use all these talented people, of not just throwing them into the classroom—that first got me involved in the Baltimore Teachers Union.

It wasn't until 1967, when the Elementary and Secondary Education Act had gotten signed into law by President Johnson, that the bulk of teachers' assistants, paraprofessionals, came into the schools. Until then, a lot of us were paid with local funds, not federal.

No matter how we were paid, paraprofessionals wanted to do a good job, but we also wanted training and wanted to work well with teachers and help students in the areas where they most needed help. Being organized with the Baltimore Teachers Union helped us achieve this and then more.

Once I became a para, I wasn't assigned to my son's school; I was assigned to one of the top schools in the city. We had so many bright

287

kids there. We had all the doctors' and lawyers' and editors' children in our school. I left that school and worked at others, even a school that was called a model school. It had a paraprofessional in every classroom and two in kindergarten classes.

My husband was such a help through these years. Without his support, I would never would have been able to continue my education and have a career in education and organized labor.

I helped Baltimore's paras secure their first contract in September 1970. And that wasn't easy because there had been a split between federally funded paras and locally funded paras. I had shown everyone that we were doing the same jobs and the boss was taking advantage of both of us. We ended up fighting together and winning together.

Along the way, I worked with the A. Philip Randolph Institute and became the president of Baltimore A. Philip Randolph Institute. That's when I met Norman Hill, a wonderful man who has given his life to this work.

Through the 1970s I began to rise through the teachers' union, holding various executive posts and working closely with the American Federation of Teachers. Later I became the executive vice president and the secretary-treasurer of the American Federation of Teachers, AFL-CIO, and a member of the executive council of the AFL-CIO.

The AFT and the union movement gave me such an opportunity. It humbles me. I would never have had these opportunities as just a general citizen.

## Patricia Jones: From Paraprofessional to National AFL-CIO Field Representative and Organized Labor Activist

I'm from a small town near Burlington, North Carolina, a place where I was sharecropping tobacco. That was the worst there was. Terrible work. This was especially true because I was never that great with the sun. I simply was not cut out for farm life.

When I was ten years old, my mother died. The decision was made that I would go to live in a boardinghouse with a friend of my mother's father. It turned out to be a life I was eager to escape. When I was a young woman, I read an ad that was promising work to people who came to New York. The pay was $50 a week. That sounded good to me, so I answered the ad and landed in Brooklyn to be a domestic worker. But my job ended up being more a babysitter than anything else. I'll tell you one thing: I worked like a slave. It was a degrading job.

After that, I found other jobs, even working ten years at an insurance company as a claim adjustor. I had gotten married and had twin daughters. When my children started school, I wasn't thinking about being a paraprofessional, although that is what I eventually became. At the time, I just volunteered to work in the school because I wanted to see how my children were being treated there. They were two Black kids in a mostly Jewish school, and they were always kept together.

For the next six years I was in the classroom working as a para. Then there was a time when it looked like the paras were going to lose our funding. At around the same time, Eleanor Holmes Norton, the head of the Human Rights Commission, was holding hearings on domestic workers, and I was asked to testify because of my experience in that work.

I told that commission just how bad it was being a maid and that I had a better job as a para in the schools but sure didn't want to lose it and go back to that life.

As a paraprofessional, I got to join the United Federation of Teachers and began to fight for a better life. Albert Shanker, its president back then, not only helped that fight, he led it with Velma Hill. Because of them, I earned a decent salary. I got paid vacations, sick leave, health insurance, and other benefits. And with the para contract, I eventually got to go to college. My mother used to tell me to get an education and take care of your teeth. I did both.

I went to Kingsborough Community College and got my associate degree. Then I did additional course work at Brooklyn College and the City University of New York. In time, I went from a paraprofessional to coordinator for the paras in Brooklyn.

Being a paraprofessional really affected me. It made me more independent and gave me more pride in myself. It was like my outreach into the larger community, too. Being a para to me was being a part of something.

289

Through my association with Velma, who did so much to organize us and get us our contract, I was able to get a post working for the AFL-CIO as a national field representative. I also got opportunities to work with Bayard Rustin and join the leadership of Black Americans in Support of Israel Committee, which Mr. Rustin helped to start.

Through some of this work, I even had a chance to work in Washington, DC. I'd say that's a long way from my start as a teacher's aide.

## Maria Portalatin: From Paraprofessional to Union Leader

I was born in Puerto Rico but came to New York looking to make a life there. At one time, I was a hairdresser. But I had children, and like a lot of mothers who became paraprofessionals, I liked the idea of having a job that put me in neighborhood schools, and better yet, I could be home by the time my children were getting out of the school.

I first became a para in District 15 in Brooklyn, where I lived. And soon, I became part of the first waves to organize paras into a labor union. I was lucky—Jeanette Delorenzo, a very smart and seasoned labor woman, saw something in me and sort of took me under her wing.

Jeanette introduced me to all these women, like Sandy Feldman and Ann Kessler, who were all so bright and committed to organizing the paras in the United Federation of Teachers. I found that I had an instant rapport with these organizers and that I also had a talent for this sort of work.

The paras not only unionized but also got a series of good, solid contracts that deeply improved how they worked and what they could achieve, like become full-fledged teachers themselves. In time, I became the second person to occupy the chair of the UFT's Paraprofessional Chapter, succeeding Velma Hill. This post gave me an automatic seat on the executive council of the American Federation of Teachers.

I went on to continue my labor work, becoming one of the founders and vice president of the Labor Council for Latin American Advancement, the Hispanic counterpart of the A. Philip Randolph Institute. The council is affiliated with the AFL-CIO and was organized to, among other things, bring Hispanic trade unionists together.

I also took part in voter registration and get-out-the-vote drives in New York and nationally. Along the way, I was very happy to see that members of my own family followed in my footsteps and became paras. I continued my work until heath issues led me to retire in 2014.

## Anna Giles-Wells: From Paraprofessional to Principal

I was raised in New Orleans, although I have deep roots in Tennessee, and African, Irish, and Cherokee Indian origins, too. When my parents separated when I was quite young, I went to live with my mother's mother. It wasn't a bad life, especially when I started going to school. I loved my teachers. I loved them so much that I decided back then that I wanted to be a teacher someday.

By the time I was twenty-one, I had moved to New York City. That was 1962. It wasn't long before I started volunteering to work with children in the schools. A guidance counselor at Public School 189 in Brooklyn noticed how well I worked with children. I was married and a mother myself; I love children.

This counselor began encouraging me to go to college, to get my degree and work in education. She even took me to Brooklyn College, and I was hooked. I knew I was going to get my degree. And by the time I was thirty years old, I did.

While I was working as a paraprofessional at PS 189, I met Velma Hill. Right away, it was as if our spirits met. We began working together to persuade paraprofessionals to organize and join the United Federation of Teachers. A lot of the paraprofessionals wanted to belong to the same union as the teachers did, but some of the paras were very nervous.

The work of trying to organize the paras reminded me of when I was much younger and watching the civil rights activists who came to New Orleans from the east. That's when I saw my first demonstration. It was urging Black people to register to vote, and I was like, "Oh, boy, I can't wait until I make it to twenty-one so I can go out and vote."

Velma was convinced that we could organize the paras. I became one of three paras who were asked to organize in Brooklyn; [the other two were] Velma Hill and Maria Portalatin. Sandy Feldman represented the

UFT headquarters, which supported us. Ann Kessler was our District 15 rep. Because some school principals were reluctant to let us meet, we'd meet with paras on their lunch breaks and after school.

One of the things Velma pushed us hard to get in our contract was a "career ladder," a way for paras to go to college and become teachers themselves. But I didn't wait for that. I went on to graduate from Brooklyn College with a BS degree in education. Eventually, I earned postgraduate degrees and left college a few credits shy of a doctorate. The next thing I did was to start working my way up to being an assistant acting principal at Intermediate School 394 in 1992, and then the principal of IS 390 in the Crown Heights section of Brooklyn. I was the principal there for almost twenty years.

At the onset of the organizing drive, I was very active, serving as vice chair to Velma Hill, who was chair of the paraprofessional division of the United Federation of Teachers. It was all very gratifying work.

## Priscilla Castro: Smallheiser Award Winner Becomes the Paraprofessional Chapter Chair

I began my career as a paraprofessional in 2000. I was in college full-time and became a substitute para. I did that for a year. Then I was laid off. The Department of Education called me back in October and informed me the only position available was in the five boroughs of District 75. I remember the staff members informing everyone that District 75 is a special-education district, and all the students have disabilities, and you will have to change diapers, and so on. Many people walked out, but I stayed and took a position at 226 Manhattan in Harlem, working as a crisis paraprofessional. I learned a lot from senior paraprofessionals as well as the teachers at that site. I wore many hats in D 75—classroom para, health para, and inclusion para for grades four and five. I enjoyed working with the students there. They had so much potential and were so eager to learn despite their disabilities. It was rewarding to see the students write their name for the first time and even learn how to read an entire book.

At 226M I became a union activist. The former para representative was retiring, and she called me and said, "Priscilla, I am retiring in June, and you should be the para representative."

I asked, "What is a para representative?"

She said, "Going to Shelvey's citywide para representative meeting and once a month you will turn over all key information to the paraprofessionals at the school."

I said okay. I learned a lot in that role and gained contractual knowledge to assist all the paraprofessionals in my school. I was a member of the school consultation team and brought any para concerns monthly, which was great because many things were resolved.

During my time at the school my chapter leader went on sabbatical, and I became chapter leader for a term, becoming much more involved with union activities. Moreover, I received chapter leader training and arbitration training as well. My passion was to advocate and ensure that the members' contractual rights were not being violated at work. It became union work that I enjoyed doing, which made me decide to apply for a master's degree in the urban studies program at Queens College in 2016. I learned a lot in all my courses about public policy and grievance. Becoming a borough advocate in 2013 for District 75 was the best challenge and prepared me for my current position as paraprofessional chapter chair. The union has helped me grow as a leader. Every day I learn from the members and my union family. I am grateful to have the opportunity to lead the largest chapter of the United Federation of Teachers, numbering 27,000.

# A Vision of Racial and Economic Justice

(From *Dissent* magazine, May 19, 2021)

More than a year into a national reckoning over racism, two heroes in the struggle for racial justice have received little national attention. A. Philip Randolph and Bayard Rustin were mentor and student, friends and colleagues—eventually, their relationship was like father and son. They were two giants who contributed greatly to the advancement of civil and human rights, economic justice, and coalition politics for the democratization of America. Although younger generations are often unaware of their contributions, it is on their shoulders that today's activists stand.

Five principles animated their lives of struggle and achievement.

## Self-Liberation

Both Randolph and Rustin were committed to self-liberation. For them, that meant that any group that is mistreated or oppressed, that is treated unfairly and unjustly, that is discriminated against, should challenge the status quo. In short, they asked, "If you don't fight for yourself, who will?"

Raised in segregated Jacksonville, Florida, A. Philip Randolph took that self-liberating principle, learned from his parents, to New York. He organized Black hotel workers, established a trade union and a socialist newspaper, *The Messenger*, and then headed the effort to organize the Brotherhood of Sleeping Car Porters, the first major union with Black leadership. A twelve-year struggle for recognition and full membership in the American Federation of Labor, plus a union contract with the Pullman Company, established the union as the nation's strongest mass Black organization. It lifted tens of thousands of workers from poverty; offered educational opportunities to their children; and provided local bases for civil rights and labor rights struggles, from Chicago to Oakland. As the Brotherhood's national leader, Randolph made the union "the advance guard" (as he later called it) of a sweeping campaign for racial equality that began with the goal of integrating the labor movement and led to the passage of national civil rights legislation.

Bayard Rustin, raised by his Quaker grandmother in a small town in Pennsylvania, took the principle of self-liberation from his upbringing and faith to a life of protest for equality. A pacifist and early practitioner of nonviolent resistance, he led the first "freedom ride" on interstate transportation to the South in 1947 as an organizer for the interracial Fellowship of Reconciliation (FOR) and Congress on Racial Equality (CORE). Later rejected by the fellowship for his homosexuality, Rustin was welcomed by Randolph, who tasked him with organizing support in the North for the emerging civil rights movement in the South. One assignment was to go to Montgomery, Alabama, in 1955 to aid the bus boycott led by Martin Luther King Jr. He organized the Prayer Pilgrimage for Freedom in Washington, DC (when Dr. King made his "Give Us the Ballot" speech) in order to press the Eisenhower administration to implement the *Brown v. Board of Education* Supreme Court decision ending segregation in public education. This was followed by Youth Marches for Integrated Schools in 1958 and 1959.

In between, Rustin developed the plan for Dr. King to create the Southern Christian Leadership Conference, but there, too, his homosexuality meant rejection. (In the 1980s, Rustin expressed the same self-liberation principle in standing up for gay rights.) The most important of Randolph's assignments, though, was when he asked Rustin to organize the 1963 March on Washington for Jobs and Freedom.

## Mass Action and Nonviolence

Randolph and Rustin's commitments to nonviolence and mass action were interrelated principles that gave success to actions for Black self-liberation. Mass actions—the picket line, the boycott, the march—were organized by the mistreated and their allies, regardless of education level or social and economic status, for the purpose of confronting key decision–makers and demanding real change. Nonviolence did not just mean passive non-resistance (a tactic) but rather an integral principle for self-liberating actions geared toward achieving major goals. Randolph argued that violence was self-defeating for any minority seeking redress of grievances from the majority. Its use generally led to greater oppression, not liberation. And while individual or local action can gain attention—even notoriety—only collective, mass action can achieve goals for overcoming inequality and injustice or improving social and economic conditions.

Randolph used the strike and the threat of a strike to win recognition and gain a contract for the Brotherhood of Sleeping Car Porters. With the Brotherhood as a base, Randolph adopted a bold mass action: the initial 1941 March on Washington. As the organization of the March proceeded, the prospect of masses of unemployed Black workers marching on the capital forced Roosevelt's reluctant hand to sign an executive order banning discrimination in the burgeoning defense industries' federal contracts.

Randolph kept the March on Washington Movement as a tool—and the threat of mass protest in reserve—to press for the successful implementation of Executive Order 8802 through the Fair Employment Practices Committee structure (leading to hundreds of thousands of jobs and expanded union membership for Black workers). He later used the MOW Movement to pressure President Truman to desegregate the armed forces. Randolph articulated his basic principles in the first call to March on Washington:

> [N]othing counts but pressure, more pressure, and still more pressure, through the tactic and strategy of broad, organized, aggressive mass action behind the vital and important issues of the Negro.

Rustin brought the principles of nonviolence and mass action to Montgomery to aid Dr. King and others as they undertook what became a year-long bus boycott. Rustin helped develop a private transportation system to allow people to get to their jobs, communications for organization and maintaining unity, and promoted the abandonment of weapons for self-defense in favor of joint nonviolent resistance. These principles were adopted by Dr. King, already inspired by the work of Black theologian Howard Thurman, and became the foundation of the modern civil rights movement.

## Achieving Racial Equality and Economic Justice Through Coalition Politics

The fourth and fifth principles were interrelated. Randolph and Rustin were committed to a society in which racial equality and economic justice would prevail, not just for Blacks but for all people. They believed that full racial equality and justice could be achieved only through demands for economic equality. It was Randolph and Rustin who insisted on the broader demands of "Jobs and Justice" among the "Big Six" civil rights leaders that came together in coalition to issue the call for the 1963 March on Washington. Randolph and Rustin initiated the program for a Freedom Budget, which King and a broad coalition adopted in 1965, and pressed for its passage by the Johnson administration.

In the pursuit of racial equality and economic justice, Randolph and Rustin believed in a basic democratic principle: the necessity for a majoritarian strategy involving coalition politics. The coalition for racial and economic justice had to be broad, encompassing different faith organizations—Catholic, Protestant, Jewish, and Muslim—as well as those of ethnic and minority groups. In their view, the core of the coalition was an alliance between the trade union and civil rights movements. It was on this basis that Randolph brought the Brotherhood of Sleeping Car Porters, the NAACP, and the National Jewish Community Relations Advisory Council together to establish the Leadership Conference on Civil Rights. (The Conference added many more trade unions and civil rights and religious organizations over time.)

Randolph's insistence on a coalition between the civil rights and trade union movements meant a long struggle for integration and the adoption of equal employment opportunities. It proved a difficult task within the white-dominated American Federation of Labor. But Randolph's many years of effort, joined by others, ultimately pushed George Meany, the president of a united AFL-CIO, to strongly support the inclusion of Title VII, or equal employment provisions, in the Civil Rights Act, and an Equal Employment Opportunity Commission to enforce these conditions. Today, the trade union movement, together with the civil service and armed forces, are among the most integrated institutions in American society.

## Moving Forward

The March on Washington in 1963, which brought a quarter million people to the capital in protest for the first time in the nation's history, wove these five principles together. Randolph and Rustin established a broad alliance uniting the major civil rights groups, religious organizations, and the trade union movement. This coalition demanded both national civil rights legislation *and* a living wage, fair and affordable housing, and full employment. Before Dr. King's famous "I Have a Dream" oration, Randolph told the marchers, "We are the advanced guard of a massive moral revolution for jobs and freedom."

The March on Washington succeeded in building a majoritarian consensus around civil rights and voting rights legislation. But the "class dimension" of the march was never fulfilled. The goals of the Freedom Budget—full employment, living wages, and universal housing and educational opportunities—were only partially addressed by President Johnson's War on Poverty.

Rustin and Randolph's engagement with freedom and the class dimension are fiercely relevant sixty years later. Randolph predicted as early as 1960 that, in an age of greater and greater automation, the failure to achieve broad economic equality across all races would mean that freedom for Blacks would be stalled. Racial inequalities in employment and housing would necessarily mean the persistence of inequalities in the justice system, education, health, and other areas.

The progress hoped for in 1963—the great "moral revolution for jobs and freedom"—has been undone by a reactionary backlash. Today, however, a younger generation is building on Randolph and Rustin's legacy—even if they don't always know their names. The Movement for Black Lives, the Fight for $15, and Reverend William J. Barber's Poor People's Campaign all have roots that stretch back to these two monumental figures. It was as a result of these efforts that a multiracial coalition led by Black voters succeeded in propelling Joe Biden to electoral victory on a platform to reverse the reactionary and authoritarian politics of Donald Trump and to renew a broad agenda for achieving progressive change.

Evidence is all around us that a majority coalition now exists for racial and economic justice. As before, it can be achieved only through the nexus of civil rights and trade union struggles—expanding the right to vote and the right to union organization, integrating schools and increasing the minimum wage, ending mass incarceration and achieving full employment for all. Looking back at the radical struggles of A. Philip Randolph and Bayard Rustin points the way forward.

# APPENDIX C

# A 2017 Conversation with William Julius Wilson

At home, in the comfort of familiar things—our books, our African art, our artifacts of our long lives together as civil rights and labor movement activists—Norman and I sometimes find ourselves simply thinking. We don't reflect so much on the physical demands of trying to change the world as we, instead, do on the very hard work of hammering out the ideas that fuel positive and lasting change.

*Velma and I agree that the work of the activist is frequently upstaged by news reels and photographs of civil rights workers committing acts of nonviolent protest, like marching and demonstrating, of sitting in and sitting down in protest at a lunch counter, in a racially segregated school, in the streets calling for justice while holding hands, holding signs, and shouting slogans of equality and justice.*

*What Norman and I know without question is that effective activism begins in the universe of ideas.* For example, much has been made of Martin Luther King Jr. being a Christian minister, a man of God. Yet, much less is often made of the fact that he was also a scholar. Dr. King was an extremely well-read intellectual who could just as easily quote Socrates, the Magna Carta, Mahatma Gandhi, and John Locke as he could Jesus Christ and the Bible. He was a thinker. Much the same was true of people such as Bayard

Rustin, A. Philip Randolph, Thurgood Marshall, Eleanor Holmes Norton, Dorothy Height, Albert Shanker, and Lane Kirkland. It is hard to believe that there could ever have been a successful movement without brilliant strategists and tacticians, political and social philosophers, and writers like the novelist and essayist James Baldwin, for instance.

*Velma and I have been fortunate to know, and to have known, such people, to have discussed, examined, and debated the animating bedrock movement concepts and approaches with many such people.* And from time to time, we call upon some of them for their expertise and insights and stimulating conversations as we continue our work.

The renowned Harvard sociologist William Julius Wilson, who for years served on the board of the A. Philip Randolph Institute, is such a person. As the nation moved into the second half of the Trump presidency, we spoke at length with Dr. Wilson, whom we affectionately know as Bill. We asked him about some the most pressing woes facing the Black community and what might be done to address issues like systematic joblessness, widening income inequality, and the hollowing out of hope for far too many. And while we might not agree on every point, like the role of charter schools in reforming public education, we always welcome his honest, thorough, and provocative analysis and point of view.

This is an excerpt of our conversation with him. It has been edited and condensed.

NORMAN: Of the problems facing the Black community, not merely racial, but economic and social, what are the challenges to resolving them today?

WILSON: To answer this first question, it's going to take some time. I want you to bear with me.

VELMA: We're going to bear with you.

WILSON: Let me begin by saying that the major problems facing the Black community have not changed significantly in the past decades. The challenges, in many cases, have become more difficult. The problems I have in mind are residential segregation; poverty, including concentrated poverty; joblessness; public school education—blacks are overwhelmingly in public schools; health issues, especially physical health issues; crime and incarceration; income inequality and wealth disparities. There's a lot. I think it is important that I address these points.

NORMAN: Yes.

WILSON: Of these problems, the problem of health in the African-American community, especially physical health, has been lessened somewhat by the passage of the Affordable Care Act. Over the long term, Obamacare will significantly help low-income African Americans. There is no doubt about it. In fact, the Affordable Care Act has disproportionately affected Blacks and Hispanics, who had much lower rates of health insurance prior to the passage of this legislation. Overall, however, I might add, the share of Americans who are uninsured has declined significantly since the passage of the Affordable Care Act. As you noticed, this improvement was in part due to a provision of the health care bill that allows children to remain on their parents' health plan until they reach age twenty-six.

However, the challenges facing Blacks in other major areas have increased. Let me begin by talking about the challenges related to residential segregation.

Robert Sampson and I—he's a sociologist here at Harvard—pointed out in a 1995 paper titled "Toward a Theory of Race, Crime, and Urban Inequality" that it is difficult or in some cases impossible to reproduce in white communities the structural circumstances under which many Black Americans live, including of course the historical legacy of extended racial segregation and discrimination across generations.

Consider what cities like Chicago, Baltimore, Milwaukee, Philadelphia, Pittsburgh, St. Louis, Cleveland, Detroit have in common. They include many poor Black neighborhoods that have undergone significant depopulation since 1970. And the most visible symbols of this depopulation are abandoned buildings and vacant lots.

HBO's *The Wire*, David Simon's brilliant series, really captured this dynamic. Depopulation. Remember the vacant buildings? The abandoned buildings and the vacant lots?

The fundamental cause of this depopulation was the end of the Great Migration, the cessation of Black migration from the South in the early 1970s. Simultaneously, the gradual movement of higher-income Blacks from inner-city neighborhoods to other parts of the metro area, including other parts of the city, which I discuss in my book *The Truly Disadvantaged*, published in 1987.

When the Great Migration ended, the ranks of those who abandoned these Black neighborhoods—people have always been moving in and moving out—they were always replenished with poor migrants moving in. Some higher-income Blacks might move out of the neighborhoods to other parts of the city, or maybe to the suburbs, but up through the first half of the twentieth century, until the early 1970s, their ranks were replenished with poor migrants flowing in.

Something is happening in some of the neighborhoods now, where other groups are moving in. Places like New York and Seattle are experiencing the growth of high-scale industries that are attracting young people who don't want to commute anymore, and so many of these inner-city neighborhoods are being redeveloped.

Some changes are beginning to occur. Now, the point that I was making—this depopulation makes it more difficult to sustain basic institutions, to achieve adequate levels of neighborhood social organization, factors that are also related to greater joblessness and higher crime rates.

Drawing upon my article with Sampson, very few urban white neighborhoods, even those with the same poverty rates as Blacks, approximate these conditions. These depopulated neighborhoods tend to lack the organizational capacity that's necessary because they suffer from what we call a weak institutional resource base. Now, what do I mean by that?

I mean the links between churches, businesses, political organizations, schools, civic clubs, health organizations, recreational facilities are unstable or insecure. And a weak institutional research base is what distinguishes these depopulated communities from more stable communities.

Because of a weakened Institutional resource base, problems like crime and gangs, drug addiction, prostitution, and other forms of social dislocation can take root in the community. It's captured in *The Wire*.

Depopulated neighborhoods tend to have really high rates of joblessness, which trigger other problems in the neighborhood, such as the focus of my book *When Work Disappears*. You can say that there is a high relationship between joblessness and a weak organizational or resource base. One of the top challenges we face is how to strengthen the institutional resource base, and this has to go hand in hand with increasing employment opportunities and access to employment.

VELMA: My question is what has been the effect of gentrification?

WILSON: Some inner-city neighborhoods are improving mainly because of gentrification. There seems to be an increasing desire by many couples—I see this in Boston—especially younger, childless couples, to live in the center of the city as opposed to the suburbs. I have a condo on the Charles River, and all these high-tech industries around are really driving up rentals. My condo's appreciation has just gone through the roof.

Long commutes to and from the suburbs are increasingly inconvenient. Traffic congestion. So you have this problem of traffic, driven by the fact of the demand for housing. There are higher-paying and attractive jobs developing in these cities, in creative industries and other sectors—research, finance and so on. You see it in New York, you see it in Seattle, you see it in San Francisco. However, here's the point. The costs of housing and rentals are increasing sharply in these cities, and couples who are seeking modest-cost accommodations are ready to relocate to inner-city neighborhoods where redevelopment projects are underway. Now, as these neighborhoods gentrify, their resources improve, including the creation of shopping centers and large chain grocery stores, and, moreover, these neighborhoods become more desirable places to live. The costs of housing, taxes, and rental properties increase.

VELMA: The cities do not become places for the middle class.

WILSON: That's right. And so you're getting a lot of these really higher-income people living in the cities, and the middle class and working class commuting. And some higher-income people can avoid that commute because they can afford to live in the cities. So you have the displacement with this gentrification taking place; you have the displacement of many low-income residents who can no longer afford to live there. Low-income families respond to the rising cost of living in the city by relocating to peripheral areas beyond the urban core, areas that have seen a rapid growth of concentrated poverty, by the way. There have been increases in suburban poverty, in what you call the inner suburbs. Yet, despite the increase in poverty in the suburbs, three-quarters of high-poverty neighborhoods in metro areas—by high poverty I mean neighborhoods with poverty rates of about 40 percent—are located in big cities.

The low-income families who are able to remain in inner areas that are gentrified, sometimes through rent subsidies and tax abatements, definitely benefit from the improvements. But given the present political climate, I have no reason to feel hopeful.

NORMAN: Is there an international model for what you are describing like North Africans forced to live on the periphery of Paris because they cannot afford to live in the center of this very expensive city?

WILSON: Yes, what's happening is that central cities of the United States are becoming like central cities in Europe. You go to Paris. Who is living in downtown Paris? Not the working class.

Another major and challenging problem is joblessness in the inner city. I've said this many times. It's important for Blacks to recognize that their economic fate is inextricably tied up with the structure and function of the modern economy. A great deal has to be done to address the continuing fundamental changes in the economy, especially the impact of these changes on the African-American community.

And I think that the impact is particularly acute for most young Black males. Many turn to crime, end up in prison, which further marginalizes them and decreases their employment opportunities. And as we all know, the big, disproportionate number of low-skilled Black males in this country is one of the legacies of historic segregation and discrimination. Now, Black women face problems, too. And I don't want to minimize all the challenges and problems that they're facing. But inner-city Black males are in a crisis.

VELMA: What about automation and the role higher technologies might have on job opportunities for these young Black males?

WILSON: We also have to look at the impersonal, in some cases economic, forces. The computer revolution. The globalization and economic activity. The declining manufacturing sector. And the growth of service industries where most of the new jobs for workers with limited skills and education are concentrated.

I would like to focus for a moment on this last factor associated with the relatively high jobless rate of low-skill Black men, and that is the gradual shift from manufacturing to service industries. And this shift has created a new set of problems for low-skilled Black men.

VELMA: And women.

WILSON: Well, not so much. In fact, I'm basing this on research that we did interviewing employers of entry-level positions in Chicago. This is research that was conducted in the early 1990s, and the findings are still relevant today. Those [service] industries feature jobs that require workers to serve and relate to consumers. The employers that we interviewed said they don't consider Black women a problem in that sense because they are not considered dangerous. Many employers favor women, including Black women, and recent immigrants of both genders—you know immigrants have come to populate the labor pool for the low-level service sector in recent decades—over Black males for entry-level service jobs. This is a problem for Black males because of the declining manufacturing industry where they were once concentrated. And employers in the service industry that we interviewed felt that consumers perceived inner-city Black males to be dangerous or threatening in part because of their perceived high incarceration rates.

So here's the point I'm trying to make. In the past, African-American men simply had to demonstrate a strong back and muscle to be hired for physical labor in a factory or at a construction site or, thinking of Detroit, on an assembly line. They interacted with peers and foremen, not consumers. Today they have to increasingly search for work in a service sector where employers are less likely to hire them because they are seen as unable to sustain positive contact with the public.

The employers we interviewed talked about Black males lacking soft skills that the jobs require. What do we mean by soft skills? Things like keeping eye contact, the ability to carry on light and friendly conversations with the customers, with consumers. The inclination to smile, to be responsive to customer requests. Body language—even though some of these requests seem to be demanding or unreasonable, you still smile. The employers said Black male job seekers don't have these traits and therefore face rising rates of rejection.

By the way, we interviewed both white employers and Black employers. And Black employers said the same thing. The difference between the Black employers and the white employers is that the Black employers had a greater understanding of what they said was the nefarious and deleterious conditions of the inner city that cause these problems. But the Black employers are reluctant to hire these workers as well. So when you take such attitudes, combined with the physical and social isolation of living in these inner-city areas of concentrated poverty, it severely limits the access that poor Black men have to getting jobs, including access to what we call the informal job network, the casual network of people or acquaintances who can pass along information about employment prospects. This is a considerable problem for Black males, especially when you consider the fact that many low-skill employees first learn about their jobs through an acquaintance, or they were recommended by someone associated with the company. And research suggest that only a small percentage of low-skill employees are hired through advertised job openings, or what we call cold calls, just coming in knocking on the door.

NORMAN: And this makes many of the low-skill Black males unmarriageable.

WILSON: Right. The findings of the research that we conducted in the early 1990s, to repeat, are still relevant today. The net effect is that many of the inner-city Black male applicants are never really given the opportunity to prove themselves. It's what economists call statistical discrimination. That is to say, they look at a category—Black male—and they just sort of think, *Well, what are the odds this person is going to create problems for me?*

I remember this one interview we had with one of the employers and he was talking about why he was reluctant to hire Black males. But then he says he just hired this kid. And he says, my colleague called and recommended this kid. And you know what? He was good.

The only reason he hired that kid was because his colleague said he's good.

VELMA: What are the service industries? There's education, there's health. You don't see a lot of working-class Black men in education and health. I organized paraprofessionals in the 1960s, and they were mostly Black and Hispanic women. Where the jobs got to the point when they were paying a little more money in New York, you had some men who applied for those jobs. But people felt uncomfortable with Black men being paraprofessionals in the classroom because they felt threated by them. I think that's true for health, too, by the way.

WILSON: That's a very good point. You know nurses, practitioners, and so on—I talked to some Black men in our research who talked about the problems they had to overcome getting these positions. The point is that the employers of these entry-level positions in the service sector believe that women and recent immigrants of both genders are better suited than Black men, especially those with prison records.

VELMA: Oh, yes.

WILSON: As you well know, this has been partly created by a kind of cultural shift in national attitudes, sort of reflected concerns about the hiring of violence. In other words, in the eyes of many Americans, Black males symbolize this violence. I see this in my own condo when I'm dressed casually. I remember one time it was after midnight and I had gotten on the elevator because I had a headache and I wanted to go to an all-night drugstore for some aspirins.

I stepped on the elevator, casually dressed, and people freaked out. I said, "It's not to worry. I'm a Harvard professor, and I've been in this building for ten years." I was so damn upset.

NORMAN: It sounds as if you are saying that these Black men are being redlined, the way residential segregation had been maintained in real estate by redlining entire Black neighborhoods.

WILSON: Absolutely. Absolutely. They have this high jobless rate and this high incarceration rate that is very much connected to their high jobless rate. We all know what being without a job can encourage. Sometimes illegal money-making activities can make ends meet, which, of course, increases the risk of incarceration. All this is captured in HBO's *The Wire*. That's really a brilliant show. Incarceration carries a stigma in the eyes of employers and decreases the probability that an ex-offender will be hired, resulting in a greater likelihood of even greater joblessness.

VELMA: We live in a middle-class housing cooperative in Manhattan that is mostly white. When Ernie Green, who integrated Little Rock High School in the 1950s, first moved in, he got on the elevator and some of the residents got off because he was Black. And this happens a lot. I'm a psychotherapist, and when my patients come here, white residents would open the door for them but not for Black patients. And this is a liberal-to-progressive development. It's less now, but it was certainly like that in the beginning. You could even be a Black person dressed well, and that made no difference.

WILSON: And it's not just whites. In my condo there are people from the Middle East and Asians and so on. They turn on TV, and they see all the violence, of Blacks being arrested and so on.

Based on our interviews, the men complain and otherwise manifest a dissatisfaction with seeming even more unattractive to employers and, therefore, encountering even more discrimination when they search for employment. This is how I would sum this up. The feelings many inner-city Black males express about their jobs and their job prospects reflect their plummeting position in a changing economy. It's really important to link their attitudes with the opportunity structure—that is, a spectrum of life chances available to them in the greater society.

This is the problem, and how do we attack it? And it is one of the reasons why I've been in favor of public sector jobs. I would strongly recommend legislation that would target areas of high unemployment with job creation strategies, including the creation of public sector jobs. Such a program would not only address unemployment in, say, Black inner-city neighborhoods, which are areas of high rates of joblessness, but also unemployment in white, Latino, and Asian areas with high jobless rates. I suggest such legislation with few allusions that it can be achieved without facing stern political opposition given the power the Republicans now have with control of the Senate and the White House. But I think about it with the hope that it would, indeed, receive serious consideration by members of Congress and the American public in the future, perhaps, and hopefully when a new president is in office.

VELMA: I know a little bit about education. Black teachers are in education more than they have ever been, and this is all over. Not just New York. But I'd like to know when you say public sector jobs, what should be one of the targets? Give me an example.

WILSON: Cleaning streets once a day. Cleaning parks and playgrounds improves the infrastructure, cutting grass, shrubbery. Stuff like that. Now, you were talking about education. There's one problem I mentioned that I want to return to because, again, we're facing a major challenge here.

VELMA: Yes.

WILSON: Blacks are overwhelmingly populated in public schools. Research by a sociologist at Stanford, Sean Reardon, and other scholars reveals that schools with high proportions of Black students, or high proportions of Hispanic students, typically tend to be schools with high proportions of poor students. In other words, these schools tend to have high rates of concentrated poverty.

VELMA: Yes, they are Title I schools, which receive federal funds to support low-income students.

WILSON: So this suggests a strong association between residential segregation and a racial achievement gap. A key dimension that is driving the problem is the proportion of a student's classmates who are poor and in concentrated poverty. Indeed, you could say that a school's poverty rate could be a proxy for general school quality. Schools with high poverty rates, they have fewer resources. Research is being conducted to explain the impact of concentrated poverty on urban public schools. There are a number of factors to be considered. First of all, that schools may experience greater difficulty in attracting and retaining competent or skilled teachers. And also, the parents of the students in these schools generally have fewer resources, what we call cultural capital and human capital, beneficial to their children's academic achievement. Well, this means that schools with a high percentage of poor students tend to have a higher percentage of low-performing students, which may result in the school offering less advanced curricula. In other words, having low-performing classmates may have an adverse effect on learning by altering the instruction or the processes in the classroom.

A study by Robert Sampson and his colleagues revealed that—and this is based on a set of longitudinal research that they conducted in Chicago—"residing in a severely disadvantaged neighborhood cumulatively impedes the development of academically relevant verbal ability in children." Which, of course, affects school performance. And, of course, you also have to consider the direct and the indirect effect of peer influence. Students from disadvantaged backgrounds are not likely to see a strong association between schooling and post-school employment. Finally, we have to factor in other conditions that we don't usually associate with school performance, but research suggest that these factors are important—for example, the impact of lead contamination on school performance of poor children who live in dilapidated buildings. The effect of evictions on children's school performance. A former colleague, Matt Desmond, talks about this in his book. And the impact, we think we see in *The Wire*, of psychological trauma of witnessing a killing in your neighborhood on school performance.

One of the problems that we have to overcome in addressing these problems is institutional entrenchment in the public schools. By that I mean the need to change long-accepted ways of allocating resources and staffing, which have become normal and gained constituencies willing to fight to maintain the current privileges. I remember Geoffrey Canada talking about this in his Harlem Children's Zone when he was trying to create some schools. Despite decades of federal support, public education continues to deteriorate primarily because, I believe, such funding is not confronting the problem of institutional entrenchment. The problem of institutional entrenchment is one of the reasons why I don't categorically reject charter schools like a number of my progressive colleagues.

I'm not talking about private charters. The creation of public charter schools puts pressure on traditional public schools to reform. And this is clearly revealed in Boston, where a group of successful charter schools—and these are public charter schools, by the way—are overwhelmingly populated by students of color from low-income backgrounds. The success of the public charter schools in Boston triggered a historic public education reform law. And the law includes, among other things, a new pay-for-excellence plan that allows public schools to grant special rewards to exceptional teachers and grants principals in what they call turnaround schools the authority to adopt schedules that best address the needs of the students and to choose the best teachers across the school district.

I will never forget Ernie Duncan telling me, when I had him over at my house for dinner when I lived in Chicago, that a lot of the public schools in Chicago, they'd become dumping grounds for some of the worst teachers.

I'm not saying that charter schools are the solution to the problem. Hell no, I'd rather see something else. But until we do something, I'm not going to systematically reject those that are doing well. And if you look at the research, there are many charter schools that are not doing very well.

VELMA: Yes, we know that. But I don't want to get into a battle about charter schools.

WILSON: I don't want you to, either. I'm just telling you that I am just so frustrated with what we're trying to do in the public schools that I'm willing to consider different things until we move on.

VELMA: One can consider different things in the context of the schools being unionized and still being a charter school. There are some of those.

WILSON: Yeah. That's a very good point. That would be great if you could have charter schools that were unionized to protect the teachers. You just gave me a research idea that I am going to pass on to my students. To look at these unionized charter schools.

NORMAN: Income segregation has increased in recent years, but statistics indicate that this phenomenon has been accelerated for Black America. Why has it been so entirely difficult for leadership to put this issue on the table?

WILSON: There was a 2014 study by the sociologist Kendra Bischoff of Cornell and Sean Reardon of Stanford that shows income segregation, the separation of families by income.

The most rapid gains have been since 2000, especially among Black and Hispanic men. Here's the point: whereas Black American families, according to their study, in 1970 recorded the least income segregation of all major racial and ethnic groups, they now register the highest income segregation. Now, I'm talking about separation of families of the same race by income. I'm not talking about segregation between Black and white families, but separation of Black families by income. When you consider a person's life trajectory, what I call life chances, the differences in the quality of one's daily life residing in a predominantly affluent neighborhood and a poor Black neighborhood are huge. It's important to note that today, poor Black families, overall—this wouldn't be true in places like New York—but overall, poor Black families have fewer Black middle-class neighbors than they had in 1970. And the rising income segregation in the Black community is driven by both the growth of affluent Blacks and the deteriorating conditions of poor Blacks. And this reminds me of the research by Anne Owens, a sociologist at the University of Southern California. She reexamined some of the longitudinal data on income segregation that Kendra Bischoff and Sean Reardon presented.

She published an article in the *American Sociological Review*, and she found that families with children had a much higher level of income segregation than childless couples. And she hypothesizes that this is because families with children tend to seek out neighborhoods with the best schools. I think this hypothesis really applies to higher-income Black families, higher-income families in the Black community. They tried to escape neighborhoods with the poorest schools. Neighborhoods in which poor Blacks suffer from the combination of income segregation and racial segregation. It's interesting that these data update some of the earlier arguments that I developed in my book *The Declining Significance of Race*, which was published in 1978. They also remind me of a recent book you may have read by the Harvard political scientist Robert Putnam titled *Our Kids: The American Dream in Crisis*. Now, according to Putnam, although racial barriers to success remain powerful, they represent less burdensome impediments than they did in the 1950s. By contrast, he maintains, class barriers in America loom much larger than they did back then.

And this is reflected not only in growing income inequality among all racial and ethnic groups in America but also increasing disparities in other aspects of well-being—accumulated wealth, class segregation across neighborhoods, quality of primary and secondary education, enrollment in highly selective colleges, and even life expectancy.

One of the major underlying themes of *The Declining Significance of Race*—that is, the changing relative significance of race and class on a Black person's life trajectory—has been extended to all US racial and ethnic groups in Putnam's book. In order to keep things in proper perspective, when talking about the relative gains in more privileged starts—and I wish I had some income data in my head to show you the growing income gap in the Black community between more affluent Blacks and the rest of the adult population—let me just say this: The Gini index is the major income inequality measure, which ranges from zero—maximum equality—to one, maximum inequality. And when you use the Gini index coefficient, believe it or not, Blacks have a higher coefficient than whites or Hispanics—differences of income within the Black group. The differences of income within the white group, the differences of income within the Hispanic group or any Asians—Blacks have the highest Gini index. That addresses your question.

VELMA: Higher than in Hispanics?

WILSON: Yes. I'm talking about within. I'm not talking about between Blacks and Hispanics. The separation of affluent Blacks from poorer Blacks is higher in the Black community. We have to keep things in proper perspective when talking about the relative gains of more privileged Blacks because we cannot overlook the continuing and severe internal racial disparities. For example, researchers at the Pew Research Center released data in 2013 showing that the median financial wealth of white households exceeded that of Black households by almost $131,000. And you've heard about the research I'm sure of Raj Chetty on neighborhoods. The economist Chetty and his colleagues reveal really sharp interracial differences in neighborhoods and neighborhood effects, saying some of the ideas I talked about in my book *The Truly Disadvantaged*.

And even when you compare the more affluent Black neighborhoods with the more affluent white neighborhoods, there are significant differences. The affluent Black neighborhoods are a hell of a lot better than their working-class and lower-middle-class, poor Black neighborhoods. But when you compare them with affluent white neighborhoods, they fall apart.

I've started to write a book on this particular point. So despite sharp increases in income inequality and income segregation among Blacks, the interracial disparities between Blacks and whites remain huge. On the one hand, race trumps class when the focus is on the longstanding interracial differences between Blacks and whites. Race trumps class. Then on the other hand, class trumps race when the focus is on changing intraracial income and neighborhood differences, especially in the Black community.

To really capture the dynamic, you have to make a distinction between the interracial differences and the intra differences when you're talking about race and class. Because Black people get suspicious of the idea that class is becoming a significant variable in the Black community because they say race overwhelms class. Yeah, but between Blacks and whites, race is the variable. It trumps class. When you look within the Black community, class is the significant factor.

NORMAN: Bill, what are the most severe implications of this intra difference of class?

BILL: A growing income inequality is resulting in the separation of families, growing social isolation, greater divisions in society, less interaction across class lines.

NORMAN: Coming back to the last part of my last question, why has it been so difficult for Black leadership to put these issues on the table?

VELMA: I don't think they understand the question facing the community.

WILSON: Yeah, that's the point. I think the main reason why the Black leadership has not put the growing income segregation among Blacks on the table is because of the continuing *interracial* differences that have only rescinded in a very few areas. And they don't want to focus on the growing *intraracial* differences where class trumps race, I believe—this is just my opinion—because of a fear that this would distract our attention away from the important and longstanding interracial differences. But if they are going to talk about the overall well-being of the community, and particular to poor Blacks, they are going to have to address this issue; it's going to have to be put on the table.

VELMA: The Occupy Wall Street movement at its peak was a single-issue movement. Much of the same can be said for the Black Lives Matter movement, and the MeToo movement. Does the popularity of these expressions of activism signal a larger question of whether coalition politics has run its course in addressing the larger and persistent needs of the Black community?

WILSON: Another thoughtful question. You know I wrote a book titled *The Bridge Over the Racial Divide: Rising Inequality and Coalition Politics*, which was published in 1999. And when I was writing that book, I was hopeful that a constructive dialogue would emerge about how problems of ordinary Americans can be addressed in a period of rising inequality. In that book, I highlighted concerns the poor, working middle classes of all races and ethnic groups share, including concerns about declining real wages, job security, unemployment, escalating medical and housing costs, the availability of affordable childcare programs, and pensions or retirement security. These are common things all people are concerned about. Commonalities.

And I also argued that programs created in response to these concerns despite being race neutral would disproportionately benefit the inner-city poor; they also benefit large segments of the remaining population, including the white population. And I pointed out that national opinion polls in the United States suggest—and I believe this even more strongly now—that careful framing of issues to address the problems of ordinary Americans could enhance the possibility of a new alignment in support of major social rights initiatives, such as universal health care, or childcare subsidies for working parents, affordable higher education, things of this sort. If such an alignment is attempted, by reason, it ought to highlight a new public rhetoric that focuses on and addresses the problems of all groups, a public rhetoric that would tend to mobilize these groups through coalition politics. And I stated that the bringers of this message should be cognizant of the fact that—and I'm quoting myself—these groups, although seen as adversaries, are potential allies in a reform coalition because they suffer from a common problem: the stress and anxiety caused by forces outside their control. Unquote. This argument is being repeated by some observers in their postelection analysis and debates.

The Democrats' emphasis on identity politics in attempts to mobilize people of color, women, immigrants, and the LGBT community tended to ignore the problems of poor white Americans. One notable exception, they point out, is Bernie Sanders.

Democrats tend to reflect on what happened. They go back to the primaries; they talk about what happened…. Different messages were advanced. They point out that what was unique about Bernie was that he had a progressive and unifying populist economic message in Democratic primaries, a message that resonated with significant segments of the white, lower-working-class populations. But Sanders was not the Democratic nominee. If he was, he would be able to capture notable support of this population.

Trump was smart. The racial divide in America reduces the political effectiveness of ordinary citizens. With that said, racial political cooperation could be enhanced if different groups focused more on the interests that their individual members hold in common, addressing economic insecurity resulting from political and economic forces beyond their control. And if they could develop a sense of interdependence in trying to develop a coalition, then you make people aware that they have commonality. There are certain goals that they all have in common. There are differences, but there are a lot of goals in common.

To achieve these goals, they need the support of other groups. Interdependence. You make other groups be aware of common interests, norms, values, aspirations, and goals, and then help them appreciate the importance of intergroup, interracial, interactive cooperation to achievement. If I had to develop a basic theoretical argument about coalitions, it would be this: a necessary condition for the development of multiracial cooperation is perceived interdependence among potential participants whereby the interests of a particular group come to recognize that they cannot achieve their common goals without the help of members of other groups.

Here you need visionary group leaders to promote this sense of interdependence, especially those who have strong community organizations. They are very important for articulating and communicating this vision, as well as developing and sustaining a multiracial coalition.

There's this article in the *Washington Post*, published May 4, 2017. The point I'm leading up to is that in the age of Trump, we may have created a situation where the framing of issues to identify and promote a common goal, like coalition, may be less challenging. This article is titled "Turning Away from Street Protests—Black Lives Matter Tries a New Tactic in the Age of Trump."

As I recall, they interviewed half a dozen of the leaders of Black Lives Matter, and the article reported that the election of Donald Trump has led to them to shift focus from street protests to joining others in a political coalition and would collectively fight Donald Trump, who has pledged to roll back Obama's efforts to change policing practices.

VELMA: It sounds like Bayard Rustin's "From Protest to Politics" to me.

WILSON: Yes. Now, that's interesting. I mean you're talking about Black Lives Matter. Another indication of the potential of such a coalition in the age of Trump is the successful grassroots organizing against the Republican-drafted health care bill by a group such as the Center for Community Change, which is a community grassroots organization. I'm on their advisory research board in Washington, DC, the West Virginia Healthy Kids, the Progressive Leadership Alliance of

Nevada. These are just some of these groups I've mentioned. And these are multiracial coalitions, by the way. Their efforts included organizing in white working-class, rural communities, where they were knocking on doors and educating people about the Affordable Care Act. I've often wondered about how over a relatively brief period, attitudes toward the Affordable Care Act went from negative to positive. They don't read the *New York Times*. They don't read the *Washington Post*. How are they getting this? And I think a major reason is the efforts of these grassroots organizations.

I just mention these two developments because they suggest that conditions may now be conducive for launching a progressive, national, multiracial political coalition not only to bring down the Trump administration, but also to overcome the congressional gridlock. Who would be in this coalition as I perceive it? Grassroots community organizations, civil rights groups, women's rights groups, labor unions, religious organizations, immigrant groups. These groups would begin developing interconnected local, regional, and national networks to advance the feeling of perceived interdependence and thereby reduce racial and ethnic antagonisms in pursuit of highly valued common goals. That's my goal. I would like to see more of that in the campaign. Elizabeth Warren is my friend. And I'm going to try to sit down with her at some point and talk to her a little bit more about some of this stuff.

VELMA: I want to add to that. Norman and I met with the leadership of the Black Lives Matter movement. We talked with a young woman who was at Harvard's law school and was a Black Lives Matter leader. I indicated to her that the problem with her movement was that there was no underlying feeling about democracy. There are all these groups that wanted to be on their own, that didn't want leadership. Democracy is very important to me, and Norman. One of the things we want our memoir to do is to talk about why democracy is relevant, why the civil rights and labor movements are instruments of democracy, and to give these groups a little history lesson.

NORMAN: I agree, Velma. But I have another question. What is the tactical and strategic framework for addressing the pressing problems facing the Black community?

WILSON: Again, another great question. To me, it comes down to the issue of framing. Allow me to elaborate. During periods when people are beset with multiple anxieties, they become more receptive to political messages. I remember in 1991 when President Clinton was campaigning. I was watching him on C-Span, and he was at a Black church. And he was talking about, you know, they think we're fools. And they want us to turn on each other, race against race, citizens against immigrants in order to deflect attention away from failed political policies and failed economic policies. They think we're stupid.

And Blacks stood up and clapped.

The next day in Baton Rouge, Louisiana, in a white church, the same message, and the whites stood up and clapped.

I called up the editors of the *New York Times* and said, you know, something is happening here. I think Clinton is developing a biracial coalition. And I said I'd like to write an op-ed piece on this. And they said, please do. So, I wrote this piece, it was titled "The Right Message." It generated a lot of discussion. Some even called my house and thanked me for it.

I think it's very, very important for political leaders to develop the right message to channel citizens' frustrations in positive, constructive directions. As you know, unfortunately, in the past two years, we've had this mean-spirited and divisive rhetoric that has been on dramatic display.

VELMA: And the current president's framing of issues is set around everything being a zero-sum game—one's gain is another's loss.

WILSON: That's right. Look. The world is very complex; there are a lot of things happening that we don't fully understand. The average person doesn't understand what the hell is going on. And when you have a charismatic, articulate person with a hateful message, it's bound to resonate. That's why you need to counter with progressive, populist messages to channel people's frustrations in the right direction.

I was thinking about this. I was reminded of a study by the social scientist Carol Graham, who's at the Brookings Institution. She maintained in a book that was published in 2017 that whites who were experiencing downward mobility were likely to support Trump. She made this assertion based in part on her analysis of a national survey's micro-data from 2008 to 2013 that revealed that poor whites were the most pessimistic group in America about their future. And there was a 2011 survey by the Pew Charitable Trusts' Economic Mobility Project, and they came to a similar conclusion. More recent studies also capture the growing pessimism of noneducated whites. In this Pew Research study, a majority of them, believe it or not, didn't expect their economic situation to improve in the next ten years. And almost half said they weren't better off than their parents were at the same age. Only one-third believe that their children will live better lives than they do. One-third.

No other group in the survey, neither Blacks nor Hispanics nor educated whites, reported such gloomy outlooks. Other recent research reveals that non-Hispanic white men and women with only a high school degree or less are experiencing marked declines in life expectancy due to the increasing deaths from drug and alcohol poisoning, chronic liver disease, cirrhosis. In fact, one of the reasons why the gap in life expectancy between Blacks and whites is narrowing is because they are worrying so much.

VELMA: How do you account for a large number of working white men who voted for Trump who were members of unions? The labor movement should be the matrix, along with civil rights, of any coalition that we have.

WILSON: Why Trump's divisive messages seem to resonate with poor and working-class whites, and some other whites? The point is that the voices of progressives are more likely to associate the problems of these citizens with complex changes in our global economy and the failed economic and social policies, with the notable exception of Bernie Sanders.

I think progressives are going to have to pay much more attention to developing messages that resonate. And they are going to have to be more skillful in how they frame these messages; they're going to have to have really effective sound bites that resonate.

NORMAN: Where should the initiative come from for addressing the problems of the Black community?

WILSON: The short answer is from different quarters, because these issues will not be seriously addressed if the issues only come from Blacks alone. Efforts to address problems in the Black community should be based in significant ways on coalition politics and a focus on helping people to help themselves. When you frame it that way, how can we help people to help themselves garners much more support.

Americans worry about quotas and numerical guidelines. They worry about unqualified people being hired or being promoted, admitted to colleges and universities, but they also recognize that the playing field is often not level and that we should make efforts to make the playing field level, that is, to provide opportunities for people of color and women so they can help themselves.

VELMA: And this should not be framed as only helping Blacks, but also helping the poor. We have to be very careful about that.

WILSON: I support that. You're really talking about making opportunities for all people....

People should be made aware that the unemployment rate only represents the percentage of workers in the labor force—that is, those who are actively looking for work. A more significant measure appears in my book *When Work Disappears*—the employment-to-population ratio, which corresponds to the percentage of adults who are working.

The point I made, which is still very true today, is that in previous years, labor market demand stimulated by fiscal or monetary policy not only absorbs what we call the technically unemployed—that is, jobless workers who are in the official labor force—but also enlarges the employment ranks by drawing back workers who were not in or who had dropped out of the labor force.

Today, it appears that many inner-city workers, particularly the Black men I talked about previously, who are not in the labor force, tend to be out of the reach of monetary or fiscal policy. Here's the problem. Over the years, tight labor markets, and the kind we are now in, tend to be of relatively short duration. Tight labor markets and low unemployment are frequently followed by a recession that either wipes out previous gains of many workers or didn't allow others to fully recover from a period of previous economic stagnation. And the point I made in *When Work Disappears* is that it would take sustained tight labor markets over many years to draw back discouraged inner-city workers who have dropped out of the labor market all together, and some for very long periods of time. This presents a serious challenge because the consequences of such joblessness are not restricted to the inner city; they affect the quality of life and race relations in the larger city as well.

Oh, my God, it's so important to feel that we can affect some change, to not throw up our hands in despair, to overcome the pessimism.

VELMA: Absolutely. That's one of the reasons Norman and I are writing this book. There is this pessimism. And we thought that by going around to book parties, public readings, college campuses, we could help generate some real optimism and enthusiasm and understanding about the movement and the past and where we have to go in the future.

WILSON: It was good for me to reflect on these thoughtful questions because I've been fighting pessimism about the future of low-income people. I'm really worried about the future, and I keep thinking, how can I generate some optimism, and then I started thinking about Bayard Rustin and coalition politics and reflecting on your questions.

NORMAN: Velma and I thank you for your thoroughly insightful and intellectually generous conversation with us.

# Acknowledgments

Thanks to our family members: parents, siblings, nieces, and nephews—those who have passed and those who are still with us. You have given us a lifetime of love and support as we climbed the mountain as civil and labor rights activists.

To Michel Marriott, for your skill and expertise. You were not able to see this memoir make it to the bookshelves, but you brought us right up to the finish line. We miss you.

To the late Rep. John Lewis and Vernon Jordan, exactly the right individuals to write our foreword.

To our literary agent Jennifer Lyons for her steadfast support and skill in finding just the right publisher, and to Gretchen Young at Regalo Press for welcoming our book warmly to her inaugural catalog.

Putting a four-hundred-plus-page book together is an exciting but complex endeavor. We thank the following people who also saw us through the process:

Sandy Byers, for her expert editing, always with an eye toward making our memoir better.

Shartina Thompson, for designing our wonderful book cover.

Madeline Sturgeon, managing editor at Post Hill Press, for keeping the production of our book on track and on time.

Our publicist Louise Crawford from Brooklyn Social Media, for her skill in getting the word out far and wide.

Ronn Taylor, for his faithful assistance.

Leslie Santora, our friend, supporter, and marvelous hair stylist.

Larry Strauss for his bookkeeping services.

And thanks to our friend and editorial liaison officer Audrey Peterson, who connected everyone to everyone else when needed and believed in this book from the beginning.

Special thanks to Fred Redmond, secretary-treasurer of the AFL-CIO, and Clayola Brown, president of the A. Philip Randolph Institute and senior advisor for Strategic Partnerships and Racial Justice, AFL-CIO. We also thank all our brothers and sisters who are leaders in the labor movement, including:

| | | |
|---|---|---|
| Edgar Romney | Don Slaiman | Kevin Mapp |
| Anthony Harmon | Virginia Diamond | Priscilla Castro |
| Nick Juravich | Clint Brown | Kathryn Thomas |
| LeRoy Barr | Doug Moore | Melvin Montford |
| Carlos Wilson | James Andrews | Randi Weingarten |
| Robert Reiter | MaryBe McMillan | Liz Shuler |
| Mary Crayton | Vinny Alvarez | Lee Saunders |

Additional thanks to:

Walter Naegle, partner of the late Bayard Rustin.

Ambur Nicosia, chair of the board of Penn South, where we have made our home since the 1960s.

Eric Chenoweth and his entire family.

Alex Hinton for his film *Freedom Waders*.

Dr. Otis Moss III, senior pastor of Trinity United Church of Christ, Chicago.

Last, and certainly not least, thanks to our friends and colleagues who previewed our manuscript and called it good with their generous blurbs:

| | |
|---|---|
| Charlayne Hunter-Gault | Carl Gershman |
| Rev. Al Sharpton | Clayola Brown |
| Congresswoman Maxine Waters | Liz Shuler |
| Congresswoman Barbara Lee | Lee Saunders |
| Congressman Robert C. "Bobby" Scott | Richard L. Trumka |
| Abraham H. Foxman | Mary Kay Henry |
| Marc Morial | William Julius Wilson |

# About the Authors

**Norman Hill** was the national program director of the Congress of Racial Equality (CORE), staff coordinator for the 1963 March on Washington for Jobs and Freedom, staff representative of the Industrial Union Department of the AFL-CIO, and president of the A. Philip Randolph Institute from 1980 to 2004, the longest tenure in the organization's history. He remains its president emeritus.

**Velma Murphy Hill**, a graduate of the Harvard Graduate School of Education, was a leader of the Chicago Wade-In to integrate Rainbow Beach, East Coast field secretary for CORE, and assistant to the president of the United Federation of Teachers, where she unionized 10,000 paraprofessionals, mostly Black and Hispanic, working in New York public schools. She was vice president of the American Federation of Teachers and International Affairs and civil rights director of the Service Employees International Union.

The Hills were the only Black couple to hold leadership positions in the civil rights and labor movements.